D0612615

Social Class
and Stratification

Social Class and Stratification

*Classic Statements
and Theoretical Debates*

edited by
Rhonda F. Levine

ROWMAN & LITTLEFIELD PUBLISHERS, INC.
Lanham • Boulder • New York • Oxford

ROWMAN & LITTLEFIELD PUBLISHERS, INC.

Published in the United States of America
by Rowman & Littlefield Publishers, Inc.
4720 Boston Way, Lanham, Maryland 20706

12 Hid's Copse Road
Cumnor Hill, Oxford OX2 9JJ, England

Copyright © 1998 by Rowman & Littlefield Publishers, Inc.

British Library Cataloguing in Publication Information Available

Library of Congress Cataloging-in-Publication Data

Social class and stratification : classic statements and theoretical
  debates / edited by Rhonda F. Levine.
     p. cm.
   Includes bibliographical references and index.
   ISBN 0-8476-8542-X (cloth : alk. paper). — ISBN 0-8476-8543-8
(pbk. : alk. paper)
    1. Social classes. 2. Social classes in literature. 3. Social
classes—United States. 4. Social structure—United States.
5. Equality. 6. United States—Social conditions. I. Levine,
Rhonda F.
HT609.S6215   1998
305.5'0973—dc21   98-14690
                                                       CIP

ISBN 0-8476-8542-X (cloth : alk. paper)
ISBN 0-8476-8543-8 (pbk. : alk. paper)

Printed in the United States of America

♾ ™ The paper used in this publication meets the minimum requirements of
American National Standard for Information Sciences—Permanence of Paper for
Printed Library Materials, ANSI Z39.48-1984.

To Jeremy and Andrew

Contents

Preface   ix

Introduction   1

Part I. Classical Perspectives on Social Class

1. Manifesto of the Communist Party   12
   Karl Marx and Friedrich Engels

2. On Classes   41
   Karl Marx

3. Class, Status, Party   43
   Max Weber

   Related Readings   57

Part II. American Stratification Theory

4. What Social Class Is in America   60
   W. Lloyd Warner, Marchia Meeker, and Kenneth Eells

5. Some Principles of Stratification   86
   Kingsley Davis and Wilbert E. Moore

6. Some Principles of Stratification: A Critical Analysis   99
   Melvin M. Tumin

   Related Readings   111

Part III: Neo-Marxian and Neo-Weberian Perspectives on Social Class

7. Marx and Weber: Problems of Class Structure   114
   Anthony Giddens

8. Marxism and Class Theory: A Bourgeois Critique   119
   Frank Parkin

9. Class Analysis   141
   Erik Olin Wright

   Related Readings   166

Part IV: Nonclass Forms of Inequality: Statements on Gender and Racial Stratification

10 The Patriarchal Family   169
    Friedrich Engels

11. The Position of Women   173
    Juliet Mitchell

12. Class, Status, and Gender   192
    David Lockwood

13. Double-Consciousness and the Veil   208
    W. E. B. Du Bois

14. Facets of the Negro Problem   215
    Gunnar Myrdal

15. Race and Class   227
    Oliver Cox

16. Toward a New Vision: Race, Class, and Gender as
    Categories of Analysis and Connection   231
    Patricia Hill Collins

    Related Readings   248

Conclusion   249

Index   261

About the Editor   269

Preface

The idea for this collection grew out of my experience teaching courses on social inequality at least sixteen times over the past twenty years. Each time I teach the course, I change the syllabus, adding new books and topics for discussion but always including selections from classic statements on social class and stratification. Since there is no text containing the materials I always assign, I would find myself putting readings on reserve reading lists and hoping students would eventually find their way to the library. This collection, I hope, will be welcomed by teachers and students of social inequality, who would like to have the classic statements in one convenient place, and also by reserve librarians, who will no longer need to keep track of numerous folders containing the same articles year after year.

The selections were chosen on the basis of their lasting impact on the study of social class and stratification. My aim was to keep this volume short, and certainly other readings could have been included to represent the varied approaches to the study of social inequality. I have purposely focused on inequality in the industrial and so-called postindustrial areas of the world. It is my hope that students and teachers will be stimulated to read beyond the selections in this volume. To that end, I have included a short list of related readings at the end of each part of the book.

Many people have helped me to see this work to fruition. Dean Birkenkamp, executive editor at Rowman & Littlefield, supported the project from its inception. His guidance and excellent editorial advice were essential in helping me shape the list of readings and making my own contributions "reader friendly." I am thankful for discussions with Mort Wenger, Erik Olin Wright, and Jim Geschwender that helped me clarify my own views on differences between abstract theory and empirical research. My thanks to Joe Feagin, Craig Jenkins, Tom Hall, and Mary Romero for their extremely helpful comments on the Introduction and Conclusion. Very special thanks to Bill Domhoff for his constant support, his careful reading of and valued comments on the Introduction and Conclusion, and his reminder that I was writing for students. And finally, my thanks to Jeremy and Andrew for helping me, however unwittingly, to structure my time so that my work did not take away from the joy of being their mother.

Rhonda F. Levine

Introduction

W hy are some people rich and others poor? Why do some young people go to private schools and others to public schools, some to private colleges and others to state universities, while still others receive no formal education past high school? Why do some people rent apartments while others own houses? Why do some folks shop at Bloomingdales and others at Wal-Mart? Why are some people more likely than others to become homeless and seek public assistance? Why are some people more likely than others to become corporate executives and professionals rather than skilled or unskilled laborers? How do we explain the "pecking order" in contemporary society and make sense of its various social and economic hierarchies?

Social stratification is about making sense of, or at least trying to explain and understand, the various hierarchies that exist within societies. We could say that social stratification is the study of the unequal distribution of societal resources. Stratification theory and research seek to understand who gets what and attempt to explain why.

Students interested in why there are rich and poor, and the social consequences of inequality, often question the relevance of reading "the classics." They might wonder why views of "dead white men" need to be taken seriously or even read at all. Most students take sociology courses because of an interest in contemporary societies, and foremost on their minds is an understanding of the nature and consequences of social inequality in the present. Professors are urged to teach the newest approaches to the study of inequality, to present the latest in both research and theory, and to pay due attention to current controversial topics such as welfare reform and affirmative action programs. Having to read the classics, or anything written more than a decade ago, seems like an intellectual exercise that many students would prefer to avoid. Classical theorists, especially ones like Karl Marx and Max Weber, are excessively wordy and employ a nineteenth-century German academic style that is sometimes quite difficult to read, let alone comprehend. Beyond that, students may argue, our world is far different from the world of nineteenth- and twentieth-century social theorists; we have electricity, television, cars, computers, and much more. We have many more opportunities than people did nearly a century ago; our standard of living would have been unheard of even fifty years ago. The class structure is much more complicated than it was then. Race and gender appear to many students as more salient and relevant bases for inequality than simply occupation and/or income. What can the classics possibly tell us about our world and our society?

The purpose of this book is to show that reading the classics is much more than an intellectual exercise. The classic statements on both social class and stratification provide the foundation from which we can fully appreciate current social dynamics and new directions in the study of social inequality. This collection of essays brings together important contributions to ongoing debates on the nature of class, race, and gender inequality in contemporary societies. Only by reading the classics can we understand both the thinking and the historical events that led to today's complex global economy, social structure, and culture.

Social class is one of the most widely used concepts in modern sociology and social science, yet little agreement exists as to its exact meaning or its usefulness for understanding contemporary inequalities. Nevertheless, class, whether it refers to those who share similar experiences and social networks, or to a position in the social structure, is an important variable in understanding how resources are distributed and who has access to them. The boundaries of classes and the way class is experienced have profound implications for public policy directed at reducing social inequality as well as political strategy for altering existing stratification systems. Much debate has developed over conceptualizing class independently from other social positions, such as age, race, gender, marital status, or even sexual preference. Is class, for example, as powerful a variable as race and/or gender in explaining the extent of and the experience of inequality?

Most analyses of class take the lifetime of thought and writing by Karl Marx as the point of departure. Understanding the basics of Marx's ideas will help us to appreciate all subsequent writings on inequality. Conflicts between high and low social classes are of critical importance in Marx's view of history and the development of capitalism. He thinks such conflicts are the engines that make history. Marx himself, however, offers no systematic analysis of the concept of class, and generations of scholars since Marx have yet to arrive at a consensus over the various aspects of the concept of class. Most of Marx's writings were concerned with critiquing the emerging industrial capitalist society rather than building theories of socialism. As such, his work on class was not fully developed. Marx, in effect, explains classes in terms of the relationship of individuals to the structure of ownership and paid labor, what he referred to as *social relations of production*. This aspect of Marx's analysis of classes is different from the common understanding of social classes in terms of income and purchasing power, or what Marx might have called *market* or *exchange relations*.

On the abstract level, capitalist society, for Marx, was composed of three fundamental classes: the capitalists (owners of the means of production), the workers (nonpropertied wage-labor), and the petty-bourgeois (those outside of capitalist social relations of production, the self-employed, professionals, and so on). Classes were conceptualized as relational categories. Capitalists could not exist without workers, for all value was produced by the labor of workers. For Marx, what distinguished these two classes was their relationship to the production process, what Marx called the *means of production*. The defining characteristics of the relationship between labor and capital can be understood by the nature of the capitalist production system, which for Marx was based on exploitation. For Marx, exploitation had a very specific meaning that referred to the nature of a relationship. Workers own no capital; they start out with only a commodity—their labor power, or capacity to work. They in turn sell their labor power for money, or wages. With that money, they buy more commodities, such as food, clothing, housing, and other consumer goods. Capitalists, on the other hand, start out with capital, or money. With that money they buy labor power. With the purchase of labor power, the capitalist ends up with more money, or profit. In the course of a working day, the worker produces commodities, which contain value. The wage the worker receives is not equivalent to the total value being produced. In other words, part of the working day goes to the production of value, which the worker receives in terms of wages. The other part of the working day goes toward the production of what Marx called *surplus value,* or value that goes to the capitalist in terms of profit. Without the production of surplus value, the capitalist could not remain a capitalist. With the profit made from the labor of workers, the capitalist lives on, reinvests, and makes more money—what Marx referred to as *capital accumulation*. Exploitation, in the Marxist sense, refers to the production of surplus value. For Marx, the process of exploitation is not only what defines capitalism but also the root of basic inequality in capitalist society.

Moreover, given the exploitative nature of capitalism, social classes are in contradictory and antagonistic relation with one another. It is in the interest of workers to receive the full value of what is being produced. It is in the interest of the owners to accumulate as much profit as possible.

Since profit comes from surplus value, and surplus value is the value labor produces but does not get compensated for in the form of wages, then it follows that workers cannot receive the full value of what is being produced if capitalists are to receive a profit. This is what Marx meant when he said workers and owners are in a relationship of contradiction, since labor cannot receive the full value of labor power while capitalists make a profit. Workers can receive higher wages and enjoy a higher standard of living at the same time capitalists can increase profits, if the *rate of exploitation* is increased. For example, the introduction of labor-saving machinery can increase labor productivity in such a way that workers may double the value they produce in an even shorter period of time, enabling capitalists to increase wages while still increasing their own profit, provided that workers are still producing surplus value, the source of profit.

It is this "hidden" contradiction that results in the antagonistic relationship between labor and capital and forms the basis for conflict in capitalist society. Hence, the opposing interests of the two different classes (the interest of the capitalists being the increase in profits and the interest of the working class being the increase in wages) lead the two classes to objective conflict. It is this objective conflict, or antagonistic, contradictory relationship, which Marx called *class struggle,* that defines the basic historical process of change for Marx. The Marxist concern for a precise definition of class and an analysis of particular class structures stems from the proposition that members of the same class have the potential to engage in common collective action. For Marxists this means forming unions, joining a socialist political party, or even revolutionizing the entire social system so that exploitation and unequal property relations no longer exist.

Hence, a central Marxist premise is that capitalism is a contradictory system and that a basic contradiction of capitalism is the conflict between labor and capital. This conflict is an antagonistic one because the survival of one class (the capitalist class) depends upon the exploitation of another (the working class). This contradiction reveals itself in conflict between labor and capital over hours and working conditions, or what Marx called the *rate of exploitation.* The debate over the precise boundaries of classes is important not merely as an esoteric, theoretical exercise but in a very practical sense with respect to locating the class that is most likely to be the historical agent for changing a system based on exploitation. One of the most complete statements on the continued significance of understanding classes in terms of relations of exploitation is Erik Olin Wright's essay in this volume. Wright elaborates on the significance of class boundaries and also extends the Marxist analysis of class to account for those who neither own capital nor produce surplus value, such as managers, professionals, clerical workers, and others who comprise the large segment of "middle classes."

Whereas Marx and those following the Marxist tradition argue that exploitation is the key to understanding social inequality in capitalist society and that an understanding of social classes based on property relations is a necessary ingredient in understanding this process, Max Weber and those who followed his lead elaborate on Marx and define classes primarily in terms of *exchange relations* or *market situation*. For Weber, classes are stratified in terms of the production process and the manner in which goods and services are acquired. Market situation for Weber is closely related to what we call today socioeconomic status. One's market situation depends to a great extent on the resources one possesses, such as certain skills, education, or even inherited wealth, and how these resources translate into purchasing power. The Weberian alternative to Marxist class analysis is based on the critique of defining class solely in terms of production relations and the insistence that production relations are only relative and not absolute in understanding one's standing in the social structure. For example, education, and not ownership of capital, may lead to certain occupations with high incomes, enabling one to live a comfortable lifestyle. While Weberians do not deny the importance of class conflict in understanding the trajectory of social change, Weberian conceptualizations do not adhere to the view of the antagonistic character of capitalist social relations of production. Class divisions and the conditions for class self-identity and therefore class-oriented activity are understood primarily in terms of different *life chances*—the chances an individual has for sharing in the economic and sociocultural goods of a society, such as income and education. Technical factors are argued to shape the form of the market and relations of exchange. For example, the development of various technologies has transformed the way goods are produced, resulting in fewer workers involved in skilled labor-intensive work. The introduction of computers, to take just one example, has transformed the newspaper industry. Whereas printers used to set type, compose the page, and run the presses, the advent of new technologies has made printing as a skilled trade obsolete. Newspaper stories can now go almost directly from the computer to the printing press. Forty years ago, being able to set type and mix inks was a skill that led to certain life chances, that is, they secured a certain job with a certain income. Today, different skills are in demand. Obsolete skills like printing do not lead to the same life chances they did forty years ago. New skills—knowledge of computers, for example—are necessary to secure a high-paying job in the newspaper industry today. The objective formation of classes, that is, classes that are shaped by the structure of ownership and work, whether or not individuals are aware of it, are defined in accordance with the subjective self-identity of the class, or how the individuals understand their own class position. Common life chances are what often give rise to *collective action,* such as protest, lobbying, or other forms of organized advocacy. People do not normally act in accordance with their class position but rather in terms of their *status group,* the collectivity of individuals who share similar consumption patterns and lifestyles.

For Weber, stratification results from more than unequal property relations. Living in a time when industrial capitalism was more developed than when Marx was writing, Weber witnessed a more complex class structure. Social stratification, he argued, is a result of the unequal distribution of power. Power derives from three different sources: class (economic power), status (social power), and parties (political power). Weber encompasses Marx on economic factors, but adds social and political factors—factors that cannot simply be derived from the economic. Weber's discussion of class and status groups is most relevant for a discussion of the American stratification system. Economic class refers to "market situation," not just property relations as in the Marxist view but also skill and education. For Weber, skills and education that were scarce on the market commanded high salaries and constituted a class.

It is Weber's discussion of status groups that is probably the clearest divergence from Marx. For Weber, status groups are collectivities of people with similar lifestyles, and they often overlap with economic class position. Whereas an economic class is an aggregate of individuals with similar market situations, a status group is a community of people who share similar lifestyles and interact as equals. People act in accordance with their status group, not necessarily their economic class. Status groups often encompass ecomomic classes, however, so the two concepts are not necessarily mutually exclusive. The process of *social closure,* embracing both *inclusionary* and *exclusionary principles,* is what maintains status differences and helps to explain status-based stratification. Groups attempt to improve or maintain their position, or life chances, by restricting access to rewards and privileges to those who share similar lifestyles and other socially defined characteristics. People are either included or excluded based on these status similarities and/or differences. Racially exclusive country clubs, for example, may be understood as having both inclusionary and exclusionary principles. Although whites and people of color may be in the same economic class position sponsorship may be forthcoming only for whites and absent for people of color. White people are included, whereas people of color are excluded on the basis of race. Frank Parkin's selection in this volume elaborates on the Weberian notion of status groups and social closure.

The Weberian perspective on social class has raised serious challenges to the usefulness of the Marxist concept of class in understanding inequality and processes of social change. If class in the Marxist sense is a viable concept, then why hasn't the working class instigated revolutionary movements throughout the world? For critics of the Marxist view, the answer is quite simple. There is either no necessary correspondence between economics and politics in general, or the entire premise of Marxist class analysis, one based on conflict and exploitation, is simply not valid.

Early American stratification theory was based on this very critique. Sociologists such as Lloyd Warner and his associates completely rejected Marx's way of looking at inequality. In their work reprinted in this volume, Warner, Meeker, and Eells implicitly argue that stratification systems arise out of different styles of life, that all complex societies have rank orderings because of the division of labor, and, furthermore, stratification is a result of how communities judge individual lifestyles. Moreover, class conflict, central to Marx's view, was seen as both unnecessary and undesirable. American stratification theory, while paying little attention to macrotheories of social class, did provide insight into how class and status operate in everyday lives. With its focus on status and community judgments, early stratification theory based its analysis on why class, in the Marxist view, was not relevant in the American case. Written in the early post–World War II period, early stratification theory stressed that conflict was not integral to the economic or political system but was reduced to a multitude of lifestyle differences.

Whereas conflict may not be necessary, according to Warner, functionalist theories of stratification stressed that inequality was indeed necessary in all industrialized societies. Again, rejecting the Marxist view that the economic system of capitalism required exploitation leading to inequalities, functionalist theories argued that all industrial societies, not just capitalist ones, required a differential system of rewards. In their article reprinted in this volume, Kingsley Davis and Wilbert Moore argue that differential rewards are necessary to motivate the best people to occupy the most important and difficult positions that are required in complex industrialized societies. Differential rewards are also necessary to motivate people to perform the duty of the position. As a result, stratification systems and the extent of inequality are justified as necessary to the functioning of complex societies.

The functionalist theory of stratification has come under great criticism, first and most notably by Melvin Tumin. In his article reprinted here, Tumin questions the assumptions that Davis and Moore make, such as the necessity and universality of inequality. In addition, taking a somewhat Weberian view, Tumin argues that inequality does not result from differential motivations, skills, or talents but from power differences. He calls into question the functional necessity of stratification and argues that stratification systems may actually be dysfunctional because they bar societies from discovering the talents of a wide range of individuals.

Most early research and theory on inequality largely ignored nonclass forms of stratification, namely, race and gender, which were seen as secondary forms of inequality within a general class analytic framework, no matter how class was defined. It was not until well into the 1970s that books began to pay due attention to these nonclass forms of stratification. This is not to say, however, that scholars had not dealt with issues of racial and gender inequality. Friedrich Engels, for example, in his classic work on the family and private property, laid out a materialist conception of women's subservience to men under capitalism, linking the development of capitalism with the subordination of women's roles to those of men. As the selections in this volume by W. E. B. Du Bois, Oliver Cox, and Gunnar Myrdal illustrate, scholars were concerned for some time about how to conceptualize racial inequality, particularly the peculiarities of race relations in the United States. The historical experience of slavery and its lingering consequences produced a complex stratification system kept in place not only by social and economic factors but by ideological factors as well. Nevertheless, most of the analyses of gender and racial inequality were still framed within an overall class analysis of the social structure, with racial and gender stratification being understood as a consequence of the class system. The civil rights movement and the women's movement of the late 1960s and early 1970s made it clear that racial and gender inequality could no longer be ignored or treated as secondary variables in understanding systems of inequality. Now, it is rare for standard social stratification textbooks to ignore the complexities of these nonclass forms of inequality.

The concern with gender and racial inequality, and corresponding political movements that stressed diversity and multiculturalism, had a continuous effect on the world of academia, but it was not until the late 1980s that sociologists began conceptualizing the intersection of class, gender, and race. In her essay in this volume, Patricia Hill Collins outlines a model to conceptualize class, race, and gender as interconnected systems that shape relationships of inequality. Collins's conceptual piece is but one example of the tremendous body of work that has been produced in the past decade that attempts both to conceptualize and to research the intersection of race, class, and gender inequality. Although this new work challenges the traditional approaches to the study of inequality, it is nevertheless an elaboration of the foundations set by Marx and Weber in their classical perspectives on the nature of inequality. Marx's view of class, for example, provides a basis for understanding that although it may be true that women, in general, still earn less money than men, the degree of inequality a woman experiences depends upon her class position. Hence, a female factory worker is in a very different position from the wife of a corporate executive. The former probably experiences gender inequality in a way that cannot be separated from her class position and that is in stark contrast to the gender inequality that a female corporate lawyer may face. In a similar vein, Weber's discussion of social closure provides great insight as to how racial and gender inequality are maintained through inclusionary and exclusionary principles, as the previous example of a racially exclusive country club suggests.

We can see how today's debates on class, race, and gender are rooted in thinkers all the way back to Karl Marx. In fact, the structure of today's world rests on the social relations of the recent past—of industrialization and its corresponding structures of inequality. This history of events, politics, economic transformations, and social thought will open a window onto the present and help us understand current debates and new directions in the study of class, race, and gender, and their intersection, in the context of the persistence of inequality.

Part I

Classical Perspectives on Social Class

"Manifesto of the Communist Party," written in 1848 by Karl Marx and Friedrich Engels, is the classic Marxist statement on the nature of class conflict under capitalism. The work is both a political tract and a piece of social theory. Students should keep in mind that the Manifesto was written at a time when democratic revolutions were occurring throughout Europe, which explains its rather optimistic tone. Marx and Engels were radical democrats promoting as well as analyzing these revolutions. For the purposes of class analysis, Marx and Engels's predictions are far less important than the method of analysis that they present. Marx's "On Classes" is an unfinished piece written as a chapter in Volume III of *Capital,* published in 1886. In this selection, Marx acknowledges that there are a multitude of class strata in existing capitalist societies. Nevertheless, he indicates that on a general level of abstraction, we can speak of three major classes with intermediary class strata. In this short piece, Marx gives an indication of his own distinction between a theoretical analysis of class on the most abstract level of the mode of production, and the concrete analysis of classes in actually existing societies. Max Weber's classic work "Class, Status, Party" is excerpted from his *Economy and Society,* Volume II, left unfinished when he died in 1920. This piece offers Weber's most systematic effort to elaborate on Marx's notion of class with a discussion of the importance of status groups and political parties for an understanding of the unequal distribution of power. This selection also makes clear that what marked the major distinction between Marx and Weber was that Marx viewed classes in terms of their relations to the production process, whereas Weber conceptualized social class in terms of "market situation" or exchange relations.

→ 1 ←

Manifesto of the Communist Party

Karl Marx and Friedrich Engels

A spectre is haunting Europe—the spectre of Communism. All the Powers of old Europe have entered into a holy alliance to exorcise this spectre: Pope and Czar, Metternich and Guizot, French Radicals and German police-spies.

Where is the party in opposition that has not been decried as Communistic by its opponents in power? Where the Opposition that has not hurled back the branding reproach of Communism, against the more advanced opposition parties, as well as against its reactionary adversaries?

Two things result from this fact.

I. Communism is already acknowledged by all European Powers to be itself a Power.

II. It is high time that Communists should openly, in the face of the whole world, publish their views, their aims, their tendencies, and meet this nursery tale of the Spectre of Communism with a Manifesto of the party itself.

To this end, Communists of various nationalities have assembled in London, and sketched the following Manifesto, to be published in the English, French, German, Italian, Flemish and Danish languages.

Reprinted from Karl Marx and Friedrich Engels, *Selected Works in One Volume* (New York: International Publishers, 1970): 35–63, by permission of the publisher.

I. Bourgeois and Proletarians[1]

The history of all hitherto existing society[2] is the history of class struggles.

Freeman and slave, patrician and plebeian, lord and serf, guild-master[3] and journeyman, in a word, oppressor and oppressed, stood in constant opposition to one another, carried on an uninterrupted, now hidden, now open fight, a fight that each time ended, either in a revolutionary reconstitution of society at large, or in the common ruin of the contending classes.

In the earlier epochs of history, we find almost everywhere a complicated arrangement of society into various orders, a manifold gradation of social rank. In ancient Rome we have patricians, knights, plebeians, slaves; in the Middle Ages, feudal lords, vassals, guild-masters, journeymen, apprentices, serfs; in almost all of these classes, again, subordinate gradations.

The modern bourgeois society that has sprouted from the ruins of feudal society has not done away with class antagonisms. It has but established new classes, new conditions of oppression, new forms of struggle in place of the old ones.

Our epoch, the epoch of the bourgeoisie, possesses, however, this distinctive feature: it has simplified the class antagonisms. Society as a whole is more and more splitting up into two great hostile camps, into two great classes directly facing each other: Bourgeoisie and Proletariat.

From the serfs of the Middle Ages sprang the chartered burghers of the earliest towns. From these burgesses the first elements of the bourgeoisie were developed.

The discovery of America, the rounding of the Cape, opened up fresh ground for the rising bourgeoisie. The East-Indian and Chinese markets, the colonisation of America, trade with the colonies, the increase in the means of exchange and in commodities generally, gave to commerce, to navigation, to industry, an impulse never before known, and thereby, to the revolutionary element in the tottering feudal society, a rapid development.

The feudal system of industry, under which industrial production was monopolised by closed guilds, now no longer sufficed for the growing wants of the new markets. The manufacturing system took its place. The guild-masters were pushed on one side by the manufacturing middle class; division of labour between the different corporate guilds vanished in the face of division of labour in each single workshop.

Meantime the markets kept ever growing, the demand ever rising. Even manufacture no longer sufficed. Thereupon, steam and machinery revolutionised industrial production. The place of manufacture was taken by the giant, Modern Industry, the place of the industrial middle class, by industrial millionaires, the leaders of whole industrial armies, the modern bourgeois.

Modern industry has established the world-market, for which the discovery of American paved the way. This market has given an immense development to commerce, to navigation, to communication by land. This develoment has, in its turn, reacted on the extension of industry; and in proportion as industry, commerce, navigation, railways extended, in the same proportion the bourgeoisie developed, increased its capital, and pushed into the background every class handed down from the Middle Ages.

We see, therefore, how the modern bourgeoisie is itself the product of a long course of development, of a series of revolutions in the modes of production and of exchange.

Each step in the development of the bourgeoisie was accompanied by a corresponding political advance of that class. An oppressed class under the sway of the feudal nobility, an armed and self-governing association in the mediaeval commune[4]; here independent urban republic (as in Italy and Germany), there taxable "third estate" of the monarchy (as in France), afterwards, in the period of manufacture proper, serving either the semi-feudal or the absolute monarchy as a counterpoise against the nobility, and, in fact, corner-stone of the great monarchies in general, the bourgeoisie has at last, since the establishment of Modern Industry and of the world-market, conquered for itself, in the modern representative State, exclusive political sway. The executive of the modern State is but a committee for managing the common affairs of the whole bourgeoisie.

The bourgeoisie, historically, has played a most revolutionary part.

The bourgeoisie, wherever it has got the upper hand, has put an end to all feudal, patriarchal, idyllic relations. It has pitilessly torn asunder the motley feudal ties that bound man to his "natural superiors," and has left remaining no other nexus between man and man than naked self-interest, than callous "cash payment." It has drowned the most heavenly ecstasies of religious fervour, of chivalrous enthusiasm, of philistine sentimentalism, in the icy water of egotistical calculation. It has resolved personal worth into exchange value, and in place of the numberless indefeasible chartered freedoms, has set up that single, unconscionable freedom—Free Trade. In one word, for exploitation, veiled by religious and political illusions, it has substituted naked, shameless, direct, brutal exploitation.

The bourgeoisie has stripped of its halo every occupation hitherto honoured and looked up to with reverent awe. It has converted the physician, the lawyer, the priest, the poet, the man of science, into its paid wage-labourers.

The bourgeoisie has torn away from the family its sentimental veil, and has reduced the family relation to a mere money relation.

The bourgeoisie has disclosed how it came to pass that the brutal display of vigour in the Middle Ages, which Reactionists so much admire, found its fitting complement in the most slothful indolence. It has been the first to show what man's activity can bring about. It has accomplished wonders far surpassing Egyptian pyramids, Roman aqueducts, and Gothic cathedrals; it has conducted expeditions that put in the shade all former Exoduses of nations and crusades.

The bourgeoisie cannot exist without constantly revolutionising the instruments of production, and thereby the relations of production, and with them the whole relations of society. Conservation of the old modes of production in unaltered form, was, on the contrary, the first condition of existence for all earlier industrial classes. Constant revolutionising of production, uninterrupted disturbance of all social conditions, everlasting uncertainty and agitation distinguish the bourgeois epoch from all earlier ones. All fixed, fast-frozen relations, with their train of ancient and venerable prejudices and opinions, are swept away, all new-formed ones become antiquated before they can ossify. All that is solid melts into air, all that is holy is profaned, and man is at last compelled to face with sober senses, his real conditions of life, and his relations with his kind.

The need of a constantly expanding market for its products chases the bourgeoisie over the whole surface of the globe. It must nestle everywhere, settle everywhere, establish connexions everywhere.

The bourgeoisie has through its exploitation of the world-market given a cosmopolitan character to production and consumption in every country. To the great chagrin of Reactionists, it has drawn from under the feet of industry the national ground on which it stood. All old-established national industries have been destroyed or are daily being destroyed. They are dislodged by new industries, whose introduction becomes a life and death question for all civilised nations, by industries that no longer work up indigenous raw material, but raw material drawn from the remotest zones; industries whose products are consumed, not only at home, but in every quarter of the globe. In place of the old wants, satisfied by the productions of the country, we find new wants, requiring for their satisfaction the products of distant lands and climes. In place of the old local and national seclusion and self-sufficiency, we have intercourse in every direction, universal inter-dependence of nations. And as in material, so also in intellectual production. The intellectual creations of individual nations become common property. National one-sidedness and narrow-mindedness become more and more impossible, and from the numerous national and local literatures, there arises a world literature.

The bourgeoisie, by the rapid improvement of all instruments of production, by the immensely facilitated means of communication, draws all, even the most barbarian, nations into civilisation. The cheap prices of its commodities are the heavy artillery with which it batters down all Chinese walls, with which it forces the barbarians' intensely obstinate hatred of foreigners to capitulate. It compels all nations, on pain of extinction, to adopt the bourgeois mode of production; it compels them to introduce what it calls civilisation into their midst, *i.e.,* to become bourgeois themselves. In one word, it creates a world after its own image.

The bourgeoisie has subjected the country to the rule of the towns. It has created enormous cities, has greatly increased the urban population as compared with the rural, and has thus rescued a considerable part of the population from the idiocy of rural life. Just as it has made the country dependent on the towns, so it has made barbarian and semi-barbarian countries dependent on the civilised ones, nations of peasants on nations of bourgeois, the East on the West.

The bourgeoisie keeps more and more doing away with the scattered state of the population, of the means of production, and of property. It has agglomerated population, centralised means of production, and has concentrated property in a few hands. The necessasry consequence of this was political centralisation. Independent, or but loosely connected provinces, with separate interests, laws, governments and systems of taxation, became lumped together into one nation, with one government, one code of laws, one national class-interest, one frontier and one customs-tariff.

The bourgeoisie, during its rule of scarce one hundred years, has created more massive and more colossal productive forces than have all preceding generations together. Subjection of Nature's forces to man, machinery, application of chemistry to industry and agriculture, steam-navigation, railways, electric telegraphs, clearing of whole continents for cultivation, canalisation of rivers, whole populations conjured out of the ground—what earlier century had even a presentiment that such productive forces slumbered in the lap of social labour?

We see then: the means of production and of exchange, on whose foundation the bourgeoisie built itself up, were generated in feudal society. At a certain stage in the development of these means of production and of exchange, the conditions under which feudal society produced and exchanged, the feudal organisation of agriculture and manufacturing industry, in one word, the feudal relations of property became no longer compatible with the already developed productive forces; they became so many fetters. They had to be burst asunder; they were burst asunder.

Into their place stepped free competition, accompanied by a social and political constitution adapted to it, and by the economical and political sway of the bourgeois class.

A similar movement is going on before our own eyes. Modern bourgeois society with its relations of production, of exchange and of property, a society that has conjured up such gigantic means of production and of exchange, is like the sorcerer, who is no longer able to control the powers of the nether world whom he has called up by his spells. For many a decade past the history of industry and commerce is but the history of the revolt of modern productive forces against modern conditions of production, against the property relations that are the conditions for the existence of the bourgeoisie and of its rule. It is enough to mention the commerical crises that by their periodical return put on its trial, each time more threateningly, the existence of the entire bourgeois society. In these crises a great part not only of the existing products, but also of the previously created productive forces, are periodically destroyed. In these crises there breaks out an epidemic that, in all earlier epochs, would have seemed an absurdity—the epidemic of over-production. Society suddenly finds itself put back into a state of momentary barbarism; it appears as if a famine, a universal war of devastation had cut off the supply of every means of subsistence; industry and commerce seem to be destroyed; and why? Because there is too much civilisation, too much means of subsistence, too much industry, too much commerce. The productive forces at the disposal of society no longer tend to further the development of the conditions of bourgeois property; on the contrary, they have become too powerful for these conditions, by which they are fettered, and so soon as they overcome these fetters, they bring disorder into the whole of bourgeois society, endanger the existence of bourgeois property. The conditions of bourgeois society are too narrow to comprise the wealth created by them. And how does the bourgeoisie get over these crises? On the one hand by enforced destruction of a mass of productive forces; on the other, by the conquest of new markets, and by the more thorough exploitation of the old ones. That is to say, by paving the way for more extensive and more destructive crises, and by diminishing the means whereby crises are prevented.

The weapons with which the bourgeoisie felled feudalism to the ground are now turned against the bourgeoisie itself.

But not only has the bourgeoisie forged the weapons that bring death to itself; it has also called into existence the men who are to wield those weapons—the modern working class—the proletarians.

In proportion as the bourgeoisie, i.e., capital, is developed, in the same proportion is the proletariat, the modern working class, developed—a class of labourers, who live only so long as they find work, and who find work only so long as their labour increases capital. These labourers, who must sell themselves piecemeal, are a commodity, like every other article of commerce, and are consequently exposed to all the vicissitudes of competition, to all the fluctuations of the market.

Owing to the extensive use of machinery and to division of labour, the work of the proletarians has lost all individual character, and, consequently, all charm for the workman. He becomes an appendage of the machine, and it is only the most simple, most monotonous, and most easily acquired knack, that is required of him. Hence, the cost of production of a workman is restricted, almost entirely, to the means of subsistence that he requires for his maintenance, and for the propagation of his race. But the price of a commodity, and therefore also of labour, is equal to its cost of production. In proportion, therefore, as the repulsiveness of the work increases, the wage decreases. Nay more, in proportion as the use of machinery and division of labour increases, in the same proportion the burden of toil also increases, whether by prolongation of the working hours, by increase of the work exacted in a given time or by increased speed of the machinery, etc.

Modern industry has converted the little workshop of the patriarchal master into the great factory of the industrial capitalist. Masses of labourers, crowded into the factory, are organised like soldiers. As privates of the industrial army they are placed under the command of a perfect hierarchy of officers and sergeants. Not only are they slaves of the bourgeois class, and of the bourgeois State; they are daily and hourly enslaved by the machine, by the overlooker, and, above all, by the individual bourgeois manufacturer himself. The more openly this despotism proclaims gain to be its end and aim, the more petty, the more hateful and the more embittering it is.

The less the skill and exertion of strength implied in manual labour, in other words, the more modern industry becomes developed, the more is the labour of men superseded by that of women. Differences of age and sex have no longer any distinctive social validity for the working class. All are instruments of labour, more or less expensive to use, according to their age and sex.

No sooner is the exploitation of the labourer by the manufacturer, so far, at an end, and he receives his wages in cash, than he is set upon by the other portions of the bourgeoisie, the landlord, the shopkeeper, the pawnbroker, etc.

The lower strata of the middle class—the small tradespeople, shopkeepers, and retired tradesmen generally, the handicraftsmen and peasants—all these sink gradually into the proletariat, partly because their diminutive capital does not suffice for the scale on which Modern Industry is carried on, and is swamped in the competition with the large capitalists, partly because their specialised skill is rendered worthless by new methods of production. Thus the proletariat is recruited from all classes of the population.

The proletariat goes through various stages of development. With its birth begins its struggle with the bourgeoisie. At first the contest is carried on by individual labourers, then by the workpeople of a factory, then by the operatives of one trade, in one locality, against the individual bourgeois who directly exploits them. They direct their attacks not against the bourgeois conditions of production, but against the instruments of production themselves; they destroy imported wares that compete with their labour, they smash to pieces machinery, they set factories ablaze, they seek to restore by force the vanished status of the workman of the Middle Ages.

At this stage the labourers still form an incoherent mass scattered over the whole country, and broken up by their mutual competition. If anywhere they unite to form more compact bodies, this is not yet the consequence of their own active union, but of the union of the bourgeoisie, which class, in order to attain its own political ends, is compelled to set the whole proletariat in motion, and is moreover yet, for a time, able to do so. At this stage, therefore, the proletarians do not fight their enemies, but the enemies of their enemies, the remnants of absolute monarchy, the landowners, the non-industrial bourgeois, the petty bourgeoisie. Thus the whole historical movement is concentrated in the hands of the bourgeoisie; every victory so obtained is a victory for the bourgeoisie.

But with the development of industry the proletariat not only increases in number; it becomes concentrated in greater masses, its strength grows, and it feels that strength more. The various interests and conditions of life within the ranks of the proletariat are more and more equalised, in proportion as machinery obliterates all distinctions of labour, and nearly everywhere reduces wages to the same low level. The growing competition among the bourgeois, and the resulting commercial crises, make the wages of the workers ever more fluctuating. The unceasing improvement of machinery, ever more rapidly developing, makes their livelihood more and more precarious; the collisions between individual workmen and individual bourgeois take more and more the character of collisions between two classes. Thereupon the workers begin to form combinations (Trades' Unions) against the bourgeois; they club together in order to keep up the rate of wages; they found permanent associations in order to make provision beforehand for these occasional revolts. Here and there the contest breaks out into riots.

Now and then the workers are victorious, but only for a time. The real fruit of their battles lies, not in the immediate result, but in the ever-expanding union of the workers. This union is helped on by the improved means of communication that are created by modern industry and that place the workers of different localities in contact with one another. It was just this contact that was needed to centralise the numerous local struggles, all of the same character, into one national struggle between classes. But every class struggle is a political struggle. And that union, to attain which the burghers of the Middle Ages, with their miserable highways, required centuries, the modern proletarians, thanks to railways, achieve in a few years.

This organisation of the proletarians into a class, and consequently into a political party, is continually being upset again by the competition between the workers themselves. But it ever rises up again, stronger, firmer, mightier. It compels legislative recognition of particular interests of the workers, by taking advantage of the divisions among the bourgeoisie itself. Thus the ten-hours' bill in England was carried.

Altogether collisions between the classes of the old society further, in many ways, the course of development of the proletariat. The bourgeoisie finds itself involved in a constant battle. At first with the aristocracy; later on, with those portions of the bourgeoisie itself, whose interests have become antagonistic to the progress of industry; at all times, with the bourgeoisie of foreign countries. In all these battles it sees itself compelled to appeal to the proletariat, to ask for its help, and thus, to drag it into the political arena. The bourgeoisie itself, therefore, supplies the proletariat with its own elements of political and general education, in other words, it furnishes the proletariat with weapons for fighting the bourgeoisie.

Further, as we have already seen, entire sections of the ruling classes are, by the advance of industry, precipitated into the proletariat, or are at least threatened in their conditions of existence. These also supply the proletariat with fresh elements of enlightenment and progress.

Finally, in times when the class struggle nears the decisive hour, the process of dissolution going on within the ruling class, in fact within the whole range of old society, assumes such a violent, glaring character, that a small section of the ruling class cuts itself adrift, and joins the revolutionary class, the class that holds the future in its hands. Just as, therefore, at an earlier period, a section of the nobility went over to the bourgeoisie, so now a portion of the bourgeoisie goes over to the proletariat, and in particular, a portion of the bourgeois ideologists, who have raised themselves to the level of comprehending theoretically the historical movement as a whole.

Of all the classes that stand face to face with the bourgeoisie today, the proletariat alone is a really revolutionary class. The other classes decay and finally disappear in the face of Modern Industry; the proletariat is its special and essential product.

The lower middle class, the small manufacturer, the shopkeeper, the artisan, the peasant, all these fight against the bourgeoisie, to save from extinction their existence as fractions of the middle class. They are therefore not revolutionary, but conservative. Nay more, they are reactionary, for they try to roll back the wheel of history. If by chance they are revolutionary, they are so only in view of their impending transfer into the proletariat, they thus defend not their present, but their future interests, they desert their own standpoint to place themselves at that of the proletariat.

The "dangerous class," the social scum, that passively rotting mass thrown off by the lowest layers of old society, may, here and there, be swept into the movement by a proletarian revolution, its conditions of life, however, prepare it far more for the part of a bribed tool of reactionary intrigue.

In the conditions of the proletariat, those of old society at large are already virtually swamped. The proletarian is without property; his relation to his wife and children has no longer anything in common with the bourgeois family-relations; modern industrial labour, modern subjection to capital, the same in England as in France, in America as in Germany, has stripped him of every trace of national character. Law, morality, religion, are to him so many bourgeois prejudices, behind which lurk in ambush just as many bourgeois interests.

All the preceding classes that got the upper hand, sought to fortify their already acquired status by subjecting society at large to their conditions of appropriation. The proletarians cannot become masters of the productive forces of society, except by abolishing their own previous mode of appropriation, and thereby also every other previous mode of appropriation. They have nothing of their own to secure and to fortify; their mission is to destroy all previous securities for, and insurances of, individual property.

All previous historical movements were movements of minorities, or in the interests of minorities. The proletarian movement is the self-conscious, independent movement of the immense majority, in the interests of the immense majority. The proletariat, the lowest stratum of our present society, cannot stir, cannot raise itself up, without the whole superincumbent strata of official society being sprung into the air.

Though not in substance, yet in form, the struggle of the proletariat with the bourgeoisie is at first a national struggle. The proletariat of each country must, of course, first of all settle matters with its own bourgeoisie.

In depicting the most general phases of the development of the proletariat, we traced the more or less veiled civil war, raging within existing society, up to the point where that war breaks out into open revolution, and where the violent overthrow of the bourgeoisie lays the foundation for the sway of the proletariat.

Hitherto, every form of society has been based, as we have already seen, on the antagonism of oppressing and oppressed classes. But in order to oppress a class, certain conditions must be assured to it under which it can, at least, continue its slavish existence. The serf, in the period of serfdom, raised himself to membership in the commune, just as the petty bourgeois, under the yoke of feudal absolutism, managed to develop into a bourgeois. The modern labourer, on the contrary, instead of rising with the progress of industry, sinks deeper and deeper below the conditions of existence of his own class. He becomes a pauper, and pauperism develops more rapidly than population and wealth. And here it becomes evident, that the bourgeoisie is unfit any longer to be the ruling class in society, and to impose its conditions of existence upon society as an over-riding law. It is unfit to rule because it is incompetent to assure an existence to its slave within his slavery, because it cannot help letting him sink into such a state, that it has to feed him, instead of being fed by him. Society can no longer live under this bourgeoisie, in other words, its existence is no longer compatible with society.

The essential condition for the existence, and for the sway of the bourgeois class, is the formation and augmentation of capital; the condition for capital is wage-labour. Wage-labour rests exclusively on competition between the labourers. The advance of industry, whose involuntary promoter is the bourgeoisie, replaces the isolation of the labourers, due to competition, by their revolutionary combination, due to association. The development of Modern Industry, therefore, cuts from under its feet the very foundation on which the bourgeoisie produces and appropriates products. What the bourgeoisie, therefore, produces, above all, is its own grave-diggers. Its fall and the victory of the proletariat are equally inevitable.

II. Proletarians and Communists

In what relation do the Communists stand to the proletarians as a whole?

The Communists do not form a separate party opposed to other working-class parties.

They have no interests separate and apart from those of the proletariat as a whole.

They do not set up any sectarian principles of their own, by which to shape and mould the proletarian movement.

The Communists are distinguished from the other working-class parties by this only: 1. In the national struggles of the proletarians of the different countries, they point out and bring to the front the common interests of the entire proletariat, independently of all nationality. 2. In the various stages of development which the struggle of the working class against the bourgeoisie has to pass through, they always and everywhere represent the interests of the movement as a whole.

The Communists, therefore, are on the one hand, practically, the most advanced and resolute section of the working-class parties of every country, that section which pushes forward all others; on the other hand, theoretically, they have over the great mass of the proletariat the advantage of clearly understanding the line of march, the conditions, and the ultimate general results of the proletarian movement.

The immediate aim of the Communists is the same as that of all the other proletarian parties: formation of the proletariat into a class, overthrow of the bourgeois supremacy, conquest of political power by the proletariat.

The theoretical conclusions of the Communists are in no way based on ideas or principles that have been invented, or discovered, by this or that would-be universal reformer.

They merely express, in general terms, actual relations springing from an existing class struggle, from a historical movement going on under our very eyes. The abolition of existing property relations is not at all a distinctive feature of Communism.

All property relations in the past have continually been subject to historical change consequent upon the change in historical conditions.

The French Revolution, for example, abolished feudal property in favour of bourgeois property.

The distinguishing feature of Communism is not the abolition of property generally, but the abolition of bourgeois property. But modern bourgeois private property is the final and most complete expression of the system of producing and appropriating products, that is based on class antagonisms, on the exploitation of the many by the few.

In this sense, the theory of the Communists may be summed up in the single sentence: Abolition of private property.

We Communists have been reproached with the desire of abolishing the right of personally acquiring property as the fruit of a man's own labour, which property is alleged to be the groundwork of all personal freedom, activity and independence.

Hard-won, self-acquired, self-earned property! Do you mean the property of the petty artisan and of the small peasant, a form of property that preceded the bourgeois form? There is no need to abolish that; the development of industry has to a great extent already destroyed it, and is still destroying it daily.

Or do you mean modern bourgeois private property?

But does wage-labour create any property for the labourer? Not a bit. It creates capital, *i.e.,* that kind of property which exploits wage-labour, and which cannot increase except upon condition of begetting a new supply of wage-labour for fresh exploitation. Property, in its present form, is based on the antagonism of capital and wage-labour. Let us examine both sides of this antagonism.

To be a capitalist, is to have not only a purely personal, but a social *status* in production. Capital is a collective product, and only by the united action of many members, nay, in the last resort, only by the united action of all members of society, can it be set in motion.

Capital is, therefore, not a personal, it is a social power.

When, therefore, capital is converted into common property, into the property of all members of society, personal property is not thereby transformed into social property. It is only the social character of the property that is changed. It loses its class-character.

Let us now take wage-labour.

The average price of wage-labour is the minimum wage, *i.e.,* that quantum of the means of subsistence, which is absolutely requisite to keep the labourer in bare existence as a labourer. What, therefore, the wage-labourer appropriates by means of his labour, merely suffices to prolong and reproduce a bare existence. We by no means intend to abolish this personal appropriation of the products of labour, an appropriation that is made for the maintenance and reproduction of human life, and that leaves no surplus wherewith to command the labour of others. All that we want to do away with, is the miserable character of this appropriation, under which the labourer lives merely to increase capital, and is allowed to live only in so far as the interest of the ruling class requires it.

In bourgeois society, living labour is but a means to increase accumulated labour. In Communist society, accumulated labour is but a means to widen, to enrich, to promote the existence of the labourer.

In bourgeois society, therefore, the past dominates the present; in Communist society, the present dominates the past. In bourgeois society capital is independent and has individuality, while the living person is dependent and has no individuality.

And the abolition of this state of things is called by the bourgeois, abolition of individuality and freedom! And rightly so. The abolition of bourgeois individually, bourgeois independence, and bourgeois freedom is undoubtedly aimed at.

By freedom is meant, under the present bourgeois conditions of production, free trade, free selling and buying.

But if selling and buying disappears, free selling and buying disappears also. This talk about free selling and buying, and all the other "brave words" of our bourgeoisie about freedom in general, have a meaning, if any, only in contrast with restricted selling and buying, with the fettered traders of the Middle Ages, but have no meaning when opposed to the Communistic abolition of buying and selling, of the bourgeois conditions of production, and of the bourgeoisie itself.

You are horrified at our intending to do away with private property. But in your existing society, private property is already done away with for nine-tenths of the population; its existence for the few is solely due to its non-existence in the hands of those nine-tenths. You reproach us, therefore, with intending to do away with a form of property, the necessary condition for whose existence is the non-existence of any property for the immense majority of society.

In one word, you reproach us with intending to do away with your property. Precisely so; that is just what we intend.

From the moment when labour can no longer be converted into capital, money, or rent, into a social power capable of being monopolised, *i.e.*, from the moment when individual property can no longer be transformed into bourgeois property, into capital, from that moment, you say, individuality vanishes.

You must, therefore, confess that by "individual" you mean no other person than the bourgeois, than the middle-class owner of property. This person must, indeed, be swept out of the way, and made impossible.

Communism deprives no man of the power to appropriate the products of society; all that it does is to deprive him of the power to subjugate the labour of others by means of such appropriation.

It has been objected that upon the abolition of private property all work will cease, and universal laziness will overtake us.

According to this, bourgeois society ought long ago to have gone to the dogs through sheer idleness; for those of its members who work, acquire nothing, and those who acquire anything, do not work. The whole of this objection is but another expression of the tautology: that there can no longer be any wage-labour when there is no longer any capital.

All objections urged against the Communistic mode of producing and appropriating material products, have, in the same way, been urged against the Communistic modes of producing and appropriating intellectual products. Just as, to the bourgeois, the disappearance of class property is the disappearance of production itself, so the disappearance of class culture is to him identical with the disappearance of all culture.

That culture, the loss of which he laments, is, for the enormous majority, a mere training to act as a machine.

But don't wrangle with us so long as you apply, to our intended abolition of bourgeois property, the standard of your bourgeois notions of freedom, culture, law, &c. Your very ideas are but the outgrowth of the conditions of your bourgeois production and bourgeois property, just as your jurisprudence is but the will of your class made into a law for all, a will, whose essential character and direction are determined by the economical conditions of existence of your class.

The selfish misconception that induces you to transform into eternal laws of nature and of reason, the social forms springing from your present mode of production and form of property—historical relations that rise and disappear in the progress of production—this misconception you share with every ruling class that has preceded you. What you see clearly in the case of ancient property, what you admit in the case of feudal property, you are of course forbidden to admit in the case of your own bourgeois form of property.

Abolition of the family! Even the most radical flare up at this infamous proposal of the Communists.

On what foundation is the present family, the bourgeois family, based? On capital, on private gain. In its completely developed form this family exists only among the bourgeoisie. But this state of things finds its complement in the practical absence of the family among the proletarians, and in public prostitution.

The bourgeois family will vanish as a matter of course when its complement vanishes, and both will vanish with the vanishing of capital.

Do you charge us with wanting to stop the exploitation of children by their parents? To this crime we plead guilty.

But, you will say, we destroy the most hallowed of relations, when we replace home education by social.

And your education! Is not that also social, and determined by the social conditions under which you educate, by the intervention, direct or indirect, of society, by means of schools, &c.? The Communists have not invented the intervention of society in education; they do but seek to alter the character of that intervention, and to rescue education from the influence of the ruling class.

The bourgeois clap-trap about the family and education, about the hallowed co-relation of parent and child, becomes all the more disgusting, the more, by the action of Modern Industry, all family ties among the proletarians are torn asunder, and their children transformed into simple articles of commerce and instruments of labour.

But you Communists would introduce community of women, screams the whole bourgeoisie in chorus.

The bourgeois sees in his wife a mere instrument of production. He hears that the instruments of production are to be exploited in common, and, naturally, can come to no other conclusion than that the lot of being common to all will likewise fall to the women.

He has not even a suspicion that the real point aimed at is to do away with the status of women as mere instruments of production.

For the rest, nothing is more ridiculous than the virtuous indignation of our bourgeois at the community of women which, they pretend, is to be openly and officially established by the Communists. The Communists have no need to introduce community of women; it has existed almost from time immemorial.

Our bourgeois, not content with having the wives and daughters of their proletarians at their disposal, not to speak of common prostitutes, take the greatest pleasure in seducing each other's wives.

Bourgeois marriage is in reality a system of wives in common and thus, at the most, what the Communists might possibly be reproached with, is that they desire to introduce, in substitution for a hypocritically concealed, an openly legalised community of women. For the rest, it is self-evident that the abolition of the present system of production must bring with it the abolition of the community of women springing from that system, *i.e.,* of prostitution both public and private.

The Communists are further reproached with desiring to abolish countries and nationality.

The working men have no country. We cannot take from them what they have not got. Since the proletariat must first of all acquire political supremacy, must rise to be the leading class of the nation, must constitute itself *the* nation, it is, so far, itself national, though not in the bourgeois sense of the word.

National differences and antagonisms between peoples are daily more and more vanishing, owing to the development of the bourgeoisie, to freedom of commerce, to the world-market, to uniformity in the mode of production and in the conditions of life corresponding thereto.

The supremacy of the proletariat will cause them to vanish still faster. United action, of the leading civilised countries at least, is one of the first conditions for the emancipation of the proletariat.

In proportion as the exploitation of one individual by another is put an end to, the exploitation of one nation by another will also be put an end to. In proportion as the antagonism between classes within the nation vanishes, the hostility of one nation to another will come to an end.

The charges against Communism made from a religious, a philosophical, and, generally, from an ideological standpoint, are not deserving of serious examination.

Does it require deep intuition to comprehend that man's ideas, views and conceptions, in one word, man's consciousness, changes with every change in the conditions of his material existence, in his social relations and in his social life?

What else does the history of ideas prove, than that intellectual production changes its character in proportion as material production is changed? The ruling ideas of each age have ever been the ideas of its ruling class.

When people speak of ideas that revolutionise society, they do but express the fact, that within the old society, the elements of a new one have been created, and that the dissolution of the old ideas keeps even pace with the dissolution of the old conditions of existence.

When the ancient world was in its last throes, the ancient religions were overcome by Christianity. When Christian ideas succumbed in the 18th century to rationalist ideas, feudal society fought its death battle with the then revolutionary bourgeoisie. The ideas of religious liberty and freedom of conscience merely gave expression to the sway of free competition within the domain of knowledge.

"Undoubtedly," it will be said, "religious, moral, philosophical and juridical ideas have been modified in the course of historical development. But religion, morality, philosophy, political science, and law, constantly survived this change.'

"There are, besides, eternal truths, such as Freedom, Justice, etc., that are common to all states of society. But Communism abolishes eternal truths, it abolishes all religion, and all morality, instead of constituting them on a new basis; it therefore acts in contradiction to all past historical experience."

What does this accusation reduce itself to? The history of all past society has consisted in the development of class antagonisms, antagonisms that assumed different forms at different epochs.

But whatever form they may have taken, one fact is common to all past ages, *viz.*, the exploitation of one part of society by the other. No wonder, then, that the social consciousness of past ages, despite all the multiplicity and variety it displays, moves within certain common forms, or general ideas, which cannot completely vanish except with the total disappearance of class antagonisms.

The Communist revolution is the most radical rupture with traditional property relations; no wonder that its development involves the most radical rupture with traditional ideas.

But let us have done with the bourgeois objections to Communism.

We have seen above, that the first step in the revolution by the working class, is to raise the proletariat to the position of ruling class, to win the battle of democracy.

The proletariat will use its political supremacy to wrest, by degrees, all capital from the bourgeoisie, to centralise all instruments of production in the hands of the State, *i.e.*, of the proletariat organised as the ruling class; and to increase the total of productive forces as rapidly as possible.

Of course, in the beginning, this cannot be effected except by means of

despotic inroads on the rights of property, and on the conditions of bourgeois production; by means of measures, therefore, which appear economically insufficient and untenable, but which, in the course of the
movement, outstrip themselves, necessitate further inroads upon the old
social order, and are unavoidable as a means of entirely revolutionising
the mode of production.

These measures will of course be different in different countries.

Nevertheless in the most advanced countries, the following will be
pretty generally applicable.

1. Abolition of property in land and application of all rents of land
   to public purposes.
2. A heavy progressive or graduated income tax.
3. Abolition of all right of inheritance.
4. Confiscation of the property of all emigrants and rebels.
5. Centralisation of credit in the hands of the State, by means of a
   national bank with State capital and an exclusive monopoly.
6. Centralisation of the means of communication and transport in
   the hands of the State.
7. Extension of factories and instruments of production owned by
   the State; the bringing into cultivation of waste-lands, and the improvement of the soil generally in accordance with a common
   plan.
8. Equal liability of all to labour. Establishment of industrial armies,
   especially for agriculture.
9. Combination of agriculture with manufacturing industries; gradual abolition of the distinction between town and country, by a
   more equable distribution of the population over the country.
10. Free education for all children in public schools. Abolition of chil-
    dren's factory labour in its present form. Combination of educa-
    tion with industrial production, &c., &c.

When, in the course of development, class distinctions have disappeared, and all production has been concentrated in the hands of a vast
association of the whole nation, the public power will lose its political
character. Political power, properly so called, is merely the organised
power of one class for oppressing another. If the proletariat during its
contest with the bourgeoisie is compelled, by the force of circumstances,
to organise itself as a class, if, by means of a revolution, it makes itself
the ruling class, and, as such, sweeps away by force the old conditions of
production, then it will, along with these conditions, have swept away
the conditions for the existence of class antagonisms and of classes generally, and will thereby have abolished its own supremacy as a class.

In place of the old bourgeois society, with its classes and class antagonisms, we shall have an association, in which the free development of each is the condition for the free development of all.

III. Socialist and Communist Literature

1. Reactionary Socialism

A. *Feudal Socialism*

Owing to their historical position, it became the vocation of the aristocracies of France and England to write pamphlets against modern bourgeois society. In the French revolution of July 1830, and in the English reform agitation, these aristocracies again succumbed to the hateful upstart. Thenceforth, a serious political contest was altogether out of question. A literary battle alone remained possible. But even in the domain of literature the old cries of the restoration period[5] had become impossible.

In order to arouse sympathy, the aristocracy were obliged to lose sight, apparently, of their own interests, and to formulate their indictment against the bourgeoisie in the interest of the exploited working class alone. Thus the aristocracy took their revenge by singing lampoons on their new master, and whispering in his ears sinister prophecies of coming catastrophe.

In this way arose Feudal Socialism: half lamentation, half lampoon; half echo of the past, half menace of the future; at times, by its bitter, witty and incisive criticism, striking the bourgeoisie to the very heart's core; but always ludicrous in its effect, through total incapacity to comprehend the march of modern history.

The aristocracy, in order to rally the people to them, waved the proletarian alms-bag in front for a banner. But the people, so often as it joined them, saw on their hindquarters the old feudal coats of arms, and deserted with loud and irreverent laughter.

One section of the French Legitimists and "Young England" exhibited this spectacle.

In pointing out that their mode of exploitation was different to that of the bourgeoisie, the feudalists forget that they exploited under circumstances and conditions that were quite different, and that are now antiquated. In showing that, under their rule, the modern proletariat never existed, they forget that the modern bourgeoisie is the necessary offspring of their own form of society.

For the rest, so little do they conceal the reactionary character of their criticism that their chief accusation against the bourgeoisie amounts to this, that under the bourgeois *régime* a class is being developed, which is destined to cut up root and branch the old order of society.

What they upbraid the bourgeoisie with is not so much that it creates a proletariat, as that it creates a *revolutionary* proletariat.

In political practice, therefore, they join in all coercive measures against the working class; and in ordinary life, despite their high-falutin phrases, they stoop to pick up the golden apples dropped from the tree of industry, and to barter truth, love, and honour for traffic in wool, beetroot-sugar, and potato spirits.[6]

As the parson has ever gone hand in hand with the landlord, so has Clerical Socialism with Feudal Socialism.

Nothing is easier than to give Christian asceticism a Socialist tinge. Has not Christianity declaimed against private property, against marriage, against the State? Has it not preached in the place of these, charity and poverty, celibacy and mortification of the flesh, monastic life and Mother Church? Christian Socialism is but the holy water with which the priest consecrates the heart-burnings of the aristocrat.

B. Petty-Bourgeois Socialism

The feudal aristocracy was not the only class that was ruined by the bourgeoisie, not the only class whose conditions of existence pined and perished in the atmosphere of modern bourgeois society. The mediaeval burgesses and the small peasant proprietors were the precursors of the modern bourgeoisie. In those countries which are but little developed, industrially and commercially, these two classes still vegetate side by side with the rising bourgeoisie.

In countries where modern civilisation has become fully developed, a new class of petty bourgeois has been formed, fluctuating between proletariat and bourgeoisie and ever renewing itself as a supplementary part of bourgeois society. The individual members of this class, however, are being constantly hurled down into the proletariat by the action of competition, and, as modern industry develops, they even see the moment approaching when they will completely disappear as an independent section of modern society, to be replaced, in manufactures, agriculture and commerce, by overlookers, bailiffs and shopmen.

In countries like France, where the peasants constitute far more than half of the population, it was natural that writers who sided with the proletariat against the bourgeoisie, should use, in their criticism of the bourgeois *régime*, the standard of the peasant and petty bourgeois, and from the standpoint of these intermediate classes should take up the cudgels for the working class. Thus arose petty-bourgeois Socialism. Sismondi was the head of this school, not only in France but also in England.

This school of Socialism dissected with great acuteness the contradictions in the conditions of modern production. It laid bare the hypocritical apologies of economists. It proved, incontrovertibly, the disastrous effects of machinery and division of labour; the concentration of capital and land in a few hands; overproduction and crises; it pointed out the inevitable ruin of the petty bourgeois and peasant, the misery of the proletariat, the anarchy in production, the crying inequalities in the distribution of wealth, the industrial war of extermination between nations, the dissolution of old moral bonds, of the old family relations, of the old nationalities.

In its positive aims, however, this form of Socialism aspires either to restoring the old means of production and of exchange, and with them the old property relations, and the old society, or to cramping the modern means of production and of exchange, within the framework of the old property relations that have been, and were bound to be, exploded by those means. In either case, it is both reactionary and Utopian.

Its last words are: corporate guilds for manufacture, patriarchal relations in agriculture.

Ultimately, when stubborn historical facts had dispersed all intoxicating effects of self-deception, this form of Socialism ended in a miserable fit of the blues.

C. *German, or "True," Socialism*

The Socialist and Communist literature of France, a literature that originated under the pressure of a bourgeoisie in power, and that was the expression of the struggle against this power, was introduced into Germany at a time when the bourgeoisie, in that country, had just begun its contest with feudal absolutism.

German philosophers, would-be philosophers, and *beaux esprits*, eagerly seized on this literature, only forgetting, that when these writings immigrated from France into Germany, French social conditions had not immigrated along with them. In contact with German social conditions, this French literature lost all its immediate practical significance, and assumed a purely literary aspect. Thus, to the German philosophers of the eighteenth century, the demands of the first French Revolution were nothing more than the demands of "Practical Reason" in general, and the utterance of the will of the revolutionary French bourgeoisie signified in their eyes the laws of pure Will, of Will as it was bound to be, of true human Will generally.

The work of the German *literati* consisted solely in bringing the new

French ideas into harmony with their ancient philosophical conscience, or rather, in annexing the French ideas without deserting their own philosophic point of view.

This annexation took place in the same way in which a foreign language is appropriated, namely, by translation.

It is well known how the monks wrote silly lives of Catholic Saints *over* the manuscripts on which the classical works of ancient heathendom had been written. The German *literati* reversed this process with the profane French literature. They wrote their philosophical nonsense beneath the French original. For instance, beneath the French criticism of the economic functions of money, they wrote "Alienation of Humanity," and beneath the French criticism of the bourgeois State they wrote "Dethronement of the Category of the General," and so forth.

The introduction of these philosophical phrases at the back of the French historical criticisms they dubbed "Philosophy of Action," "True Socialism," "German Science of Socialism," "Philosophical Foundation of Socialism," and so on.

The French Socialist and Communist literature was thus completely emasculated. And, since it ceased in the hands of the German to express the struggle of one class with the other, he felt conscious of having overcome "French one-sidedness" and of representing, not true requirements, but the requirements of Truth; not the interest of the proletariat, but the interests of Human Nature, of Man in general, who belongs to no class, has no reality, who exists only in the misty realm of philosophical fantasy.

This German Socialism, which took its schoolboy task so seriously and solemnly, and extolled its poor stock-in-trade in such mountebank fashion, meanwhile gradually lost its pedantic innocence.

The fight of the German, and, especially, of the Prussian bourgeoisie, against feudal aristocracy and absolute monarchy, in other words, the liberal movement, became more earnest.

By this, the long wished-for opportunity was offered to "True" Socialism of confronting the political movement with the Socialist demands, of hurling the traditional anathemas against liberalism, against representative government, against bourgeois competition, bourgeois freedom of the press, bourgeois legislation, bourgeois liberty and equality, and of preaching to the masses that they had nothing to gain, and everything to lose, by this bourgeois movement. German Socialism forgot, in the nick of time, that the French criticism, whose silly echo it was, presupposed the existence of modern bourgeois society, with its corresponding economic conditions of existence, and the political constitution adapted thereto, the very things whose attainment was the object of the pending struggle in Germany.

To the absolute governments, with their following of parsons, professors, country squires and officials, it served as a welcome scarecrow against the threatening bourgeoisie.

It was a sweet finish after the bitter pills of floggings and bullets with which these same governments, just at that time, dosed the German working-class risings.

While this "True" Socialism thus served the governments as a weapon for fighting the German bourgeoisie, it, at the same time, directly represented a reactionary interest, the interest of the German Philistines. In Germany the *petty-bourgeois* class, a relic of the sixteenth century, and since then constantly cropping up again under various forms, is the real social basis of the existing state of things.

To preserve this class is to preserve the existing state of things in Germany. The industrial and political supremacy of the bourgeoisie threatens it with certain destruction; on the one hand, from the concentration of capital; on the other, from the rise of a revolutionary proletariat. "True" Socialism appeared to kill these two birds with one stone. It spread like an epidemic.

The robe of speculative cobwebs, embroidered with flowers of rhetoric, steeped in the dew of sickly sentiment, this transcendental robe in which the German Socialists wrapped their sorry "eternal truths," all skin and bone, served to wonderfully increase the sale of their goods amongst such a public.

And on its part, German Socialism recognised, more and more, its own calling as the bombastic representative of the petty-bourgeois Philistine.

It proclaimed the German nation to be the model nation, and the German petty Philistine to be the typical man. To every villainous meanness of this model man it gave a hidden, higher, Socialistic interpretation, the exact contrary of its real character. It went to the extreme length of directly opposing the "brutality destructive" tendency of Communism, and of proclaiming its supreme and impartial contempt of all class struggles. With very few exceptions, all the so-called Socialist and Communist publications that now (1847) circulate in Germany belong to the domain of this foul and enervating literature.[7]

2. Conservative, or Bourgeois, Socialism

A part of the bourgeoisie is desirous of redressing social grievances, in order to secure the continued existence of bourgeois society.

To this section belong economists, philanthropists, humanitarians, improvers of the condition of the working class, organisers of charity, members of societies for the prevention of cruelty to animals, temperance fanatics, hole-and-corner reformers of every imaginable kind. This form of Socialism has, moreover, been worked out into complete systems.

We may cite Proudhon's *Philosophie de la Misère* as an example of this form.

The Socialistic bourgeois want all the advantages of modern social conditions without the struggles and dangers necessarily resulting therefrom. They desire the existing state of society minus its revolutionary and disintegrating elements. They wish for a bourgeoisie without a proletariat. The bourgeoisie naturally conceives the world in which it is supreme to be the best; and bourgeois Socialism develops this comfortable conception into various more or less complete systems. In requiring the proletariat to carry out such a system, and thereby to march straightway into the social New Jerusalem, it but requires in reality, that the proletariat should remain within the bounds of existing society, but should cast away all its hateful ideas concerning the bourgeoisie.

A second and more practical, but less systematic, form of this Socialism sought to depreciate every revolutionary movement in the eyes of the working class, by showing that no mere political reform, but only a change in the material conditions of existence, in economical relations, could be of any advantage to them. By changes in the material conditions of existence, this form of Socialism, however, by no means understands abolition of the bourgeois relations of production, an abolition that can be effected only by a revolution, but administrative reforms, based on the continued existence of these relations; reforms, therefore, that in no respect affect the relations between capital and labour, but, at the best, lessen the cost, and simplify the administrative work, of bourgeois government.

Bourgeois Socialism attains adequate expression, when, and only when, it becomes a mere figure of speech.

Free trade: for the benefit of the working class. Protective duties: for the benefit of the working class. Prison Reform: for the benefit of the working class. This is the last word and the only seriously meant word of bourgeois Socialism.

It is summed up in the phrase: the bourgeois is a bourgeois—for the benefit of the working class.

3. Critical-Utopian Socialism and Communism

We do not here refer to that literature which, in every great modern revolution, has always given voice to the demands of the proletariat, such as the writings of Babeuf and others.

The first direct attempts of the proletariat to attain its own ends, made in times of universal excitement, when feudal society was being overthrown, these attempts necessarily failed, owing to the then undeveloped state of the proletariat, as well as to the absence of the economic conditions for its emancipation, conditions that had yet to be produced, and could be produced by the impending bourgeois epoch alone. The revolutionary literature that accompanied these first movements of the proletariat had necessarily a reactionary character. It inculcated universal asceticism and social leveling in its crudest form.

The Socialist and Communist systems properly so called, those of Saint-Simon, Fourier, Owen and others, spring into existence in the early undeveloped period, described above, of the struggle between proletariat and bourgeoisie (see Section I. Bourgeoisie and Proletariat).

The founders of these systems see, indeed, the class antagonisms, as well as the action of the decomposing elements, in the prevailing form of society. But the proletariat, as yet in its infancy, offers to them the spectacle of a class without any historical initiative or any independent political movement.

Since the development of class antagonism keeps even pace with the development of industry, the economic situation, as they find it, does not as yet offer to them the material conditions for the emancipation of the proletariat. They therefore search after a new social science, after new social laws, that are to create these conditions.

Historical action is to yield to their personal inventive action, historically created conditions of emancipation to fantastic ones, and the gradual, spontaneous class-organisation of the proletariat to an organisation of society specially contrived by these inventors. Future history resolves itself, in their eyes, into the propaganda and the practical carrying out of their social plans.

In the formation of their plans they are conscious of caring chiefly for the interests of the working class, as being the most suffering class. Only from the point of view of being the most suffering class does the proletariat exist for them.

The undeveloped state of the class struggle, as well as their own surroundings, causes Socialists of this kind to consider themselves far superior to all class antagonisms. They want to improve the condition of every member of society, even that of the most favoured. Hence, they habitually appeal to society at large, without distinction of class; nay, by preference, to the ruling class. For how can people, when once they understand their system, fail to see it in the best possible plan of the best possible state of society?

Hence, they reject all political, and especially all revolutionary, action; they wish to attain their ends by peaceful means, and endeavour, by small experiments, necessarily doomed to failure, and by the force of example, to pave the way for the new social Gospel.

Such fantastic pictures of future society, painted at a time when the proletariat is still in a very undeveloped state and has but a fantastic conception of its own position, correspond with the first instinctive yearnings of that class for a general reconstruction of society.

But these Socialist and Communist publications contain also a critical element. They attack every principle of existing society. Hence they are full of the most valuable materials for the enlightenment of the working class. The practical measures proposed in them—such as the abolition of the distinction between town and country, of the family, of the carrying on of industries for the account of private individuals, and of the wage system, the proclamation of social harmony, the conversion of the functions of the State into a mere superintendence of production, all these proposals point solely to the disappearance of class antagonisms which were, at that time, only just cropping up, and which, in these publications, are recognised in their earliest, indistinct and undefined forms only. These proposals, therefore, are of a purely Utopian character.

The significance of Critical-Utopian Socialism and Communism bears an inverse relation to historical development. In proportion as the modern class struggle develops and takes definite shape, this fantastic standing apart from the contest, these fantastic attacks on it, lose all practical value and all theoretical justification. Therefore, although the originators of these systems were, in many respects, revolutionary, their disciples have, in every case, formed mere reactionary sects. They hold fast by the original views of their masters, in opposition to the progressive historical development of the proletariat. They, therefore, endeavour, and that consistently, to deaden the class struggle and to reconcile the class antagonisms. They still dream of experimental realisation of their social Utopias, of founding isolated "*phalanstères*," of establishing "Home Colonies," of setting up a "Little Icaria"[8]—duodecimo editions of the New Jerusalem—and to realise all these castles in the air, they are compelled to appeal to the feelings and purses of the bourgeois. By degrees they sink into the category of the reactionary conservative Socialists depicted above, differing from these only by more systematic pedantry, and by their fanatical and superstitious belief in the miraculous effects of their social science.

They, therefore, violently oppose all political action on the part of the working class; such action, according to them, can only result from blind unbelief in the new Gospel.

The Owenites in England, and the Fourierists in France, respectively, oppose the Chartists and the *Réformistes*.

IV. Position of the Communists in Relation to the Various Existing Opposition Parties

Section II has made clear the relations of the Communists to the existing working-class parties, such as the Chartists in England and the Agrarian Reformers in America.

The Communists fight for the attainment of the immediate aims, for the enforcement of the momentary interests of the working class; but in the movement of the present, they also represent and take care of the future of that movement. In France the Communists ally themselves with the Social-Democrats,[9] against the conservative and radical bourgeoisie, reserving, however, the right to take up a critical position in regard to phrases and illusions traditionally handed down from the great Revolution.

In Switzerland they support the Radicals, without losing sight of the fact that this party consists of antagonistic elements, partly of Democratic Socialists, in the French sense, partly of radical bourgeois.

In Poland they support the party that insists on an agrarian revolution as the prime condition for national emancipation, that party which fomented the insurrection of Cracow in 1846.

In Germany they fight with the bourgeoisie whenever it acts in a revolutionary way, against the absolute monarchy, the feudal squirearchy, and the petty bourgeoisie.

But they never cease, for a single instant, to instil into the working class the clearest possible recognition of the hostile antagonism between bourgeoisie and proletariat, in order that the German workers may straightway use, as so many weapons against the bourgeoisie, the social and political conditions that the bourgeoisie must necessarily introduce along with its supremacy, and in order that, after the fall of the reactionary classes in Germany, the fight against the bourgeoisie itself may immediately begin.

The Communists turn their attention chiefly to Germany, because that country is on the eve of a bourgeois revolution that is bound to be carried out under more advanced conditions of European civilisation, and with a much more developed proletariat, than that of England was in the seventeenth, and of France in the eighteenth century, and because the bourgeois revolution in Germany will be but the prelude to an immediately following proletarian revolution.

In short, the Communists everywhere support every revolutionary movement against the existing social and political order of things.

In all these movements they bring to the front, as the leading question in each, the property question, no matter what its degree of development at the time.

Finally, they labour everywhere for the union and agreement of the democratic parties of all countries.

The Communists disdain to conceal their views and aims. They openly declare that their ends can be attained only by the forcible overthrow of all existing social conditions. Let the ruling classes tremble at a Communistic revolution. The proletarians have nothing to lose but their chains. They have a world to win.

WORKING MEN OF ALL COUNTRIES, UNITE!

Written by Marx and Engels in
December 1847–January 1848

Originally published in German
in London in February 1848

Printed according to the 1888
English edition

Notes

1. By bourgeoisie is meant the class of modern Capitalists, owners of the means of social production and employers of wage-labour. By proletariat, the class of modern wage-labourers who, having no means of production of their own, are reduced to selling their labour-power in order to live. [*Note by Engels to the English edition of 1888.*]

2. That is, all *written* history. In 1847, the pre-history of society, the social organisation existing previous to recorded history, was all but unknown. Since then, Haxthausen discovered common ownership of land in Russia, Maurer proved it to be the social foundation from which all Teutonic races started in history, and by and by village communities were found to be, or to have been the primitive form of society everywhere from India to Ireland. The inner organisation of this primitive Communistic society was laid bare, in its typical form, by Morgan's crowning discovery of the true nature of the *gens* and its relation to the *tribe.* With the dissolution of these primaeval communities society begins to be differentiated into separate and finally antagonistic classes. I have attempted to retrace this process of dissolution in: "Der Ursprung der Familie, des Privateigenthums und des Staats" [*The Origin of the Family, Private Property and the State.* See pp. 455–593 of this volume.—Ed.], 2nd edition, Stuttgart 1886. [*Note by Engels to the English edition of 1888*].

3. Guild-master, that is, a full member of a guild, a master within, not a head of a guild. [*Note by Engels to the English edition of 1888*].

4. "Commune" was the name taken, in France, by the nascent towns even before they had conquered from their feudal lords and masters local self-government and political rights as the "Third Estate". Generally speaking, for the economical development of the bourgeoisie, England is here taken as the typical country; for its political development, France. [*Note by Engels to the English edition of 1888*].

This was the name given their urban communities by the townsmen of Italy and France, after they had purchased or wrested their initial rights of self-government from their feudal lords. [*Note by Engels to the German edition of 1890*].

5. Not the English Restoration 1660 to 1689, but the French Restoration 1814 to 1830. [*Note by Engels to the English edition of 1888*].

6. This applies chiefly to Germany where the landed aristocracy and squirearchy have large portions of their estates cultivated for their own account by stewards, and are, moreover, extensive beetroot-sugar manufacturers and distillers of potato spirits. The wealthier British aristocracy are, as yet, rather above that; but they, too, know how to make up for declining rents by lending their names to floaters of more or less shady joint-stock companies. [*Note by Engels to the English edition of 1888*].

7. The revolutionary storm of 1848 swept away this whole shabby tendency and cured its protagonists of the desire to dabble further in Socialism. The chief representative and classical type of this tendency is Herr Karl Grün. [*Note by Engels to the German edition of 1890*].

8. *Phalanstères* were Socialist colonies on the plan of Charles Fourier; *Icaria* was the name given by Cabet to his Utopia and, later on, to his American Communist colony. [*Note by Engels to the English edition of 1888*].

"Home colonies" were what Owen called his Communist model societies. *Phalanstères* was the name of the public palaces planned by Fourier. *Icaria* was the name given to the Utopian land of fancy, whose Communist institutions Cabet portrayed. [*Note by Engels to the German edition of 1890*].

9. The party then represented in Parliament by Ledru-Rollin, in literature by Louis Blanc, in the daily press by the *Réforme*. The name of Social-Democracy signified, with these its inventors, a section of the Democratic or Republican party more or less tinged with Socialism. [*Note by Engels to the English edition of 1888*].

The party in France which at that time called itself Socialist-Democratic was represented in political life by Ledru-Rollin and in literature by Louis Blanc; thus it differed immeasurably from present-day German Social-Democracy. [*Note by Engels to the German edition of 1890*].

⇥ 2 ⇤

On Classes

Karl Marx

The owners merely of labour-power, owners of capital, and land-owners, whose respective sources of income are wages, profit and ground-rent, in other words, wage-labourers, capitalists and land-owners, constitute then three big classes of modern society based upon the capitalist mode of production.

In England, modern society is indisputably most highly and classically developed in economic structure. Nevertheless, even here the stratification of classes does not appear in its pure form. Middle and intermediate strata even here obliterate lines of demarcation everywhere (although incomparably less in rural districts than in the cities). However, this is immaterial for our analysis. We have seen that the continual tendency and law of development of the capitalist mode of production is more and more to divorce the means of production from labour, and more and more to concentrate the scattered means of production into large groups, thereby transforming labour into wage-labour and the means of production into capital. And to this tendency, on the other hand, corresponds the independent separation of landed property from capital and labour,[1] or the transformation of all landed property into the form of landed property corresponding to the capitalist mode of production.

The first question to be answered is this: What constitutes a class?—and the reply to this follows naturally from the reply to another question, namely: What makes wage-labourers, capitalists and landlords constitute the three great social classes?

At first glance—the identity of revenues and sources of revenue. There are three great social groups whose members, the individuals forming

---

Reprinted from Karl Marx, *Capital* (New York: International Publishers, 1973), vol. 3: 885–886, by permission of the publisher.

labour *capital* *landed*

them, live on wages, profit and ground-rent respectively, on the realisation of their labour-power, their capital, and their landed property.

However, from this standpoint, physicians and officials, e.g., would also constitute two classes, for they belong to two distinct social groups, the members of each of these groups receiving their revenue from one and the same source. The same would also be true of the infinite fragmentation of interest and rank into which the division of social labour splits labourers as well as capitalists and landlords—the latter, e.g., into owners of vineyards, farm owners, owners of forests, mine owners and owners of fisheries.

Note

1. F. List remarks correctly: "The prevalence of a self-sufficient economy on large estates demonstrates solely the lack of civilisation, means of communication, domestic trades and wealthy cities. It is to be encountered, therefore, throughout Russia, Poland, Hungary and Mecklenburg. Formerly, it was also prevalent in England; with the advance of trades and commerce, however, this was replaced by the breaking up into middle estates and the leasing of land." (*Die Ackerverfassung, die Zwergwirtschaft und die Auswanderung,* 1842, p. 10.)

⇥ 3 ⇤

Class, Status, Party

Max Weber

Economically Determined Power and the Status Order

The structure of every legal order directly influences the distribution of power, economic or otherwise, within its respective community. This is true of all legal orders and not only that of the state. In general, we understand by "power" the chance of a man or a number of men to realize their own will in a social action even against the resistance of others who are participating in the action.

"Economically conditioned" power is not, of course, identical with "power" as such. On the contrary, the emergence of economic power may be the consequence of power existing on other grounds. Man does not strive for power only in order to enrich himself economically. Power, including economic power, may be valued for its own sake. Very frequently the striving for power is also conditioned by the social honor it entails. Not all power, however, entails social honor: The typical American Boss, as well as the typical big speculator, deliberately relinquishes social honor. Quite generally, "mere economic" power, and especially "naked" money power, is by no means a recognized basis of social honor. Nor is power the only basis of social honor. Indeed, social honor, or prestige, may even be the basis of economic power, and very frequently has been. Power, as well as honor, may be guaranteed by the legal order, but, at least normally, it is not their primary source. The legal order is rather an additional factor that enhances the chance to hold power or honor; but it can not always secure them.

The way in which social honor is distributed in a community between

Reprinted from Max Weber, *Economy and Society, Vol. II* (Berkeley: University of California Press, 1978): 927–939, by permission of the publisher.

social honor

typical groups participating in this distribution we call the "status order." The social order and the economic order are related in a similar manner to the legal order. However, the economic order merely defines the way in which economic goods and services are distributed and used. Of course, the status order is strongly influenced by it, and in turn reacts upon it.

Now: "classes," "status groups," and "parties" are phenomena of the distribution of power within a community.

Determination of Class Situation by Market Situation

In our terminology, "classes" are not communities; they merely represent possible, and frequent, bases for social action. We may speak of a "class" when (1) a number of people have in common a specific causal component of their life chances, insofar as (2) this component is represented exclusively by economic interests in the possession of goods and opportunities for income, and (3) is represented under the conditions of the commodity or labor markets. This is "class situation."

It is the most elemental economic fact that the way in which the disposition over material property is distributed among a plurality of people, meeting competitively in the market for the purpose of exchange, in itself creates specific life chances. The mode of distribution, in accord with the law of marginal utility, excludes the non-wealthy from competing for highly valued goods; it favors the owners and, in fact, gives to them a monopoly to acquire such goods. Other things being equal, the mode of distribution monopolizes the opportunities for profitable deals for all those who, provided with goods, do not necessarily have to exchange them. It increases, at least generally, their power in the price struggle with those who, being propertyless, have nothing to offer but their labor or the resulting products, and who are compelled to get rid of these products in order to subsist at all. The mode of distribution gives to the propertied a monopoly on the possibility of transferring property from the sphere of use as "wealth" to the sphere of "capital," that is, it gives them the entrepreneurial function and all chances to share directly or indirectly in returns on capital. All this holds true within the area in which pure market conditions prevail. "Property" and "lack of property" are, therefore, the basic categories of all class situations. It does not matter whether these two categories become effective in the competitive struggles of the consumers or of the producers.

Within these categories, however, class situations are further differentiated: on the one hand, according to the kind of property that is usable for returns; and, on the other hand, according to the kind of services that can be offered in the market. Ownership of dwellings; workshops; warehouses; stores; agriculturally usable land in large or small holdings—a quantitative difference with possibly qualitative consequences; ownership of mines; cattle; men (slaves); disposition over mobile instruments of production, or capital goods of all sorts, especially money or objects that can easily be exchanged for money; disposition over products of one's own labor or of others' labor differing according to their various distances from consumability; disposition over transferrable monopolies of any kind—all these distinctions differentiate the class situations of the propertied just as does the "meaning" which they can give to the use of property, especially to property which has money equivalence. Accordingly, the propertied, for instance, may belong to the class of rentiers or the class of entrepreneurs.

Those who have no property but who offer services are differentiated just as much according to their kinds of services as according to the way in which they make use of these services, in a continuous or discontinuous relation to a recipient. But always this is the generic connotation of the concept of class: that the kind of chance in the *market* is the decisive moment which presents a common condition for the individual's fate. Class situation is, in this sense, ultimately market situation. The effect of naked possession *per se,* which among cattle breeders gives the non-owning slave or serf into the power of the cattle owner, is only a fore-runner of real "class" formation. However, in the cattle loan and in the naked severity of the law of debts in such communities for the first time mere "possession" as such emerges as decisive for the fate of the individual; this is much in contrast to crop-raising communities, which are based on labor. The creditor-debtor relation becomes the basis of "class situations" first in the cities, where a "credit market," however primitive, with rates of interest increasing according to the extent of dearth and factual monopolization of lending in the hands of a plutocracy could develop. Therewith "class struggles" begin.

Those men whose fate is not determined by the chance of using goods or services for themselves on the market, e.g., slaves, are not, however, a class in the technical sense of the term. They are, rather, a status group.

Social Action Flowing from Class Interest

According to our terminology, the factor that creates "class" is unambiguously economic interest, and indeed, only those interests involved in the existence of the market. Nevertheless, the concept of class-interest is an ambiguous one: even as an empirical concept it is ambiguous as soon as one understands by it something other than the factual direction of interests following with a certain probability from the class situation for a certain average of those people subjected to the class situation. The class situation and other circumstances remaining the same, the direction in which the individual worker, for instance, is likely to pursue his interests may vary widely, according to whether he is constitutionally qualified for the task at hand to a high, to an average, or to a low degree. In the same way, the direction of interests may vary according to whether or not social action of a larger or smaller portion of those commonly affected by the class situation, or even an association among them, e.g., a trade union, has grown out of the class situation, from which the individual may expect promising results for himself. The emergence of an association or even of mere social action from a common class situation is by no means a universal phenomenon.

The class situation may be restricted in its efforts to the generation of essentially *similar* reactions, that is to say, within our terminology, of "mass behavior." However, it may not even have this result. Furthermore, often merely amorphous social action emerges. For example, the "grumbling" of workers known in ancient Oriental ethics: The moral disapproval of the work-master's conduct, which in its practical significance was probably equivalent to an increasingly typical phenomenon of precisely the latest industrial development, namely, the slowdown of laborers by virtue of tacit agreement. The degree in which "social action" and possibly associations emerge from the mass behavior of the members of a class is linked to general cultural conditions, especially to those of an intellectual sort. It is also linked to the extent of the contrasts that have already evolved, and is especially linked to the transparency of the connections between the causes and the consequences of the class situation. For however different life chances may be, this fact in itself, according to all experience, by no means gives birth to "class action" (social action by the members of a class). For that, the real conditions and the results of the class situation must be distinctly recognizable. For only then the contrast of life chances can be felt not as an absolutely given fact to be accepted, but as a resultant from either (1) the given distribution of property, or (2) the structure of the concrete economic order. It is only then that people may react against the class structure not only through acts of intermittent and irrational protest, but in the form of rational association. There have been "class situations" of the first category (1), of a specifically naked and transparent sort, in the urban centers of Antiquity and during the Middle Ages; especially then when great fortunes were accumulated by factually monopolized trading in local industrial products or in foodstuffs; furthermore, under certain conditions, in the rural economy of the most diverse periods, when agriculture was increasingly exploited in a profit-making manner. The most important historical example of the second category (2) is the class situation of the modern proletariat.

Types of Class Struggle

Thus every class may be the carrier of any one of the innumerable possible forms of class action, but this is not necessarily so. In any case, a class does not in itself constitute a group (*Gemeinschaft*). To treat "class" conceptually as being equivalent to "group" leads to distortion. That men in the same class situation regularly react in mass actions to such tangible situations as economic ones in the direction of those interests that are most adequate to their average number is an important and after all simple fact for the understanding of historical events. However, this fact must not lead to that kind of pseudo-scientific operation with the concepts of class and class interests which is so frequent these days and which has found its most classic expression in the statement of a talented author, that the individual may be in error concerning his interests but that the class is infallible about its interests.

If classes as such are not groups, nevertheless class situations emerge only on the basis of social action. However, social action that brings forth class situations is not basically action among members of the identical class; it is an action among members of different classes. Social actions that directly determine the class situation of the worker and the entrepreneur are: the labor market, the commodities market, and the capitalistic enterprise. But, in its turn, the existence of a capitalistic enterprise presupposes that a very specific kind of social action exists to protect the possession of goods *per se,* and especially the power of individuals to dispose, in principle freely, over the means of production: a certain kind of legal order. Each kind of class situation, and above all when it rests upon the power of property *per se,* will become most clearly efficacious when all other determinants of reciprocal relations are, as far as possible, eliminated in their significance. It is in this way that the use of the power of property in the market obtains its most sovereign importance.

Now status groups hinder the strict carrying through of the sheer market principle. In the present context they are of interest only from this one point of view. Before we briefly consider them, note that not much of a general nature can be said about the more specific kinds of antagonism between classes (in our meaning of the term). The great shift, which has been going on continuously in the past, and up to our times, may be summarized, although at a cost of some precision: the struggle in which class situations are effective has progressively shifted from consumption credit toward, first, competitive struggles in the commodity market and then toward wage disputes on the labor market. The class struggles of Antiquity—to the extent that they were genuine class struggles and not struggles between status groups—were initially carried on by peasants and perhaps also artisans threatened by debt bondage and struggling against urban creditors. For debt bondage is the normal result of the differentiation of wealth in commerical cities, especially in seaport cities. A similar situation has existed among cattle breeders. Debt relationships as such produced class action up to the days of Catilina. Along with this, and with an increase in provision of grain for the city by transporting it from the outside, the struggle over the means of sustenance emerged. It centered in the first place around the provision of bread and determination of the price of bread. It lasted throughout Antiquity and the entire Middle Ages. The propertyless flocked together against those who actually and supposedly were interested in the dearth of bread. This fight spread until it involved all those commodities essential to the way of life and to handicraft production. There were only incipient discussions of wage disputes in Antiquity and in the Middle Ages. But they have been slowly increasing up into modern times. In the earlier periods they were completely secondary to slave rebellions as well as to conflicts in the commodity market.

The propertyless of Antiquity and of the Middle Ages protested against monopolies, pre-emption, forestalling, and the withholding of goods from the market in order to raise prices. Today the central issue is the determination of the price of labor. The transition is represented by the fight for access to the market and for the determination of the price of products. Such fights went on between merchants and workers in the putting-out system of domestic handicraft during the transition to modern times. Since it is quite a general phenomenon we must mention here that the class antagonisms that are conditioned through the market situations are usually most bitter between those who actually and directly participate as opponents in price wars. It is not the rentier, the shareholder, and the banker who suffer the ill will of the worker, but almost exclusively the manufacturer and the business executives who are the direct opponents of workers in wage conflicts. This is so in spite of the fact that it is precisely the cash boxes of the rentier, the share-holder, and the banker into which the more or less unearned gains flow, rather than into the pockets of the manufacturers or of the business executives. This simple state of affairs has very frequently been decisive for the role the class situation has played in the formation of political parties. For example, it has made possible the varieties of patriarchal socialism and the frequent attempts—formerly, at least—of threatened status groups to form alliances with the proletariat against the bourgeoisie.

Status Honor

In contrast to classes, *Stände* (*status groups*) are normally groups. They are, however, often of an amorphous kind. In contrast to the purely economically determined "class situation," we wish to designate as *status situation* every typical component of the life of men that is determined by a specific, positive or negative, social estimation of *honor*. This honor may be connected with any quality shared by a plurality, and, of course, it can be knit to a class situation: class distinctions are linked in the most varied ways with status distinctions. Property as such is not always recognized as a status qualification, but in the long run it is, and with extraordinary regularity. In the subsistence economy of neighborhood associations, it is often simply the richest who is the "chieftain." However, this often is only an honorific preference. For example, in the so-called pure modern democracy, that is, one devoid of any expressly ordered status privileges for individuals, it may be that only the families coming under approximately the same tax class dance with one another. This example is reported of certain smaller Swiss cities. But status honor need not necessarily be linked with a class situation. On the contrary, it normally stands in sharp opposition to the pretensions of sheer property.

Both propertied and propertyless people can belong to the same status group, and frequently they do with very tangible consequences. This equality of social esteem may, however, in the long run become quite precarious. The equality of status among American gentlemen, for instance, is expressed by the fact that outside the subordination determined by the different functions of business, it would be considered strictly repugnant—wherever the old tradition still prevails—if even the richest boss, while playing billiards or cards in his club would not treat his clerk as in every sense fully his equal in birthright, but would bestow upon him the condescending status-conscious "benevolence" which the German boss can never dissever from his attitude. This is one of the most important reasons why in America the German clubs have never been able to attain the attraction that the American clubs have.

In content, status honor is normally expressed by the fact that above all else a specific *style of life* is expected from all those who wish to belong to the circle. Linked with this expectation are restrictions on social intercourse (that is, intercourse which is not subservient to economic or any other purposes). These restrictions may confine normal marriages to within the status circle and may lead to complete endogamous closure. Whenever this is not a mere individual and socially irrelevant imitation of another style of life, but consensual action of this closing character, the status development is under way.

In its characteristic form, stratification by status groups on the basis of conventional styles of life evolves at the present time in the United States out of the traditional democracy. For example, only the resident of a certain street ("the Street") is considered as belonging to "society," is qualified for social intercourse, and is visited and invited. Above all, this differentiation evolves in such a way as to make for strict submission to the fashion that is dominant at a given time in society. This submission to fashion also exists among men in America to a degree unknown in Germany; it appears as an indication of the fact that a given man puts forward a *claim* to qualify as a gentleman. This submission decides, at least *prima facie*, that he will be treated as such. And this recognition becomes just as important for his employment chances in swank establishments, and above all, for social intercourse and marriage with "esteemed" families, as the qualification for dueling among Germans. As for the rest, status honor is usurped by certain families resident for a long time, and, of course, correspondingly wealthy, or by the actual or alleged descendants of the "Indian Princess" Pocahontas, of the Pilgrim fathers, or of the Knickerbockers, the members of almost inaccessible sects and all sort of circles setting themselves apart by means of any other characteristics and badges. In this case stratification is purely conventional and rests largely on usurpation (as does almost all status honor in its beginning). But the road to legal privilege, positive or negative, is easily traveled as soon as a certain stratification of the social order has in fact been "lived in" and has achieved stability by virtue of a stable distribution of economic power.

Ethnic Segregation and Caste

Where the consequences have been realized to their full extent, the status group evolves into a closed caste. Status distinctions are then guaranteed not merely by conventions and laws, but also by religious sanctions. This occurs in such a way that every physical contact with a member of any caste that is considered to be lower by the members of a higher caste is considered as making for a ritualistic impurity and a stigma which must be expiated by a religious act. In addition, individual castes develop quite distinct cults and gods.

In general, however, the status structure reaches such extreme consequences only where there are underlying differences which are held to be "ethnic." The caste is, indeed, the normal form in which ethnic communities that believe in blood relationship and exclude exogamous marriage and social intercourse usually associate with one another. As mentioned before, such a caste situation is part of the phenomenon of pariah peoples and is found all over the world. These people form communities, acquire specific occupational traditions of handicrafts or of other arts, and cultivate a belief in their ethnic community. They live in a diaspora strictly segregated from all personal intercourse, except that of an unavoidable sort, and their situation is legally precarious. Yet, by virtue of their economic indispensability, they are tolerated, indeed frequently privileged, and they live interspersed in the political communities. The Jews are the most impressive historical example.

A status segregation grown into a caste differs in its structure from a mere ethnic segregation: the caste structure transforms the horizontal and unconnected coexistences of ethnically segregated groups into a vertical social system of super- and sub-ordination. Correctly formulated: a comprehensive association integrates the ethnically divided communities into one political unit. They differ precisely in this way: ethnic coexistence, based on mutual repulsion and disdain, allows each ethnic community to consider its own honor as the highest one; the caste structure brings about a social subordination and an acknowledgement of "more honor" in favor of the privileged caste and status groups. This is due to the fact that in the caste structure ethnic distinctions as such have become "functional" distinctions within the political association (warriors, priests, artisans that are politically important for war and for building, and so on). But even pariah peoples who are most despised (for example, the Jews) are usually apt to continue cultivating the belief in their own specific "honor," a belief that is equally peculiar to ethnic and to status groups.

However, with the negatively privileged status groups the sense of dignity takes a specific deviation. A sense of dignity is the precipitation in individuals of social honor and of conventional demands which a positively privileged status group raises for the deportment of its members. The sense of dignity that characterizes positively privileged status groups is naturally related to their "being" which does not transcend itself, that is, it is related to their "beauty and excellence" ($\kappa\alpha\lambda o\kappa\dot{\alpha}\gamma\alpha\theta\dot{\iota}\alpha$). Their kingdom is "of this world." They live for the present and by exploiting their great past. The sense of dignity of the negatively privileged strata naturally refers to a future lying beyond the present, whether it is of this life or of another. In other words, it must be nurtured by the belief in a providential mission and by a belief in a specific honor before God. The chosen people's dignity is nurtured by a belief either that in the beyond "the last will be the first," or that in this life a Messiah will appear to bring forth into the light of the world which has cast them out the hidden honor of the pariah people. This simple state of affairs, and not the resentment which is so strongly emphasized in Nietzsche's much-admired construction in the *Genealogy of Morals,* is the source of the religiosity cultivated by pariah status groups; moreover, resentment applies only to a limited extent; for one of Nietzsche's main examples, Buddhism, it is not at all applicable.

For the rest, the development of status groups from ethnic segregations is by no means the normal phenomenon. On the contrary. Since objective "racial differences" are by no means behind every subjective sentiment of an ethnic community, the question of an ultimately racial foundation of status structure is rightly a question of the concrete individual case. Very frequently a status group is instrumental in the production of a thoroughbred anthropological type. Certainly status groups are to a high degree effective in producing extreme types, for they select personally qualified individuals (e.g. the knighthood selects those who are fit for warfare, physically and psychically). But individual selection is far from being the only, or the predominant, way in which status groups are formed: political membership or class situation has at all times been at least as frequently decisive. And today the class situation is by far the predominent factor. After all, the possibility of a style of life expected for members of a status group is usually conditioned economically.

Status Privileges

For all practical purposes, stratification by status goes hand in hand with a monopolization of ideal and material goods or opportunities, in a manner we have come to know as typical. Besides the specific status honor, which always rests upon distance and exclusiveness, honorific preferences may consist of the privilege of wearing special costumes, of eating special dishes taboo to others, of carrying arms—which is most obvious in its consequences—, the right to be a dilettante, for example, to play certain musical instruments. However, material monopolies provide the most effective motives for the exclusiveness of a status group; although, in themselves, they are rarely sufficient, almost always they come into play to some extent. Within a status circle there is the question of inter-marriage: the interest of the families in the monopolization of potential bridegrooms is at least of equal importance and is parallel to the interest in the monopolization of daughters. The daughters of the members must be provided for. With an increased closure of the status group, the conventional preferential opportunities for special employment grow into a legal monopoly of special offices for the members. Certain goods become objects for monopolization by status groups, typically, entailed estates, and frequently also the possession of serfs or bondsmen and, finally, special trades. This monopolization occurs positively when the status group is exclusively entitled to own and to manage them; and negatively when, in order to maintain its specific way of life, the status group must *not* own and manage them. For the decisive role of a style of life in status honor means that status groups are the specific bearers of all conventions. In whatever way it may be manifest, all stylization of life either originates in status groups or is at least conserved by them. Even if the principles of status conventions differ greatly, they reveal certain typical traits, especially among the most privileged strata. Quite generally, among privileged status groups there is a status disqualification that operates against the performance of common physical labor. This disqualification is now "setting in" in America against the old tradition of esteem for labor. Very frequently every rational economic pursuit, and especially entrepreneurial activity, is looked upon as a disqualification of status. Artistic and literary activity is also considered degrading work as soon as it is exploited for income, or at least when it is connected with hard physical exertion. An example is the sculptor working like a mason in his dusty smock as over against the painter in his salon-like studio and those forms of musical practice that are acceptable to the status group.

Economic Conditions and Effects of Status Stratification

The frequent disqualification of the gainfully employed as such is a direct result of the principle of status stratification, and of course, of this principle's opposition to a distribution of power which is regulated exclusively through the market. These two factors operate along with various individual ones, which will be touched upon below.

We have seen above that the market and its processes knows no personal distinctions: "functional" interests dominate it. It knows nothing of honor. The status order means precisely the reverse: stratification in terms of honor and styles of life peculiar to status groups as such. The status order would be threatened at its very root if mere economic acquisition and naked economic power still bearing the stigma of its extra-status origin could bestow upon anyone who has won them the same or ever greater honor as the vested interests claim for themselves. After all, given equality of status honor, property *per se* represents an addition even if it is not overtly acknowledged to be such. Therefore all groups having interest in the status order react with special sharpness precisely against the pretensions of purely economic acquisition. In most cases they react the more vigorously the more they feel themselves threatened. Calderon's respectful treatment of the peasant, for instance, as opposed to Shakespeare's simultaneous ostensible disdain of the *canaille* illustrates the different way in which a firmly structured status order reacts as compared with a status order that has become economically precarious. This is an example of a state of affairs that recurs everywhere. Precisely because of the rigorous reactions against the claims of property *per se,* the "parvenu" is never accepted, personally and without reservation, by the privileged status groups, no matter how completely his style of life has been adjusted to theirs. They will only accept his descendants who have been educated in the conventions of their status group and who have never besmirched its honor by their own economic labor.

As to the general *effect* of the status order, only one consequence can be stated, but it is a very important one: the hindrance of the free development of the market. This occurs first for those goods that status groups directly withhold from free exchange by monopolization, which may be effected either legally or conventionally. For example, in many Hellenic cities during the "status era" and also originally in Rome, the inherited estate (as shown by the old formula for placing spendthrifts under a guardian) was monopolized, as were the estates of knights, peasants, priests, and especially the clientele of the craft and merchant guilds. The market is restricted, and the power of naked property *per se,* which gives its stamp to class formation, is pushed into the background. The results of this process can be most varied. Of course, they do not necessarily weaken the contrasts in the economic situation. Frequently they strengthen these contrasts, and in any case, where stratification by status permeates a community as strongly as was the case in all political communities of Antiquity and of the Middle Ages, one can never speak of a genuinely free market competition as we understand it today. There are wider effects than this direct exclusion of special goods from the market. From the conflict between the status order and the purely economic order mentioned above, it follows that in most instances the notion of honor peculiar to status absolutely abhors that which is essential to the market: hard bargaining. Honor abhors hard bargaining among peers and occasionally it taboos it for the members of a status group in general. Therefore, everywhere some status groups, and usually the most influential, consider almost any kind of overt participation in economic acquisition as absolutely stigmatizing.

With some over-simplification, one might thus say that classes are stratified according to their relations to the production and acquisition of goods; whereas status groups are stratified according to the principles of their *consumption* of goods as represented by special styles of life.

An "occupational status group," too, is a status group proper. For normally, it successfully claims social honor only by virtue of the special style of life which may be determined by it. The differences between classes and status groups frequently overlap. It is precisely those status communities most strictly segregated in terms of honor (viz. the Indian castes) who today show, although within very rigid limits, a relatively high degree of indifference to pecuniary income. However, the Brahmins seek such income in many different ways.

As to the general economic conditions making for the predominance of stratification by status, only the following can be said. When the bases of the acquisition and distribution of goods are relatively stable, stratification by status is favored. Every technological repercussion and economic transformation threatens stratification by status and pushes the class situation into the foreground. Epochs and countries in which the naked class situation is of predominant significance are regularly the periods of technical and economic transformations. And every slowing down of the change in economic stratification leads, in due course, to the growth of status structures and makes for a resuscitation of the important role of social honor.

Parties

Whereas the genuine place of classes is within the economic order, the place of status groups is within the social order, that is, within the sphere of the distribution of honor. From within these spheres, classes and status groups influence one another and the legal order and are in turn influenced by it. "*Parties*" reside in the sphere of power. Their action is oriented toward the acquisition of social power, that is to say, toward influencing social action no matter what its content may be. In principle, parties may exist in a social club as well as in a state. As over against the actions of classes and status groups, for which this is not necessarily the case, party-oriented social action always involves association. For it is always directed toward a goal which is striven for in a planned manner. This goal may be a cause (the party may aim at realizing a program for ideal or material purposes), or the goal may be personal (sinecures, power, and from these, honor for the leader and the followers of the party). Usually the party aims at all these simultaneously. Parties are, therefore, only possible within groups that have an associated character, that is, some rational order and a staff of persons available who are ready to enforce it. For parties aim precisely at influencing this staff, and if possible, to recruit from it party members.

In any individual case, parties may represent interests determined through class situation or status situation, and they may recruit their following respectively from one or the other. But they need be neither purely class nor purely status parties; in fact, they are more likely to be mixed types, and sometimes they are neither. They may represent ephemeral or enduring structures. Their means of attaining power may be quite varied, ranging from naked violence of any sort to canvassing for votes with coarse or subtle means: money, social influence, the force of speech, suggestion, clumsy hoax, and so on to the rougher or more artful tactics of obstruction in parliamentary bodies.

The sociological structure of parties differs in a basic way according to the kind of social action which they struggle to influence; that means, they differ according to whether or not the community is stratified by status or by classes. Above all else, they vary according to the structure of domination. For their leaders normally deal with its conquest. In our general terminology, parties are not only products of modern forms of domination. We shall also designate as parties the ancient and medieval ones, despite the fact that they differ basically from modern parties. Since a party always struggles for political control (*Herrschaft*), its organization too is frequently strict and "authoritarian." Because of these variations between the forms of domination, it is impossible to say anything about the structure of parties without discussing them first. Therefore, we shall now turn to this central phenomenon of all social organization.

Before we do this, we should add one more general observation about classes, status groups and parties: The fact that they presuppose a larger association, especially the framework of a polity, does not mean that they are confined to it. On the contrary, at all times it has been the order of the day that such association (even when it aims at the use of military force in common) reaches beyond the state boundaries. This can be seen in the [interlocal] solidarity of interests of oligarchs and democrats in Hellas, of Guelphs and Ghibellines in the Middle Ages, and with the Calvinist party during the age of religious struggles; and all the way up to the solidarity of landlords (International Congresses of Agriculture), princes (Holy Alliance, Karlsbad Decrees [of 1819]), socialist workers, conservatives (the longing of Prussian conservatives for Russian intervention in 1850). But their aim is not necessarily the establishment of a new territorial dominion. In the main they aim to influence the existing polity.

Part I: Related Readings

Antonio, Robert J., and Ronald M. Glassman, eds. 1985. *A Weber-Marx Dialogue*. Lawrence: University Press of Kansas.

Appelbaum, Richard P. 1988. *Karl Marx*. Newbury Park, Calif.: Sage Publications.

Parkin, Frank. 1988. *Max Weber*. New York: Routledge.

Solomos, John, and Les Black. 1995. "Marxism, Racism, and Ethnicity." *American Behavioral Scientist* 38:407–20.

Stone, John. 1995. "Race, Ethnicity, and the Weberian Legacy." *American Behavioral Scientist* 38:391–406.

Wiley, Norbert, ed. 1987. *The Marx-Weber Debate*. Newbury Park, Calif.: Sage Publications.

Part II
American Stratification Theory

In the early postwar period, American stratification theory was concerned almost exclusively with issues of status. W. Lloyd Warner, Marchia Meeker, and Kenneth Eells, in an excerpt from their book *What Social Class Is in America*, first published in 1949, argue that all complex societies must have rank orders to perform functions necessary for group survival. Certain positions carry a sense of prestige. It is community judgment as to the degree of prestige that creates certain classes. Since all complex societies must have rank orders, and prestige is merely community judgment, it follows that Marx's notion of the necessity of class conflict under capitalism and the possibility of a classless society is incorrect. For Warner et al., social class in the United States does not imply a conflictual relationship.

Kingsley Davis and Wilbert Moore, in their article "Some Principles of Stratification," build on the notion of the necessity of rank orders in complex societies and argue that the unequal distribution of rewards is one way a society can ensure that the most important positions are filled by the best people. People are rewarded according to their motivation to perform a particular task. Differential rewards are based on the functional importance of the position to the survival of the society itself. In his critique, Melvin Tumin calls into question the very assumptions on which Davis and Moore base their argument. For Tumin, Davis and Moore ignore the fundamentals of power in deciding which positions are more important than others. Tumin's critique provides a significant challenge to a functionalist theory of stratification.

⇥ 4 ⇤

What Social Class Is in America

W. Lloyd Warner, Marchia Meeker, and Kenneth Eells

The American Dream and Social Class

I n the bright glow and warm presence of the American Dream all men
are born free and equal. Everyone in the American Dream has the
right, and often the duty, to try to succeed and to do his best to reach
the top. Its two fundamental themes and propositions, that all of us are
equal and that each of us has the right to the chance of reaching the top,
are mutually contradictory, for if all men are equal there can be no top
level to aim for, no bottom one to get away from; there can be no superior or inferior positions, but only one common level into which all
Americans are born and in which all of them will spend their lives. We
all know such perfect equality of position and opportunity does not exist.
All Americans are not born into families of equal position: some are born
into a rich man's aristocracy on the Gold Coast; some into the solid comfort of Suburbia's middle classes; and others into a mean existence among
the slum families living on the wrong side of the tracks. It is common
knowledge that the sons and daughters of the Gold Coasts, the Main
Lines, and Park Avenues of America are more likely to receive recognition for their efforts than the children of the slums. The distance these
fortunate young people travel to achieve success is shorter, and the route
up easier, than the long hard pull necessary for the ambitious children of
the less fortunate middle class. Though everyone has the common right
to succeed, it is not an equal "right"; though there is equality of rank for
some of us, there is not equality of rank for all of us.

When some men learn that *all* the American Dream does not fit *all* that

Reprinted from W. Lloyd Warner, Marchia Meeker, and Kenneth Eels, "What Social
Class Is in America," in *Social Class in America* (New York: Harper & Row, 1960): 3–33.

is true about the realities of our life, they denounce the Dream and deny the truth of *any* of it. Fortunately, most of us are wiser and better adjusted to social reality; we recognize that, though it is called a Dream and though some of it is false, by virtue of our firm belief in it we have made some of it true. Despite the presence of social hierarchies which place people at higher and lower levels in American communities, the principles of democracy do operate; the Christian dogma that all men are equal in the sight of God because He is our Father and we are His spiritual children, buttressed by the democratic faith in the equality of men and the insistence on their equal rights as citizens, is a powerful influence in the daily life of America.

From grade school on, we have learned to cite chapter and verse proving from the lives of many of the great men of American history that we can start at the bottom and climb to the highest peaks of achievement when we have a few brains and a will to do. Our mass magazines and newspapers print and reprint the legendary story of rags to riches and tell over and over again the Ellis-Island-to-Park-Avenue saga in the actual lives of contemporary successful immigrant men and women. From mere repetition, it might be thought the public would tire of the theme; the names are all that vary and the stories, like those of children, remain the same. But we never do tire of this theme, for it says what we need to know and what we want to hear.

Among people around us, we sometimes recognize men who have got ahead, who have been successfully upward-mobile, and who have reached levels of achievement beyond even the dreams of most men. Many Americans by their own success have learned that, for them, enough of the Dream is true to make all of it real. The examples from history, from the world around us, and from our own experience provide convincing evidence that, although full equality is absent, opportunity for advancement is present sufficiently to permit the rise of a few from the bottom and a still larger number from the middle to the higher economic and social levels. Although we know the statement that everyone is equal but that some men are higher than others is contradictory, and although some of us smile or become angry when we hear that "all of us are equal but some are more equal than others," we still accept both parts of this proposition either by understressing one part of the proposition or by letting all of it go as a paradox we feel to be true.

Our society does an excellent job in giving us an explicit knowledge of, and good argument for, the equalitarian aspects of our life. We have much scholarly knowledge about the workings of democracy, but we have little scientific knowledge about the powerful presence of social status and how it works for good and evil in the lives of all of us. Yet to live successfully and adaptively in America, every one of us must adjust his life to each of these contradictions, not just one of them, and we must make the most of each. Our knowledge of the democratic aspects of America is learned directly as part of our social heritage, but our understanding of the principle of social status tends to be implicit and to be learned obliquely and through hard and sometimes bitter experience. The lives of many are destroyed because they do not understand the workings of social class.[1]

It is the hope of the authors that this [essay] will provide a corrective instrument which will permit men and women better to evaluate their social situations and thereby better adapt themselves to social reality and fit their dreams and aspirations to what is possible.

Our great state papers, the orations of great men, and the principles and pronouncements of politicians and statesmen tell us of the equality of all men. Each school boy learns and relearns it; but most of us are dependent upon experience and indirect statement to learn about "the wrong side of the tracks," "the Gold Coast and the slums," and "the top and bottom of the social heap." We are proud of those facts of American life that fit the pattern we are taught, but somehow we are often ashamed of those equally important social facts which demonstrate the presence of social class. Consequently, we tend to deny them or, worse, denounce them and by so doing deny their existence and magically make them disappear from consciousness. We use such expressions as "the Century of the Common Man" to insist on our democratic faith; but we know that, ordinarily, for Common Men to exist as a class, un-Common superior and inferior men must also exist. We know that every town or city in the country has its "Country Club set" and that this group usually lives on its Gold Coast, its Main Line, North Shore, or Nob Hill, and is the top of the community's social heap. Most of us know from novels such as those of Sinclair Lewis of the Main Streets that run through all our towns and cities, populated by Babbitts or, more explicitly stated, by "the substantial upper-middle class"; and by now, thanks to another group of novelists such as Erskine Caldwell, we know there is a low road, a Tobacco Road, that runs not only by the ramshackle houses of the poor whites of the South, but by the tarpaper shanties of the slums and river bottoms or Goat Hills of every town and city in the United States.

The "superior people" of Marquand's New England, "the North Shore crowd," divided into a top level of "old families" with a set of values and a way of life rated above those of the "new families," are matched by Philadelphia's "Main Line" families in Christopher Morley's *Kitty Foyle* and by similar groups in many other novels which report on the dominance of "the upper classes" in all regions of the United States. Reading them, together with similar novels reporting on Suburbia and Main Street for the middle classes and those on the Tobacco Roads and the city slums for the lower levels, gives one the understanding that throughout the towns and cities of America the inhabitants are divided into status levels which are ways of life with definite characteristics and values. Talking to and observing the people of these communities demonstrate that they, too, know how real these status levels are, and they prove it by agreeing among themselves about the levels and who belongs to them in their particular city.

Although well aware of social class, social scientists have been more concerned with their theories and with quarreling among themselves about what social class is than with studying its realities in the daily lives of the people. Until recently, they have lagged behind the novelists in investigating what our classes are, how they operate in our social life, and what effect they have on our individual lives.

But recent scientific studies of social class in the several regions of the United States demonstrate that it is a major determinant of individual decisions and social actions; that every major area of American life is directly and indirectly influenced by our class order; and that the major decisions of most individuals are partly controlled by it. To act intelligently and know consciously how this basic factor in American life affects us and our society, it is essential and necessary that we have an explicit understanding of what our class order is, how it works, and what it does to the lives and personalities who live in it. Our most democratic institutions, including our schools, churches, business organizations, government, and even our family life, are molded by its all-pervading and exceedingly subtle but powerful influence.

The researches on social class in the several regions of the United States make it possible to fill in much of the missing knowledge necessary to give Americans such explicit understanding of social class and to answer some of the important questions we raise about it when adjusting to the realities of our existence. Reduced to their simplicities these questions are: What is social class? How are social classes organized? And how do they function in the individual and the community? How do we use such knowledge to adjust ourselves more satisfactorily to the world around us? What is the effect of class on buying and selling and other problems of business enterprise, on the problems of personnel, on school and education, on the church and religion, on the acceptance and rejection of the communications of mass media such as the radio, magazine, newspaper, and motion picture? And, above all, are there effective and simple techniques of studying and applying the social-class concept so that those who are not specialized class analysts can apply such knowledge to the practical problems of their business or profession or to the research problems of the scientist?

The answer to this last important question is "yes"; the answer to the others will be found in this volume. The authors believe that they present a sufficient description here of how to do these things to enable interested people to deal with problems arising from social class. They recognize that further refinement is necessary and that modifications and improvement will have to be made, but the fundamental elements are now known sufficiently well to provide this set of instructions adequate to the identification and measurement of social class in America. Most of the book—all chapters between this and the last—will deal specifically with these instructions.

The Structural Imperative—
Why We Have a Class System

The recognition of social class and other status hierarchies in this country comes as no surprise to students of society. Research on the social life of the tribes and civilizations of the world clearly demonstrates that some form of rank is always present and a necessity for our kind of society.

Just as students of comparative biology have demonstrated that the physical structure of the higher animals must have certain organs to survive, so students of social anthropology have shown that the social structures of the "higher," the more complex, societies must have rank orders to perform certain functions necessary for group survival.

When societies are complex and service large populations, they always possess some kind of status system which, by its own values, places people in higher or lower positions. Only the very simple hunting and gathering tribes, with very small populations and very simple social problems, are without systems of rank; but when a society is complex, when there are large numbers of individuals in it pursuing diverse and complex activities and functioning in a multiplicity of ways, individual positions and behaviors are evaluated and ranked. This happens primarily because, to maintain itself, the society must co-ordinate the efforts of all its members into common enterprises necessary for the preservation of the group, and it must solidify and integrate all these enterprises into a working whole. In other words, as the division of labor increases and the social units become more numerous and diverse, the need for co-ordination and integration also increases and, when satisfied, enables the larger group to survive and develop.

Those who occupy co-ordinating positions acquire power and prestige. They do so because their actions partly control the behavior of the individuals who look to them for direction. Within this simple control there is simple power. Those who exercise such power either acquire prestige directly from it or have gained prestige from other sources sufficiently to be raised to a co-ordinating position. For example, among many primitive peoples a simple fishing expedition may be organized so that the men who fish and handle each boat are under the direction of one leader. The efforts of each boat are directed by the leader and, in turn, each boat is integrated into the total enterprise by its leader's taking orders from his superior. The same situation prevails in a modern factory. Small plants with a small working force and simple problems possess a limited hierarchy, perhaps no more than an owner who bosses all the workers. But a large industrial enterprise, with complex activities and problems, like General Motors, needs an elaborate hierarchy of supervision. The position in a great industrial empire which integrates and co-ordinates all the positions beneath it throughout all the supervising levels down to the workers has great power and prestige. The same holds true for political, religious, educational, and other social institutions; the more complex the group and the more diverse the functions and activities, the more elaborate its status system is likely to be. We will amplify this point later.

The studies of other societies have demonstrated one other basic point: the more complex the technological and economic structure, the more complex the social structure; so that some argue (the Marxians and many classical economists) that technological advancement is the cause of social complexity and all class and status systems. It cannot be denied that economic and technological factors are important in the determination of class and status orders. We must not lose sight of the fact, however, that the social system, with its beliefs, values, and rules, which governs human behavior may well determine what kind of technology and what kind of economic institutions will survive or thrive in any given tribe or nation. In any case, social complexity is necessary for economic advancement. Furthermore, social complexity is a basic factor determining the presence or absence of class.

The Marxians have argued that the economic changes our society is undergoing always result in a class war in which "the proletariat" will be triumphant and out of which a "classless society" will result. The authors do not agree with them for several reasons. The principal reasons are: (1) the presence of a class order does not necessarily mean class conflict—the relations of the classes can be and often are amiable and peaceful; (2) classless societies (without differential status systems) are impossible where there is complexity for the reasons previously given. Russia's communistic system, supposedly designed to produce a pure equalitarian society, necessarily has citizens who are ranked above and below each other. Generals, there, outrank privates; commissars, the rank and file; and members of the Politburo, the ordinary comrade. Occupants of these higher ranks in Russia tend to associate together; those of the lower ranks form their own groups. Their children are trained according to the rank of their parents. This means that the younger generation learns these status differences, thereby strengthening status differences between levels and fostering the further development of social class in Communistic Russia.

All this has occurred despite the fact that the Russians have removed the means of production from private hands and placed them under the control of the State ("the people"). The economic factor which by Marxian doctrine produced social classes is largely absent; yet social hierarchies and social classes are present for the reason that Russia is a complex society and needs them to survive.

These status trends in Russia will undoubtedly continue, for her population is vast, her peoples diverse, her problems immensely complex; and elaborate systems of co-ordination and control are necessary for such a nation to maintain itself. The Communist ideals of economic and political equality cannot produce perfect equality within the complexities of Russian life.

But let us return to the United States. We, too, have a complex, highly diverse society. We, too, possess an elaborate division of labor and a ramified technology. And we, too, possess a variety of rank orders built on the need of maintaining unity and cohesion in making our common enterprises successful. Men occupying high and low positions possess families. Their families and their activities are identified with their social position. Families of the same position tend to associate together. They do this informally or through cliques, associations, or other institutions. This social matrix provides the structure of our class system. Children are always born to their families' position. Through life they may increase or decrease their status. The family thereby strengthens and helps maintain our class order. Social status in America is somewhat like man's alimentary canal; he may not like the way it works and he may want to forget that certain parts of it are part of him, but he knows it is necessary for his very existence. So a status system, often an object of our disapproval, is present and necessary in our complex social world.

If we cannot eliminate the system of status, we can and must work to keep it as democratic and equalitarian as possible. To be successful we must see to it that each American is given his chance to move in the social scale. This ideal of equality of opportunity is essential for our democracy. To do this intelligently, we must know what our class order is and what can be done to make it conform most closely to the needs of the American people.

The remainder of this chapter will briefly summarize what we now know about our social classes and how they are organized and function in the towns and cities of the several regions of the United States. We will start with the New England Yankees and then go on to the Middle and

Far West and end up with the South before we take up the question of the common features of American class and what it is as a status system.

Class among The New England Yankees

Studies of communities in New England clearly demonstrate the presence of a well-defined social-class system.[2] At the top is an aristocracy of birth and wealth. This is the so-called "old family" class. The people of Yankee City say the families who belong to it have been in the community for a long time—for at least three generations and preferably many generations more than three. "Old family" means not only old to the community but old to the class. Present members of the class were born into it; the families into which they were born can trace their lineage through many generations participating in a way of life characteristic of the upper class back to a generation marking the lowly beginnings out of which their family came. Although the men of this level are occupied gainfully, usually as large merchants, financiers, or in the higher professions, the wealth of the family, inherited from the husband's or the wife's side, and often from both, has been in the family for a long time. Ideally, it should stem from the sea trade when Yankee City's merchants and sea captains made large fortunes, built great Georgian houses on elm-lined Hill Street, and filled their houses and gardens with the proper symbols of their high position. They became the 400, the Brahmins, the Hill Streeters to whom others looked up; and they, well-mannered or not, looked down on the rest. They counted themselves, and were so counted, equals of similar levels in Salem, Boston, Providence, and other New England cities. Their sons and daughters married into the old families from these towns and at times, when family fortune was low or love was great, they married wealthy sons and daughters from the newly rich who occupied the class level below them. This was a happy event for the fathers and mothers of such fortunate young people in the lower half of the upper class, an event well publicized and sometimes not too discreetly bragged about by the parents of the lower-upper-class children, an occasion to be explained by the mothers from the old families in terms of the spiritual demands of romantic love and by their friends as "a good deal and a fair exchange all the way around for everyone concerned."

The new families, the lower level of the upper class, came up through the new industries—shoes, textiles, silverware—and finance. Their fathers were some of the men who established New England's trading and financial dominance throughout America. When New York's Wall Street rose to power, many of them transferred their activities to this new center of dominance. Except that they aspire to old-family status, if not for themselves then for their children, these men and their families have a design for living similar to the old-family group. But they are consciously aware that their money is too new and too recently earned to have the sacrosanct quality of wealth inherited from a long line of ancestors. They know, as do those about them, that, while a certain amout of wealth is necessary, birth and old family are what really matter. Each of them can cite critical cases to prove that particular individuals have no money at all, yet belong to the top class because they have the right lineage and right name. While they recognize the worth and importance of birth, they feel that somehow their family's achievements should be better rewarded than by a mere second place in relation to those who need do little more than be born and stay alive.

The presence of an old-family class in a community forces the newly rich to wait their turn if they aspire to "higher things." Meanwhile, they must learn how to act, fill their lives with good deeds, spend their money on approved philanthropy, and reduce their arrogance to manageable proportions.

The families of the upper and lower strata of the upper classes are organized into social cliques and exclusive clubs. The men gather fortnightly in dining clubs where they discuss matters that concern them. The women belong to small clubs or to the Garden Club and give their interest to subjects which symbolize their high status and evoke those sentiments necessary in each individual if the class is to maintain itself. Both sexes join philanthropic organizations whose good deeds are an asset to the community and an expression of the dominance and importance of the top class to those socially beneath them. They are the members of the Episcopalian and Unitarian and, occasionally, the Congregational and Presbyterian churches.

Below them are the members of the solid, highly respectable upper-middle class, the people who get things done and provide the active front in civic affairs for the classes above them. They aspire to the classes above and hope their good deeds, civic activities, and high moral principles will somehow be recognized far beyond the usual pat on the back and that they will be invited by those above them into the intimacies of upper-class cliques and exclusive clubs. Such recognition might increase their status and would be likely to make them members of the lower-upper group. The fact that this rarely happens seldom stops members of this level, once activated, from continuing to try. The men tend to be owners of stores and belong to the large proprietor and professional levels. Their incomes average less than those of the lower-upper class, this latter group having a larger income than any other group, including the old-family level.

These three strata, the two upper classes and the upper-middle, constitute the levels above the Common Man. There is a considerable distance socially between them and the mass of the people immediately below them. They comprise three of the six classes present in the community. Although in number of levels they constitute half the community, in population they have no more than a sixth, and sometimes less, of the Common Man's population. The three levels combined include approximately 13 per cent of the total population.

The lower-middle class, the top of the Common Man level, is composed of clerks and other white-collar workers, small tradesmen, and a fraction of skilled workers. Their small houses fill "the side streets" down from Hill Street, where the upper classes and some of the upper-middle live, and are noticeably absent from the better suburbs where the upper-middle concentrate. "Side Streeter" is a term often used by those above them to imply an inferior way of life and an inconsequential status. They have accumulated little property but are frequently home owners. Some of the more successful members of ethnic groups, such as the Italians, Irish, French-Canadians, have reached this level. Only a few members of these cultural minorities have gone beyond it; none of them has reached the old-family level.

The old-family class (upper-upper) is smaller in size than the new-family class (lower-upper) below them. It has 1.4 per cent, while the lower-upper class has 1.6 per cent, of the total population. Ten per cent of the population belongs to the upper-middle class, and 28 per cent to the lower-middle level. The upper-lower is the most populous class, with 34 per cent, and the lower-lower has 25 per cent of all the people in the town.

The prospects of the upper-middle-class children for higher education are not as good as those of the classes above. One hundred per cent of the children of the two upper classes take courses in the local high school that prepare them for college, and 88 per cent of the upper-middle do; but only 44 per cent of the lower-middle take these courses, 28 per cent of the upper-lower, and 26 per cent of the lower-lower. These percentages provide a good index of the position of the lower-middle class, ranking it well below the three upper classes, but placing it well above the upper-lower and the lower-lower.[3]

The upper-lower class, least differentiated from the adjacent levels and hardest to distinguish in the hierarchy, but clearly present, is composed of the "poor but honest workers" who more often than not are only semi-skilled or unskilled. Their relative place in the hierarchy of class is well portrayed by comparing them with the classes superior to them and with the lower-lower class beneath them in the category of how they spend their money.

A glance at the ranking of the proportion of the incomes of each class

spent on ten items (including such things as rent and shelter, food, clothing, and education, among others) shows, for example, that this class
ranks second for the percentage of the money spent on food, the lower-
lower class being first and the rank order of the other classes following
lower-middle according to their place in the social hierarchy. The money
spent on rent and shelter by upper-lower class is also second to the lower-
lower's first, the other classes' rank order and position in the hierarchy
being in exact correspondence. To give a bird's-eye view of the way this
class spends its money, the rank of the upper-lower, for the percentage
of its budget spent on a number of common and important items, has
been placed in parentheses after every item in the list which follows: food
(2), rent (2), clothing (4), automobiles (5), taxes (5), medical aid (5),
education (4), and amusements (4–5). For the major items of expenditure
the amount of money spent by this class out of its budget corresponds
fairly closely with its place in the class hierarchy, second to the first of
the lower-lower class for the major necessities of food and shelter, and
ordinarily, but not always, fourth or fifth to the classes above for the
items that give an opportunity for cutting down the amounts spent on
them. Their feelings about doing the right thing, of being respectable
and rearing their children to do better than they have, coupled with the
limitations of their income, are well reflected in how they select and reject
what can be purchased on the American market.[4]

The lower-lower class, referred to as "Riverbrookers" or the "low-
down Yankees who live in the clam flats," have a "bad reputation"
among those who are socially above them. This evaluation includes beliefs that they are lazy, shiftless, and won't work, all opposites of the
good middle-class virtues belonging to the essence of the Protestant ethic.
They are thought to be improvident and unwilling or unable to save their
money for a rainy day and, therefore, often dependent on the philanthropy of the private or public agency and on poor relief. They are sometimes said to "live like animals" because it is believed that their sexual
mores are not too exacting and that pre-marital intercourse, post-marital
infidelity, and high rates of illegitimacy, sometimes too publicly mixed
with incest, characterize their personal and family lives. It is certain that
they deserve only part of this reputation. Research shows many of them
guilty of no more than being poor and lacking in the desire to get ahead,
this latter trait being common among those above them. For these reasons and others, this class is ranked in Yankee City below the level of the
Common Man (lower-middle and upper-lower). For most of the indexes
of status it ranks sixth and last.

Class in the Democratic Middle West and Far West

Cities large and small in the states west of the Alleghenies sometimes
have class systems which do not possess an old-family (upper-upper)

class. The period of settlement has not always been sufficient for an old-family level, based on the security of birth and inherited wealth, to entrench itself. Ordinarily, it takes several generations for an old-family class to gain and hold the prestige and power necessary to impress the rest of the community sufficiently with the marks of its "breeding" to be able to confer top status on those born into it. The family, its name, and its lineage must have had time to become identified in the public mind as being above ordinary mortals.

While such identification is necessary for the emergence of an old-family (upper upper) class and for its establishment, it is also necessary for the community to be large enough for the principles of exclusion to operate. For example, those in the old-family group must be sufficiently numerous for all the varieties of social participation to be possible without the use of new-family members; the family names must be old enough to be easily identified; and above all there should always be present young people of marriageable age to become mates of others of their own class and a sufficient number of children to allow mothers to select playmates and companions of their own class for their children.

When a community in the more recently settled regions of the United States is sufficiently large, when it has grown slowly and at an average rate, the chances are higher that it has an old-family class. If it lacks any one of these factors, including size, social and economic complexity, and steady and normal growth, the old-family class is not likely to develop.

One of the best tests of the presence of an old-family level is to determine whether members of the new-family category admit, perhaps grudgingly and enviously and with hostile derogatory remarks, that the old-family level looks down on them and that it is considered a mark of advancement and prestige by those in the new-family group to move into it and be invited to the homes and social affairs of the old families. When a member of the new-family class says, "We've only been here two generations, but we still aren't old-family," and when he or she goes on to say that "they (old family) consider themselves better than people like us and the poor dopes around here let them get away with it," such evidence indicates that an old-family group is present and able to enforce recognition of its superior position upon its most aggressive and hostile competitors, the members of the lower-upper, or new-family, class.

When the old-family group is present and its position is not recognized as superordinate to the new families, the two tend to be co-ordinate and view each other as equals. The old-family people adroitly let it be known that their riches are not material possessions alone but are old-family lineage; the new families display their wealth, accent their power, and prepare their children for the development of a future lineage by giving them the proper training at home and later sending them to the "right" schools and marrying them into the "right" families.

Such communities usually have a five-class pyramid, including an upper-class, two middle, and two lower classes.[5]

Jonesville, located in the Middle West, approximately a hundred years old, is an example of a typical five-class community. The farmers around Jonesville use it as their market, and it is the seat of government for Abraham County. Its population of over 6,000 people is supported by servicing the needs of the farmers and by one large and a few small factories.

At the top of the status structure is an upper class commonly referred to as "the 400." It is composed of old-family and new-family segments. Neither can successfully claim superiority to the other. Below this level is an upper-middle-class which functions like the same level in Yankee City and is composed of the same kind of people, the only difference being the recognition that the distance to the top is shorter for them and the time necessary to get there much less. The Common Man level, composed of lower-middle- and upper-lower-class people, and the lower-lower level are replicas of the same classes in Yankee City. The only difference is that the Jonesville ethnics in these classes are Norwegian Lutherans and Catholic Poles, the Catholic Irish and Germans having been absorbed for the most part in the larger population; whereas in Yankee City the ethnic population is far more heterogeneous, and the Catholic Irish are less assimilated largely because of more opposition to them, and because the church has more control over their private lives.

The present description of Jonesville's class order can be brief and no more than introductory because all the materials used to demonstrate how to measure social class are taken from Jonesville. The interested reader will obtain a clear picture in the chapters which follow of what the classes are, who is in them, the social and economic characteristics of each class, and how the people of the town think about their status order.

The communities of the mountain states and Pacific Coast are new, and many of them have changed their economic form from mining to other enterprises; consequently, their class orders are similar to those found in the Middle West. The older and larger far western communities which have had a continuing, solid growth of population which has not destroyed the original group are likely to have the old-family level at the top with the other classes present; the newer and smaller communities and those disturbed by the destruction of their original status structure by large population gains are less likely to have an old-family class reigning above all others. San Francisco is a clear example of the old-family type; Los Angeles, of the more amorphous, less well-organized class structure.

Class in the Deep South

Studies in the Deep South demonstrate that, in the older regions where social changes until recently have been less rapid and less disturbing to the status order, most of the towns above a few thousand population have a six-class system in which an old-family elite is socially dominant.

For example, in a study of a Mississippi community, a market town for a cotton-growing region around it, Davis and the Gardners found a six-class system.[6] Perhaps the southern status order is best described by Chart I which gives the names used by the people of the community for each class and succinctly tells how the members of each class regard themselves and the rest of the class order.

The people of the two upper classes make a clear distinction between an old aristocracy and an aristocracy which is not old. There is no doubt that the first is above the other; the upper-middle class views the two upper ones much as the upper classes do themselves but groups them in one level with two divisions, the older level above the other; the lower-middle class separates them but considers them co-ordinate; the bottom two classes, at a greater social distance than the others, group all the levels above the Common Man as "society" and one class. An examination of the terms used by the several classes for the other classes shows that similar principles are operating.

The status system of most communities in the South is further complicated by a color-caste system which orders and systematically controls the relations of those categorized as Negroes and whites.

Although color-caste in America is a separate problem and the present volume does not deal with this American status system, it is necessary that we describe it briefly to be sure a clear distinction is made between it and social class. Color-caste is a system of values and behavior which places all people who are thought to be white in a superior position and those who are thought of as black in an inferior status.

Characteristics of American Negroes vary from very dark hair and skin and Negroid features to blond hair, fair skin, and Caucasian features, yet all of them are placed in the "racial" category of Negro. The skin and physical features of American Caucasians vary from Nordic blond types to the dark, swarthy skin and Negroid features of some eastern Mediterranean stocks, yet all are classed as socially white, despite the fact that a sizable proportion of Negroes are "whiter" in appearance than a goodly proportion of whites. The members of the two groups are severely punished by the formal and informal rules of our society if they intermarry, and when they break this rule of "caste endogamy," their children suffer the penalties of our caste-like system by being placed in the lower color caste. Furthermore, unlike class, the rules of this system forbid the members of the lower caste from climbing out of it. Their status and that of their children are fixed forever. This is true no matter how much money they have, how great the prestige and power they may accumulate, or how well they have acquired correct manners and proper behavior. There

CHART I
The Social Perspectives of the Social Classes[7]

UPPER-UPPER CLASS

"Old aristocracy"	UU
"Aristocracy," but not "old"	LU
"Nice, respectable people"	UM
"Good people, but 'nobody'"	LM
	UL
"Po' whites"	LL

LOWER-UPPER CLASS

"Old aristocracy"	UU
"Aristocracy," but not "old"	LU
"Nice, respectable people"	UM
"Good people, but 'nobody'"	LM
	UL
"Po' whites"	LL

UPPER-MIDDLE CLASS

"Society"	"Old families"	UU
	"Society" but not "old familes"	LU
"People who should be upper class"		UM
"People who don't have much money"		LM
		UL
"No 'count lot"		LL

LOWER-MIDDLE CLASS

"Old aristocracy" (older)	"Broken-down aristocracy" (younger)	UU / LU
"People who think they are somebody"		UM
"We poor folk"		LM
"People poorer than us"		UL
"No 'count lot"		LL

UPPER-LOWER CLASS

	UU / LU
"Society" or the "folks with money"	UM
"People who are up because they have a little money"	LM
"Poor but honest folk"	UL
"Shiftless people"	LL

LOWER-LOWER CLASS

	UU / LU
"Society" or the "folks with money"	UM
"Way-high-ups," but not "Society"	LM
"Snobs trying to push up"	UL
"People just as good as anybody"	LL

can be no social mobility out of the lower caste into the higher one. (There may, of course, be class mobility within the Negro or white caste.) The rigor of caste rules varies from region to region in the United States.[8]

The Mexicans, Spanish Americans, and Orientals occupy a somewhat different status from that of the Negro, but many of the characteristics of their social place in America are similar.[9]

The social-class and color-caste hypotheses, inductively established as working principles for understanding American society, were developed in the researches which were reported in the "Yankee City" volumes, *Deep South,* and *Caste and Class in a Southern Town.* Gunnar Myrdal borrowed them, particularly color-caste, and made them known to a large, non-professional American audience.[10]

The Generalities of American Class

It is now time to ask what are the basic characteristics of social status common to the communities of all regions in the United States and, once we have answered this question, to inquire what the variations are among the several systems. Economic factors are significant and important in determining the class position of any family or person, influencing the kind of behavior we find in any class, and contributing their share to the present form of our status system. But, while significant and necessary, the economic factors are not sufficient to predict where a particular family or individual will be or to explain completely the phenomena of social class. Something more than a large income is necessary for high social position. Money must be translated into socially approved behavior and possessions, and they in turn must be translated into intimate participation with, and acceptance by, members of a superior class.

This is well illustrated by what is supposed to be a true story of what happened to a Mr. John Smith, a newly rich man in a far western community. He wanted to get into a particular social club of some distinction and significance in the city. By indirection he let it be known, and was told by his friends in the club they had submitted his name to the membership committee.

Mr. Abner Grey, one of the leading members of the club and active on its membership committee, was a warm supporter of an important philanthropy in this city. It was brought to his attention that Mr. Smith, rather than contributing the large donation that had been expected of him, had given only a nominal sum to the charity.

When Mr. Smith heard nothing more about his application, he again approached one of the board members. After much evasion, he was told that Mr. Grey was the most influential man on the board and he would be wise to see that gentleman. After trying several times to make an appointment with Mr. Grey, he finally burst into Grey's offices unannounced.

"Why the hell, Abner, am I being kept out of the X club?"

Mr. Grey politely evaded the question. He asked Mr. Smith to be seated. He inquired after Mr. Smith's health, about the health of his wife, and inquired about other matters of simple convention.

Finally, Mr. Smith said, "Ab, why the hell am I being kept out of your club?"

"But, John, you're not. Everyone in the X club thinks you're a fine fellow."

"Well, what's wrong?"

"Well, John, we don't think you've got the *kind* of money necessary for being a good member of the X club. We don't think you'd be happy in the X club."

"Like hell I haven't. I could buy and sell a half dozen of some of your board members."

"I know that, John, but that isn't what I said. I did not say the amount of money. I said the kind of money."

"What do you mean?"

"Well, John, my co-workers on the charity drive tell me you only gave a few dollars to our campaign, and we had you down for a few thousand."

For a moment Mr. Smith was silent. Then he grinned. So did Mr. Grey. Smith took out his fountain pen and checkbook. "How much?"

At the next meeting of the X club Mr. Smith was unanimously elected to its membership.

Mr. Smith translated his money into philanthropy acceptable to the dominant group, he received their sponsorship, and finally became a participant in the club. The "right" kind of house, the "right" neighborhood, the "right" furniture, the proper behavior—all are symbols that can ultimately be translated into social acceptance by those who have sufficient money to aspire to higher levels than they presently enjoy.

To belong to a particular level in the social-class system of America means that a family or individual has gained acceptance as an equal by those who belong in the class. The behavior in this class and the participation of those in it must be rated by the rest of the community as being at a particular place in the social scale.

Although our democratic heritage makes us disapprove, our class order helps control a number of important functions. It unequally divides the highly and lowly valued things of our society among the several classes according to their rank. Our marriage rules conform to the rules of class, for the majority of marriages are between people of the same class. No class system, however, is so rigid that it completely prohibits marriages above and below one's own class. Furthermore, an open class system such as ours permits a person during his lifetime to move up or down from the level into which he was born. Vertical social mobility for individuals or families is characteristic of all class systems. The principal forms of mobility in this country are through the use of money, education, occupation, talent, skill, philanthropy, sex, and marriage. Although economic mobility is still important, it seems likely now that more people move to higher positions by education than by any other route. We have indicated before this that the mere possession of money is insufficient for gaining and keeping a higher social position. This is equally true of all other forms of mobility. In every case there must be social acceptance.

Class varies from community to community. The new city is less likely than an old one to have a well-organized class order; this is also true for cities whose growth has been rapid as compared with those which have not been disturbed by huge increases in population from other regions or countries or by the rapid displacement of old industries by new ones. The mill town's status hierarchy is more likely to follow the occupational hierarchy of the mill than the levels of evaluated participation found in market towns or those with diversified industries. Suburbs of large metropolises tend to respond to selective factors which reduce the number of classes to one or a very few. They do not represent or express all the cultural factors which make up the social pattern of an ordinary city.

Yet systematic studies from coast to coast, in cities large and small and of many economic types, indicate that, despite the variations and diversity, class levels do exist and that they conform to a particular pattern of organization.

How Class Operates in Our Daily Lives

Because social class permeates all parts of our existence, it is impossible to do more than indicate how it enters consciously or unconsciously into the success and failure of business, professional, and other occupations or to show how knowledge of its effects is necessary for increasing the predictive qualities of much of the research done by psychologists and social scientists. Class is vitally significant in marriage and training children as well as in most social activities of a community. Status plays a decisive role in the formation of personality at the various stages of development, for if young people are to learn to live adaptively as mature people in our society they must be trained by the informal controls of our society to fit into their places.

Education is now competing with economic mobility as the principle route to success. Today fewer men rise from the bottom to the top places in industry and business than did a generation ago. More and more, the sons of executives are replacing their fathers in such positions, leaving fewer positions into which the sons of those farther down can climb from the ranks. Captains of industry educate their sons to take their places or to occupy similar places in other industries. Also, more and more top jobs in industry are being filled by men coming from the technical and engineering schools or from the universities. The route up for them is no longer through a hierarchy of increasing skill to management and ownership as it was two generations ago. The prudent mobile man today must prepare himself by education if he wishes to fill an important job and provide his family with the money and prestige necessary to get "the better things of life."

Social-class research demonstrates that our educational system performs the dual task of aiding social mobility and, at the same time, working effectively to hinder it. This ceases to be a paradox when all the facts are examined. In the lower grades, our public schools are filled by children from all walks of life. Since education is free in the public schools, since everyone has a right to it and our laws try to keep children in school, and since it is common knowledge that "if you want to get ahead you must get an education," it would be assumed that children at, and below, the Common Man level would stay in school and equip themselves for mobility. Such is not the case. The social and educational systems work to eliminate the majority of them and permit only a few to get through. It has been estimated that, whereas 80 per cent of the upper- and upper-middle-class children actually go to college, only 20 per cent of the lower-middle and five per cent of the lower-class children get there.[11] The evidence indicates that most, if not all, of the children of the top classes complete their preparation and go on to college, whereas those from the lower classes start dropping out in the grade schools and continue to do so in increasing numbers in high school. Only a very few of them go on to college. The educational conveyor belt drops lower-class children at the beginning and bottom of the educational route and carries those from the higher classes a longer distance, nearly all the upper-class children going to the end of the line.

If the teachers and school administrators in grade and high schools know the class positions of the children who enter their schools they can predict who will and will not get to college. Furthermore, with such knowledge the educator can act to change a negative prediction to a positive one for the bright, ambitious lower- and lower-middle-class children, whose chances for higher education are now very slight.

The reason for the high mortality rate among the lower-class children becomes apparent when one examines the relation of the teachers and the other children to them. We now know that the intelligence of lower-class children is not responsible for their failures in school for often their I.Q.'s are equal to those of children higher up. Although inferior intelligence has been the most frequent and plausible explanation,[12] I.Q. tests equated to social class demonstrate that differential intelligence is not the answer.

Teachers, it must be said, although one of the most democratically minded groups in America, tend to favor the children of the classes above the Common Man and to show less interest in those below that level. Studies in the Deep South, New England, and the Middle West indicate that they rate the school work of children from the higher classes in accordance with their family's social position and conversely give low ratings to the work of the lower-class children.

To illustrate how the system of rating the child's abilities and attainments is relative to his position in the social-class order, we will quote from *Who Shall Be Educated?*[13] on what happens in Old City in the Deep South.

"In some elementary schools where there is more than one classroom per grade there is a section system by which students are rated and put together into A section, B section, C section, and more if necessary. In Old City, we find such a system. Each grade is divided into three sections: A, B, and C. This division into sections pervades the whole school system but of necessity it has less formal characteristics in the later years of high school. The junior high-school principal says of these sections:

> When a child enters school he is put into one of three sections according to what the teacher thinks his ability is. When you have dealt with children much you soon find that you can pretty well separate them into three groups according to ability. Then if a child shows more ability he may be shifted into a higher group or if he fails he may be moved into a lower group.

"Sometime later when this same principal was asked whether there seemed to be any class distinctions between the sections, he answered:

> There is to some extent. You generally find that children from the best families do the best work. That is not always true but usually it is so. The children from the lower class seem to be not as capable as the others. I think it is to some extent inheritance. The others come from people who are capable and educated, and also the environment probably has a great effect. They come to school with a lot of knowledge already that the others lack.

"Whatever one may think of this principal's theory in explanation of the correlation between social position and school section, this correlation holds true. There is a strong relationship between social status and rank in school. An analysis of the classes of three years in which the social position of 103 girls was known, shows that:

(1) of the ten upper-class girls, eight were in section A, one in B, and one in C
(2) of the seven upper-middle class girls, six were in section A and one in B
(3) of the thirty-three girls from lower middle and indeterminate middle class, twenty-one were in section A, ten in section B, and two in section C
(4) of the fifty-three lower-class girls, only six were in section A, twenty-eight in section B, and nineteen in section C.

"A teacher in junior high school was willing and able to talk more explicitly about these sections than was the principal quoted above. This teacher was asked if there was 'much class feeling in the school' and she said:

Oh, yes, there is a lot of that. We try not to have it as much as we can but of course we can't help it. Now, for instance, even in the sections we have, it is evident. Sections are supposed to be made up just on the basis of records in school but it isn't and everybody knows it isn't. I know right in my own A section I have children who ought to be in B section, but they are little socialites and so they stay in A. I don't say there are children in B who should be in A but in the A section there are some who shouldn't be there. We have discussed it in faculty meetings but nothing is ever done.

"Later on, she said:

Of course, we do some shifting around. There are some border-liners who were shifted up to make the sections more nearly even. But the socialites who aren't keeping up their standard in the A section were never taken into B or C section and they never will. They don't belong there socially. Of course, there are some girls in A section who don't belong there socially, but almost everyone of the socialites is in A.

"In Old City the ranking of students in their classrooms is clearly influenced by status considerations."
The democratically minded educator asks how this can be. The answer is that most of it is done through ignorance of social class and how it operates in our lives. To be more specific, part of the general answer lies within the teacher as a product of our class system. The teacher conscientiously applies his own best values to his rating of the child. The middle-class teacher, and over three-fourths of teachers are middle-class, applies

middle-class values. For him, upper- and upper-middle-class children possess traits that rank high and are positive; lower-class children have characteristics that are negative and are ranked low.

Perhaps the most powerful influence of social class on the educational careers of our children, and certainly one of the most decisive and crucial situations in settling the ultimate class position of children from the Common Man and lower-class levels, is the influence of other children on the child's desire to stay in school. If the world of the child is pleasant, rewarding, and increases his self-esteem, he is likely to want to stay and do well. If it is punishing and decreases his self-respect, he is likely to do poorly and want to quit.

In a study of children's ratings of other children in a middle western community, Neugarten found that the children of the upper and upper-middle classes were rated high by all other children for such traits as good looks, liking for school, leadership, friendship, and many other favorable personal traits; lower-class children were ranked low or, more often than not, were given a negative rating and were said to be bad looking, dirty, and "people you would not want for friends."[14] When it is remembered that these children were only in the fifth and sixth grades and that each child in these grades was supposedly rated by all other children with no reference to status, we can see how quickly class values influence behavior and have their decisive effect in molding the personalities and influencing the life careers of Americans from their earliest years. School for the children of the populous lower classes is not the satisfactory place it is for the middle and upper classes. Given children of equal intellect, ability, and interest, it can be predicted by the use of class analysis that a large percentage of those from the lower classes will be out of school before the sophomore year in high school and that none of the upper-class children, except those physically or mentally handicapped, will quit school.

If our society is to use more effectively the brains and native talent of this great army of young people, it must learn how to train them. To do this, it must keep them in school long enough to equip them with the skills and disciplines necessary for them to function satisfactorily in our economic and social world. Children, as well as teachers and school administrators, must have a conscious and explicit understanding of social class and a simple and easy way to use such knowledge in solving problems. Personality and I.Q. tests are important instruments to guide the teacher, but unless they are supplemented with instruments to measure and count the effects of social class they are insufficient. We believe the instructions in this book for the measurement of social class provide much of the necessary information.

Studies of the relations of workers and managers in business and industry demonstrate how class continues to operate selectively when the young people leave school. Management is bringing college-trained men into the lower ranks of supervisors and promoting fewer from the ranks because it finds that the workers, while good men technically, do not have the necessary knowledge about handling men and relating themselves effectively to the higher reaches of management. Their education is often insufficient to make them good prospects for continuing advancement. The hiring of formally educated men effectively puts a ceiling over the legitimate aspirations of workers expecting to rise in the ranks. The blocking of the worker's mobility and the encouragement of college-trained men is the ultimate payoff of what began in the grade schools. Mobility for workers is becoming more difficult; this means for the United States generally that the American Dream is becoming less real.[15]

Studies of the personalities of workers and managers now being made demonstrate that the effects of social-class and mobility drives are clearly discernible and demonstrably a part of the personality of individuals.[16]

In another area, studies of magazine subscriptions show that the class factor is of real importance in the selection of magazines. Readers from different class levels prefer various magazines on the basis of the different symbolic appeal of the stories and pictures. The Yankee City research showed that class entered not only into the purchase of magazines but into newspaper reading.[17] Later research indicates it has a decided effect on radio listening.

A casual examination of the advertising displayed in various magazines demonstrates that advertising agencies and their clients often waste their money because they are ignorant of the operation of class values in their business. This is not surprising since so many status factors have to be considered. The class distribution of readers of the periodicals published in America varies enormously. The readers of certain magazines are confined to the narrow limits of the classes above the Common Man, others to the lower classes, still others to the Common Man level, but there are some who are not confined to any one segment, being well distributed throughout all class levels. The editors of the magazines last designated, intuitively, by trial and error, or some better means, have chosen reading matter which appeals to all levels. The others, not knowing how to extend their readership or appealing deliberately to a narrow range, have a status-limited range of readers.

The readers to whom the advertiser is appealing may or may not be the potential purchasers of his product. The product may be of such a nature that it appeals to only a narrow segment of the total society; to advertise in those media which have readers largely from other strata or to pay for advertising in journals which appeal to every level is a waste of money.

Although advertising agencies often spend their money foolishly when judged by class criteria, the fault is not always theirs, for frequently the manufacturer or retailer does not know how his product appeals to the different classes. Sometimes the product will appeal to but one level, but often a product might appeal to, and be used by, all class levels, were the producer aware of how his product is valued at different social levels. It is certain that the use and meaning of most objects sold on the American market shift from class to class.

The soap opera is a product of contemporary radio. The average upper-middle-class radio listener has little interest in soap operas; in fact, most of this group are actively hostile to these curious little dramas that fill the daytime air waves. Yet, millions and millions of American women listen daily to their favorite soap operas, and advertisers of certain commodities have found them invaluable in selling their products.

Research has shown that the soap opera appeals particularly to the level of the Common Man. The problems raised in these folk dramas, their characters, plot, and values have a strong positive appeal to women of this class level, whereas they have little appeal to women above the Common Man level.[18]

Other researches demonstrate that furniture, including drapes, floor coverings, chairs and other seating facilities, is class-typed.

Another phenomenon of class, social mobility, is enormously important in the daily lives of Americans and, to a very great degree, determines how they will act on the job or at home. Recent studies of executives in large business enterprises clearly demonstrate that the success or failure of all of them is partly determined by the presence or absence of a "mobility drive." Our research shows that when a family loses its desire to achieve and advance itself, this very often is reflected in the executive's "slowing down" or being unwilling to make the effort necessary for success as a manager. On the other hand, some men are too aggressively mobile and stir up trouble by their overly ambitious desires and their ruthless competition.

Tests combining knowledge of social class and personality demonstrate the necessity of knowing not only what the man's status level is, what it has been, and what he wants it to be, but how the class values and beliefs of his early training have become integral parts of his personality, and ever-present guides for what he thinks, what he feels, and how he acts. Those concerned with selecting executives need a personality inventory and a man's I.Q. to predict how a man will function in a given job; but they also need to find out what his experiences in our status order have done to his individuality and character structure.

Every aspect of American thought and action is powerfully influenced by social class; to think realistically and act effectively, we must know and understand our status system.

We now face the task of giving exact and precise instructions on how to measure social class and how to identify and locate exactly the class position of anyone in our American society. The methods presented give the reader two techniques for establishing social-class position.

Notes

1. Jurgen Ruesch, Martin B.f Loeb, *et al., Chronic Disease and Psychological Invalidism; a Psychosomatic Study* (New York: American Society for Research in Psychosomatic Problems, 1946). A research at the University of California Hospital by Ruesch and others which demonstrates that this can be literally true; their results show how certain serious physical and mental ailments are directly attributable to social class and mobility strivings and anxieties.

2. New and poorly organized towns sometimes have class systems which have no old-family (upper-upper) class.

3. See W. Lloyd Warner and Paul S. Lunt, *The Social Life of a Modern Community,* Vol. I, "Yankee City Series" (New Haven: Yale University Press, 1941), pp. 58–72.

4. The evidence for the statements in this paragraph can be found in *The Social Life of a Modern Community,* pp. 287–300.

5. It is conceivable that in smaller communities there may be only three, or even two, classes present.

6. Allison Davis, Burleigh B. Gardner, and Mary R. Gardner, *Deep South* (Chicago: University of Chicago Press, 1941). Also read: John Dollard, *Caste and Class in a Southern Town* (New Haven: Yale University Press, 1937); Mozell Hill, "The All-Negro Society in Oklahoma" (Unpublished Ph.D. dissertation, University of Chicago, 1936); Harry J. Walker, "Changes in Race Accommodation in a Southern Community" (Unpublished Ph.D. dissertation, University of Chicago, 1945).

7. Allison Davis, Burleigh B. Gardner, and Mary R. Gardner, *Deep South* (Chicago: University of Chicago Press, 1941), p. 65.

8. See St. Clair Drake and Horace R. Cayton, *Black Metropolis* (New York: Harcourt, Brace & Co., 1945), for studies of two contrasting caste orders; read the "Methodological Note" by Warner in *Black Metropolis* for an analysis of the difference between the two systems.

9. See W. Lloyd Warner and Leo Srole, *The Social Systems of American Ethnic Groups,* Vol. III, "Yankee City Series" (New Haven: Yale University Press, 1945). Chapter X discusses the similarities and differences and presents a table of predictability on their probable assimilation and gives the principles governing these phenomena.

10. Gunnar Myrdal, *An American Dilemma* (New York: Harper & Bros., 1944). For an early publication on color-caste, see W. Lloyd Warner, "American Caste and Class," *American Journal of Sociology,* XLII, No. 2 (September, 1936),

234–37, and "Formal Education and the Social Structure," *Journal of Educational-Sociology,* IX (May, 1936), 524–531.

11. Robert J. Havighurst and Hilda Taba, *Adolescent Character and Personality* (New York: John Wiley & Sons, 1948).

12. The unpublished studies of Allison Davis, Robert J. Havighurst, and their collaborators on the class bias *within* the I.Q. tests themselves provide strong evidence to show that the tests are not "culture free" but reflect the middle- and upper-class cultural bias of those who fabricate them. For example, the tests, being largely products of upper-middle-class people, reflect their biases and only middle- and higher-class children are properly prepared to take them.

13. W. Lloyd Warner, Robert J. Havighurst, and Martin B. Loeb, *Who Shall Be Educated?* (New York: Harper & Bros., 1944), pp. 73–74.

14. Bernice L. Neugarten, "Social Class and Friendship among School Children," *American Journal of Sociology,* LI, No. 4 (January, 1946), 305–13.

15. See W. Lloyd Warner and J. O. Low, *The Social System of the Modern Factory,* Vol. IV, "Yankee City Series" (New Haven: Yale University Press, 1947), for a discussion of how many of the strikes and conflicts with management are determined by the factor of workers' blocked opportunity.

16. The ordinary tests of personnel offices fail completely to account for social mobility and class factors, yet the predictive value of these factors for the success of managers in different kinds of jobs is very high.

17. See Warner and Lunt, *The Social Life of a Modern Community,* Chapter XIX; and W. Lloyd Warner and William E. Henry, "Radio Daytime Serial: A Symbolic Analysis," *Genetic Psychology Monographs,* 1948, 37, pp. 3–71.

18. *Ibid.*

⇥ 5 ⇤

Some Principles of Stratification

Kingsley Davis and Wilbert E. Moore

In a previous paper some concepts for handling the phenomena of social inequality were presented.[1] In the present paper a further step in stratification theory is undertaken—an attempt to show the relationship between stratification and the rest of the social order.[2] Starting from the proposition that no society is "classless," or unstratified, an effort is made to explain, in functional terms, the universal necessity which calls forth stratification in any social system. Next, an attempt is made to explain the roughly uniform distribution of prestige as between the major types of positions in every society. Since, however, there occur between one society and another great differences in the degree and kind of stratification, some attention is also given to the varieties of social inequality and the variable factors that give rise to them.

Clearly, the present task requires two different lines of analysis—one to understand the universal, the other to understand the variable features of stratification. Naturally each line of inquiry aids the other and is indispensable, and in the treatment that follows the two will be interwoven, although, because of space limitations, the emphasis will be on the universals.

Throughout, it will be necessary to keep in mind one thing—namely, that the discussion relates to the system of positions, not to the individuals occupying those positions. It is one thing to ask why different positions carry different degrees of prestige, and quite another to ask how certain individuals get into those positions. Although, as the argument will try to show, both questions are related, it is essential to keep them

Reprinted from Kingsley Davis and Wilbert E. Moore, "Some Principles of Stratification," *American Sociological Review* 10 (April 1945): 242–249, by permission of The American Sociological Association.

separate in our thinking. Most of the literature on stratification has tried to answer the second question (particularly with regard to the ease or difficulty of mobility between strata) without tackling the first. The first question, however, is logically prior and, in the case of any particular individual or group, factually prior.

The Functional Necessity of Stratification

Curiously, however, the main functional necessity explaining the universal presence of stratification is precisely the requirement faced by any society of placing and motivating individuals in the social structure. As a functioning mechanism a society must somehow distribute its members in social positions and induce them to perform the duties of these positions. It must thus concern itself with motivation at two different levels: to instill in the proper individuals the desire to fill certain positions, and, once in these positions, the desire to perform the duties attached to them. Even though the social order may be relatively static in form, there is a continuous process of metabolism as new individuals are born into it, shift with age, and die off. Their absorption into the positional system must somehow be arranged and motivated. This is true whether the system is competitive or non-competitive. A competitive system gives greater importance to the motivation to achieve positions, whereas a non-competitive system gives perhaps greater importance to the motivation to perform the duties of the positions; but in any system both types of motivation are required.

If the duties associated with the various positions were all equally pleasant to the human organism, all equally important to societal survival, and all equally in need of the same ability or talent, it would make no difference who got into which positions, and the problem of social placement would be greatly reduced. But actually it does make a great deal of difference who gets into which positions, not only because some positions are inherently more agreeable than others, but also because some require special talents or training and some are functionally more important than others. Also, it is essential that the duties of the positions be performed with the diligence that their importance requires. Inevitably, then, a society must have, first, some kind of rewards that it can use as inducements, and, second, some way of distributing these rewards differently according to positions. The rewards and their distribution become a part of the social order, and thus give rise to stratification.

One may ask what kind of rewards a society has at its disposal in distributing its personnel and securing essential services. It has, first of all, the things that contribute to sustenance and comfort. It has, second, the things that contribute to humor and diversion. And it has, finally, the things that contribute to self respect and ego expansion. The last, because of the peculiarly social character of the self, is largely a function of the opinion of others, but it nonetheless ranks in importance with the first two. In any social system all three kinds of rewards must be dispensed differently according to positions.

In a sense the rewards are "built into" the position. They consist in the "rights" associated with the position, plus what may be called its accompaniments or perquisites. Often the rights, and sometimes the accompaniments, are functionally related to the duties of the position. (Rights as viewed by the incumbent are usually duties as viewed by other members of the community.) However, there may be a host of subsidiary rights and perquisites that are not essential to the function of the position and have only an indirect and symbolic connection with its duties, but which still may be of considerable importance in inducing people to seek the positions and fulfil the essential duties.

If the rights and perquisites of different positions in a society must be unequal, then the society must be stratified, because that is precisely what stratification means. Social inequality is thus an unconsciously evolved device by which societies insure that the most important positions are conscientiously filled by the most qualified persons. Hence every society, no matter how simple or complex, must differentiate persons in terms of both prestige and esteem, and must therefore possess a certain amount of institutionalized inequality.

It does not follow that the amount or type of inequality need be the same in all societies. This is largely a function of factors that will be discussed presently.

The Two Determinants of Positional Rank

Granting the general function that inequality subserves, one can specify the two factors that determine the relative rank of different positions. In general those positions convey the best reward, and hence have the highest rank, which (a) have the greatest importance for the society and (b) require the greatest training or talent. The first factor concerns function and is a matter of relative significance; the second concerns means and is a matter of scarcity.

Differential Functional Importance. Actually a society does not need to reward positions in proportion to their functional importance. It merely needs to give sufficient reward to them to insure that they will be filled competently. In other words, it must see that less essential positions do not compete successfully with more essential ones. If a position is easily filled, it need not be heavily rewarded, even though important. On the other hand, if it is important but hard to fill, the reward must be high enough to get it filled anyway. Functional importance is therefore a necessary but not a sufficient cause of high rank being assigned to a position.[3]

Differential Scarcity of Personnel. Practically all positions, no matter how acquired, require some form of skill or capacity for performance. This is implicit in the very notion of position, which implies that the incumbent must, by virtue of his incumbency, accomplish certain things.

There are, ultimately, only two ways in which a person's qualifications come about: through inherent capacity or through training. Obviously, in concrete activities both are always necessary, but from a practical standpoint the scarcity may lie primarily in one or the other, as well as in both. Some positions require innate talents of such high degree that the persons who fill them are bound to be rare. In many cases, however, talent is fairly abundant in the population but the training process is so long, costly, and elaborate that relatively few can qualify. Modern medicine, for example, is within the mental capacity of most individuals, but a medical education is so burdensome and expensive that virtually none would undertake it if the position of the M.D. did not carry a reward commensurate with the sacrifice.

If the talents required for a position are abundant and the training easy, the method of acquiring the position may have little to do with its duties. There may be, in fact, a virtually accidental relationship. But if the skills required are scarce by reason of the rarity of talent or the costliness of training, the position, if functionally important, must have an attractive power that will draw the necessary skills in competition with other positions. This means, in effect, that the position must be high in the social scale—must command great prestige, high salary, ample leisure, and the like.

How Variations Are to Be Understood. In so far as there is a difference between one system of stratification and another, it is attributable to whatever factors affect the two determinants of differential reward—namely, functional importance and scarcity of personnel. Positions important in one society may not be important in another, because the conditions faced by the societies, or their degree of internal development, may be different. The same conditions, in turn, may affect the question of scarcity; for in some societies the stage of development, or the external situation, may wholly obviate the necessity of certain kinds of skill or talent. Any particular system of stratification, then, can be understood as a product of the special conditions affecting the two aforementioned grounds of differential reward.

Major Societal Functions and Stratification

Religion. The reason why religion is necessary is apparently to be found in the fact that human society achieves its unity primarily through the possession by its members of certain ultimate values and ends in common. Although these values and ends are subjective, they influence behavior, and their integration enables the society to operate as a system. Derived neither from inherited nor from external nature, they have evolved as a part of a culture by communication and moral pressure. They must, however, appear to the members of the society to have some reality, and it is the role of religious belief and ritual to supply and reinforce this appearance of reality. Through belief and ritual the common ends and values are connected with an imaginary world symbolized by concrete sacred objects, which world in turn is related in a meaningful way to the facts and trials of the individual's life. Through the worship of the sacred objects and the beings they symbolize, and the acceptance of supernatural prescriptions that are at the same time codes of behavior, a powerful control over human conduct is exercised, guiding it along lines sustaining the institutional structure and conforming to the ultimate ends and values.

If this conception of the role of religion is true, one can understand why in every known society the religious activities tend to be under the charge of particular persons, who tend thereby to enjoy greater rewards than the ordinary societal member. Certain of the rewards and special privileges may attach to only the highest religious functionaries, but others usually apply, if such exists, to the entire sacerdotal class.

Moreover, there is a peculiar relation between the duties of the religious official and the special privileges he enjoys. If the supernatural world governs the destinies of men more ultimately than does the real world, its earthly representative, the person through whom one may communicate with the supernatural, must be a powerful individual. He is a keeper of sacred tradition, a skilled performer of the ritual, and an interpreter of lore and myth. He is in such close contact with the gods that he is viewed as possessing some of their characteristics. He is, in short, a bit sacred, and hence free from some of the more vulgar necessities and controls.

It is no accident, therefore, that religious functionaries have been associated with the very highest positions of power, as in theocratic regimes. Indeed, looking at it from this point of view, one may wonder why it is that they do not get *entire* control over their societies. The factors that prevent this are worthy of note.

In the first place, the amount of technical competence necessary for the performance of religious duties is small. Scientific or artistic capacity is not required. Anyone can set himself up as enjoying an intimate relation with deities, and nobody can successfully dispute him. Therefore, the factor of scarcity of personnel does not operate in the technical sense.

One may assert, on the other hand, that religious ritual is often elaborate and religious lore abstruse, and that priestly ministrations require tact, if not intelligence. This is true, but the technical requirements of the profession are for the most part adventitious, not related to the end in the same way that science is related to air travel. The priest can never be free from competition, since the criteria of whether or not one has genuine contact with the supernatural are never strictly clear. It is this competition that debases the priestly position below what might be expected at first glance. That is why priestly prestige is highest in those societies where membership in the profession is rigidly controlled by the priestly guild itself. That is why, in part at least, elaborate devices are utilized to stress the identification of the person with his office—spectacular costume, abnormal conduct, special diet, segregated residence, celibacy, conspicuous leisure, and the like. In fact, the priest is always in danger of becoming somewhat discredited—as happens in a secularized society—because in a world of stubborn fact, ritual and sacred knowledge alone will not grow crops or build houses. Furthermore, unless he is protected by a professional guild, the priest's identification with the supernatural tends to preclude his acquisition of abundant worldly goods.

As between one society and another it seems that the highest general position awarded the priest occurs in the medieval type of social order. Here there is enough economic production to afford a surplus, which can be used to support a numerous and highly organized priesthood; and yet the populace is unlettered and therefore credulous to a high degree. Perhaps the most extreme example is to be found in the Buddhism of Tibet, but others are encountered in the Catholicism of feudal Europe, the Inca regime of Peru, the Brahminism of India, and the Mayan priesthood of Yucatan. On the other hand, if the society is so crude as to have no surplus and little differentiation, so that every priest must be also a cultivator or hunter, the separation of the priestly status from the others has hardly gone far enough for priestly prestige to mean much. When the priest actually has high prestige under these circumstances, it is because he also performs other important functions (usually political and medical).

In an extremely advanced society built on scientific technology, the priesthood tends to lose status, because sacred tradition and supernaturalism drop into the background. The ultimate values and common ends of the society tend to be expressed in less anthropomorphic ways, by officials who occupy fundamentally political, economic, or educational rather than religious positions. Nevertheless, it is easily possible for intel-

lectuals to exaggerate the degree to which the priesthood in a presumably
secular milieu has lost prestige. When the matter is closely examined the
urban proletariat, as well as the rural citizenry, proves to be surprisingly
god-fearing and priest-ridden. No society has become so completely secularized as to liquidate entirely the belief in transcendental ends and supernatural entities. Even in a secularized society some system must exist for
the integration of ultimate values, for their ritualistic expression, and for
the emotional adjustments required by disappointment, death, and di-
saster.

Government. Like religion, government plays a unique and indispensable part in society. But in contrast to religion, which provides integration in terms of sentiments, beliefs; and rituals, it organizes the society in
terms of law and authority. Furthermore, it orients the society to the
actual rather than the unseen world.

The main functions of government are, internally, the ultimate enforcement of norms, the final arbitration of conflicting interests, and the overall planning and direction of society; and externally, the handling of war
and diplomacy. To carry out these functions it acts as the agent of the
entire people, enjoys a monopoly of force, and controls all individuals
within its territory.

Political action, by definition, implies authority. An official can command because he has authority, and the citizen must obey because he is
subject to that authority. For this reason stratification is inherent in the
nature of political relationships.

So clear is the power embodied in political position that political inequality is sometimes thought to comprise all inequality. But it can be
shown that there are other bases of stratification, that the following controls operate in practice to keep political power from becoming complete:
(a) The fact that the actual holders of political office, and especially those
determining top policy must necessarily be few in number compared to
the total population. (b) The fact that the rulers represent the interest of
the group rather than of themselves, and are therefore restricted in their
behavior by rules and mores designed to enforce this limitation of interest. (c) The fact that the holder of political office has his authority by
virtue of his office and nothing else, and therefore any special knowledge,
talent, or capacity he may claim is purely incidental, so that he often has
to depend upon others for technical assistance.

In view of these limiting factors, it is not strange that the rulers often
have less power and prestige than a literal enumeration of their formal
rights would lead one to expect.

Wealth, Property, and Labor. Every position that secures for its incumbent a livelihood is, by definition, economically rewarded. For this reason
there is an economic aspect to those positions (e.g. political and religious)

the main function of which is not economic. It therefore becomes convenient for the society to use unequal economic returns as a principal means
of controlling the entrance of persons into positions and stimulating the
performance of their duties. The amount of the economic return therefore becomes one of the main indices of social status.

It should be stressed, however, that a position does not bring power
and prestige *because* it draws a high income. Rather, it draws a high
income because it is functionally important and the available personnel
is for one reason or another scarce. It is therefore superficial and erroneous to regard high income as the cause of a man's power and prestige,
just as it is erroneous to think that a man's fever is the cause of his disease.[4]

The economic source of power and prestige is not income primarily,
but the ownership of capital goods (including patents, good will, and
professional reputation). Such ownership should be distinguished from
the possession of consumers' goods, which is an index rather than a cause
of social standing. In other words, the ownership of producers' goods is
properly speaking, a source of income like other positions, the income
itself remaining an index. Even in situations where social values are
widely commercialized and earnings are the readiest method of judging
social position, income does not confer prestige on a position so much as
it induces people to compete for the position. It is true that a man who
has a high income as a result of one position may find this money helpful
in climbing into another position as well, but this again reflects the effect
of his initial, economically advantageous status, which exercises its influence through the medium of money.

In a system of private property in productive enterprise, an income
above what an individual spends can give rise to possession of capital
wealth. Presumably such possession is a reward for the proper management of one's finances originally and of the productive enterprise later.
But as social differentiation becomes highly advanced and yet the institution of inheritance persists, the phenomenon of pure ownership, and reward for pure ownership, emerges. In such a case it is difficult to prove
that the position is functionally important or that the scarcity involved is
anything other than extrinsic and accidental. It is for this reason, doubt-
less, that the institution of private property in productive goods becomes
more subject to criticism as social development proceeds toward industrialization. It is only this pure, that is, strictly legal and functionless ownership, however, that is open to attack; for some form of active ownership,
whether private or public, is indispensable.

One kind of ownership of production goods consists in rights over the
labor of others. The most extremely concentrated and exclusive of such
rights are found in slavery, but the essential principle remains in serfdom,

peonage, encomienda, and indenture. Naturally this kind of ownership has the greatest significance for stratification, because it necessarily entails an unequal relationship.

But property in capital goods inevitably introduces a compulsive element even into the nominally free contractual relationship. Indeed, in some respects the authority of the contractual employer is greater than that of the feudal landlord, inasmuch as the latter is more limited by traditional reciprocities. Even the classical economics recognized that competitors would fare unequally, but it did not pursue this fact to its necessary conclusion that, however it might be acquired, unequal control of goods and services must give unequal advantage to the parties to a contract.

Technical Knowledge. The function of finding means to single goals, without any concern with the choice between goals, is the exclusively technical sphere. The explanation of why positions requiring great technical skill receive fairly high rewards is easy to see, for it is the simplest case of the rewards being so distributed as to draw talent and motivate training. Why they seldom if ever receive the highest rewards is also clear: the importance of technical knowledge from a societal point of view is never so great as the integration of goals, which takes place on the religious, political, and economic levels. Since the technological level is concerned solely with means, a purely technical position must ultimately be subordinate to other positions that are religious, political, or economic in character.

Nevertheless, the distinction between expert and layman in any social order is fundamental, and cannot be entirely reduced to other terms. Methods of recruitment, as well as of reward, sometimes lead to the erroneous interpretation that technical positions are economically determined. Actually, however, the acquisition of knowledge and skill cannot be accomplished by purchase, although the opportunity to learn may be. The control of the avenues of training may inhere as a sort of property right in certain families or classes, giving them power and prestige in consequence. Such a situation adds an artificial scarcity to the natural scarcity of skills and talents. On the other hand, it is possible for an opposite situation to arise. The rewards of technical position may be so great that a condition of excess supply is created, leading to at least temporary devaluation of the rewards. Thus "unemployment in the learned professions" may result in a debasement of the prestige of those position. Such adjustments and readjustments are constantly occurring in changing societies; and it is always well to bear in mind that the efficiency of a stratified structure may be affected by the modes of recruitment for positions. The social order itself, however, sets limits to the inflation or deflation of the prestige of experts: an over-supply tends to debase the rewards and discourage recruitment or produce revolution, whereas an under-supply tends to increase the rewards or weaken the society in competition with other societies.

Particular systems of stratification show a wide range with respect to the exact position of technically competent persons. This range is perhaps most evident in the degree of specialization. Extreme division of labor tends to create many specialists without high prestige since the training is short and the required native capacity relatively small. On the other hand it also tends to accentuate the high position of the true experts—scientists, engineers, and administrators—by increasing their authority relative to other functionally important positions. But the idea of a technocratic social order or a government or priesthood of engineers or social scientists neglects the limitations of knowledge and skills as a basic for performing social functions. To the extent that the social structure is truly specialized the prestige of the technical person must also be circumscribed.

Variation in Stratified Systems

The generalized principles of stratification here suggested form a necessary preliminary to a consideration of types of stratified systems, because it is in terms of these principles that the types must be described. This can be seen by trying to delineate types according to certain modes of variation. For instance, some of the most important modes (together with the polar types in terms of them) seem to be as follows:

(a) *The Degree of Specialization.* The degree of specialization affects the fineness and multiplicity of the gradations in power and prestige. It also influences the extent to which particular functions may be emphasized in the invidious system, since a given function cannot receive much emphasis in the hierarchy until it has achieved structural separation from the other functions. Finally, the amount of specialization influences the bases of selection. Polar types: *Specialized, Unspecialized.*

(b) *The Nature of the Functional Emphasis.* In general when emphasis is put on sacred matters, a rigidity is introduced that tends to limit specialization and hence the development of technology. In addition, a brake is placed on social mobility, and on the development of bureaucracy. When the preoccupation with the sacred is withdrawn, leaving greater scope for purely secular preoccupations, a great development, and rise in status, of economic and technological positions seemingly takes place. Curiously, a concomitant rise in political position is not likely, because it has usually been allied with the religious and stands to gain little by the decline of the latter. It is also possible for a society to emphasize family functions—as in relatively undifferentiated societies where high morality requires high fertility and kinship forms the main basis of social organization. Main types: *Familistic, Authoritarian (Theocratic* or sacred, and *Totalitarian* or secular), *Capitalistic.*

(c) *The Magnitude of Invidious Differences.* What may be called the amount of social distance between positions, taking into account the entire scale, is something that should lend itself to quantitative measurement. Considerable differences apparently exist between different societies in this regard, and also between parts of the same society. Polar types: *Equalitarian, Inequalitarian.*

(d) *The Degree of Opportunity.* The familiar question of the amount of mobility is different from the question of the comparative equality or inequality of rewards posed above, because the two criteria may vary independently up to a point. For instance, the tremendous divergences in monetary income in the United States are far greater than those found in primitive societies, yet the equality of opportunity to move from one rung to the other in the social scale may also be greater in the United States than in a hereditary tribal kingdom. Polar types: *Mobile* (open), *Immobile* (closed).

(e) *The Degree of Stratum Solidarity.* Again, the degree of "class solidarity" (or the presence of specific organizations to promote class interests) may vary to some extent independently of the other criteria, and hence is an important principle in classifying systems of stratification. Polar types: *Class organized, Class unorganized.*

External Conditions

What state any particular system of stratification is in with reference to each of these modes of variation depends on two things: (1) its state with reference to the other ranges of variation, and (2) the conditions outside the system of stratification which nevertheless influence that system. Among the latter are the following:

(a) *The Stage of Cultural Development.* As the cultural heritage grows, increased specialization becomes necessary, which in turn contributes to the enhancement of mobility, a decline of stratum solidarity, and a change of functional emphasis.

(b) *Situation with Respect to Other Societies.* The presence or absence of open conflict with other societies, of free trade relations or cultural diffusion, all influence the class structure to some extent. A chronic state of warfare tends to place emphasis upon the military functions, especially when the opponents are more or less equal. Free trade, on the other hand, strengthens the hand of the trader at the expense of the warrior and priest. Free movement of ideas generally has an equalitarian effect. Migration and conquest create special circumstances.

(c) *Size of the Society.* A small society limits the degree to which functional specialization can go, the degree of segregation of different strata, and the magnitude of inequality.

Composite Types

Much of the literature on stratification has attempted to classify concrete systems into a certain number of types. This task is deceptively simple, however, and should come at the end of an analysis of elements and principles, rather than at the beginning. If the preceding discussion has any validity, it indicates that there are a number of modes of variation between different systems, and that any one system is a composite of the society's status with reference to all these modes of variation. The danger of trying to classify whole societies under such rubrics as *caste, feudal,* or *open class* is that one or two criteria are selected and others ignored, the result being an unsatisfactory solution to the problem posed. The present discussion has been offered as a possible approach to the more systematic classification of composite types.

Notes

1. Kingsley Davis, "A Conceptual Analysis of Stratification," *American Sociological Review.* 7: 309–321, June, 1942.

2. The writers regret (and beg indulgence) that the present essay, a condensation of a longer study, covers so much in such short space that adequate evidence and qualification cannot be given and that as a result what is actually very tentative is presented in an unfortunately dogmatic manner.

3. Unfortunately, functional importance is difficult to establish. To use the position's prestige to establish it, as is often unconsciously done, constitutes circular reasoning from our point of view. There are, however, two independent clues: (a) the degree to which a position is functionally unique, there being no other positions that can perform the same function satisfactorily; (b) the degree to which other positions are dependent on the one in question. Both clues are best exemplified in organized systems of positions built around one major function. Thus, in most complex societies the religious, political, economic, and educational functions are handled by distinct structures not easily interchangeable. In addition, each structure possesses many different positions, some clearly dependent on, if not subordinate to, others. In sum, when an institutional nucleus becomes differentiated around one main function, and at the same time organizes a large portion of the population into its relationships, the *key* positions in it are of the highest functional importance. The absence of such specialization does not

prove functional unimportance, for the whole society may be relatively unspecial-ized; but it is safe to assume that the more important functions receive the first and clearest structural differentiation.

4. The symbolic rather than intrinsic role of income in social stratification has been succinctly summarized by Talcott Parsons, "An Analytical Approach to the Theory of Social Stratification," *American Journal of Sociology.* 45: 841–862, May, 1940.

→ 6 ←

Some Principles of Stratification: A Critical Analysis

Melvin M. Tumin

T he fact of social inequality in human society is marked by its ubiquity and its antiquity. Every known society, past and present, distributes its scarce and demanded goods and services unequally. And there are attached to the positions which command unequal amounts of such goods and services certain highly morally-toned evaluations of their importance for the society.

The ubiquity and the antiquity of such inequality has given rise to the assumption that there must be something both inevitable and positively functional about such social arrangements.

Clearly, the truth or falsity of such an assumption is a strategic question for any general theory of social organization. It is therefore most curious that the basic premises and implications of the assumption have only been most casually explored by American sociologists.

The most systematic treatment is to be found in the well-known article by Kingsley Davis and Wilbert Moore, entitled "Some Principles of Stratification."[1] More than twelve years have passed since its publication, and though it is one of the very few treatments of stratification on a high level of generalization, it is difficult to locate a single systematic analysis of its reasoning. It will be the principal concern of this paper to present the beginnings of such an analysis.

The central argument advanced by Davis and Moore can be stated in a number of sequential propositions, as follows:

Reprinted from Melvin M. Tumin, "Some Principles of Stratification: A Critical Analysis," *American Sociological Review* 18 (August 1953): 387–394, by permission of The American Sociological Association.

(1) Certain positions in any society are functionally more important than others, and require special skills for their performance.

(2) Only a limited number of individuals in any society have the talents which can be trained into the skills appropriate to these positions.

(3) The conversion of talents into skills involves a training period during which sacrifices of one kind or another are made by those undergoing the training.

(4) In order to induce the talented persons to undergo these sacrifices and acquire the training, their future positions must carry an inducement value in the form of differential, i.e., privileged and disproportionate access to the scarce and desired rewards which the society has to offer.[2]

(5) These scarce and desired goods consist of the rights and perquisites attached to, or built into, the positions, and can be classified into those things which contribute to (a) sustenance and comfort, (b) humor and diversion, (c) self-respect and ego expansion.

(6) This differential access to the basic rewards of the society has as a consequence the differentiation of the prestige and esteem which various strata acquire. This may be said, along with the rights and perquisites, to constitute institutionalized social inequality, i.e., stratification.

(7) Therefore, social inequality among different strata in the amounts of scarce and desired goods, and the amounts of prestige and esteem which they receive, is both positively functional and inevitable in any society.

Let us take these propositions and examine them *seriatim.*[3]

(1) Certain positions in any society are more functionally important than others and require special skills for their performance.

The key term here is "functionally important." The functionalist theory of social organization is by no means clear and explicit about this term. The minimum common referent is to something known as the "survival value" of a social structure.[4] This concept immediately involves a number of perplexing questions. Among these are: (a) the issue of minimum vs. maximum survival, and the possible empirical referents which can be given to those terms; (b) whether such a proposition is a useless tautology since any *status quo* at any given moment is nothing more and nothing less than everything present in the *status quo.* In these terms, all acts and structures must be judged positively functional in that they constitute essential portions of the *status quo*; (c) what kind of calculus of functionality exists which will enable us, at this point in our development, to add and subtract long and short range consequences, with their mixed qualities, and arrive at some summative judgment regarding the rating an act or structure should receive on a scale of greater or lesser functionality? At best, we tend to make primarily intuitive judgments. Often enough, these judgments involve the use of value-laden criteria, or, at least, criteria which are chosen in preference to others not for any sociologically systematic reasons but by reason of certain implicit value preferences.

Thus, to judge that the engineers in a factory are functionally more important to the factory than the unskilled workmen involves a notion regarding the dispensability of the unskilled workmen, or their replace-ability, relative to that of the engineers. But this is not a process of choice with infinite time dimensions. For at some point along the line one must face the problem of adequate motivation for *all* workers at all levels of skill in the factory. In the long run, *some* labor force of unskilled work-men is as important and as indispensable to the factory as *some* labor force of engineers. Often enough, the labor force situation is such that this fact is brought home sharply to the entrepreneur in the short run rather than in the long run.

Moreover, the judgment as to the relative indispensability and replace-ability of a particular segment of skills in the population involves a prior judgment about the bargaining-power of that segment. But this power is itself a culturally shaped *consequence* of the existing system of rating, rather than something inevitable in the nature of social organization. At least the contrary of this has never been demonstrated, but only assumed.

A generalized theory of social stratification must recognize that the prevailing system of inducements and rewards is only one of many vari-ants in the whole range of possible systems of motivation which, at least theoretically, are capable of working in human society. It is quite conceiv-able, of course, that a system of norms could be institutionalized in which the idea of threatened withdrawal of services, except under the most ex-treme circumstances, would be considered as absolute moral anathema. In such a case, the whole notion of relative functionality, as advanced by Davis and Moore, would have to be radically revised.

(2) Only a limited number of individuals in any society have the tal-ents which can be trained into the skills appropriate to these positions (i.e., the more functionally important positions).

The truth of this proposition depends at least in part on the truth of proposition 1 above. It is, therefore, subject to all the limitations indi-cated above. But for the moment, let us assume the validity of the first proposition and concentrate on the question of the rarity of appropriate talent.

If all that is meant is that in every society there is a *range* of talent, and that some members of any society are by nature more talented than others, no sensible contradiction can be offered, but a question must be raised here regarding the amount of sound knowledge present in any society concerning the presence of talent in the population.

For, in every society there is some demonstrable ignorance regarding the amount of talent present in the population. *And the more rigidly stratified a society is, the less chance does that society have of discovering any new facts about the talents of its members.* Smoothly working and stable systems of stratification, wherever found, tend to build-in obstacles to the further exploration of the range of available talent. This is especially true in those societies where the opportunity to discover talent in any one generation varies with the differential resources of the parent generation. Where, for instance, access to education depends upon the wealth of one's parents, and where wealth is differentially distributed, large segments of the population are likely to be deprived of the chance even to *discover* what are their talents.

Whether or not differential rewards and opportunities are functional in any one generation, it is clear that if those differentials are allowed to be socially inherited by the next generation, then, the stratification system is specifically dysfunctional for the discovery of talents in the next generation. In this fashion, systems of social stratification tend to limit the chances available to maximize the efficiency of discovery, recruitment and training of "functionally important talent."[5]

Additionally, the unequal distribution of rewards in one generation tends to result in the unequal distribution of motivation in the succeeding generation. Since motivation to succeed is clearly an important element in the entire process of education, the unequal distribution of motivation tends to set limits on the possible extensions of the educational system, and hence, upon the efficient recruitment and training of the widest body of skills available in the population.[6]

Lastly, in this context, it may be asserted that there is some noticeable tendency for elites to restrict further access to their privileged positions, once they have sufficient power to enforce such restrictions. This is especially true in a culture where it is possible for an elite to contrive a high demand and a proportionately higher reward for its work by restricting the numbers of the elite available to do the work. The recruitment and training of doctors in modern United States is at least partly a case in point.

Here, then, are three ways, among others which could be cited, in which stratification systems, once operative, tend to reduce the survival value of a society by limiting the search, recruitment and training of functionally important personnel far more sharply than the facts of available talent would appear to justify. It is only when there is genuinely equal access to recruitment and training for all potentially talented persons that differential rewards can conceivably be justified as functional. And stratification systems are apparently *inherently antagonistic* to the development of such full equality of opportunity.

(3) The conversion of talents into skills involves a training period during which sacrifices of one kind or another are made by those undergoing the training.

Davis and Moore introduce here a concept, "sacrifice" which comes closer than any of the rest of their vocabulary of analysis to being a direct reflection of the rationalizations, offered by the more fortunate members of a society, of the rightness of their occupancy of privileged positions. It is the least critically thought-out concept in the repertoire, and can also be shown to be least supported by the actual facts.

In our present society, for example, what are the scarifices which talented persons undergo in the training period? The possibly serious losses involve the surrender of earning power and the cost of the training. The latter is generally borne by the parents of the talented youth undergoing training, and not by the trainees themselves. But this cost tends to be paid out of income which the parents were able to earn generally by virture of *their* privileged positions in the hierarchy of stratification. That is to say, the parents' ability to pay for the training of their children is part of the deferential *reward* they, the parents, received for their privileged positions in the society. And to charge this sum up against sacrifices made by the youth is falsely to perpetrate a bill or a debt already paid by the society to the parents.

So far as the sacrifice of earning power by the trainees themselves is concerned, the loss may be measured relative to what they might have earned had they gone into the labor market instead of into advanced training for the "important" skills. There are several ways to judge this. One way is to take all the average earnings of age peers who did go into the labor market for a period equal to the average length of the training period. The total income, so calculated, roughly equals an amount which the elite can, on the average, earn back in the first decade of professional work, over and above the earnings of his age peers who are not trained. Ten years is probably the maximum amount needed to equalize the differential.[7] There remains, on the average, twenty years of work during each of which the skilled person then goes on to earn far more than his unskilled age peers. And, what is often forgotten, there is then still another ten or fifteen year period during which the skilled person continues to work and earn when his unskilled age peer is either totally or partially out of the labor market by virture of the attrition of his strength and capabilities.

One might say that the first ten years of differential pay is perhaps justified, in order to regain for the trained person what he lost during his training period. But it is difficult to image what would justify continuing such differential rewards beyond that period.

Another and probably sounder way to measure how much is lost during the training period is to compare the per capita income available to the trainee with the per capita income of the age peer on the untrained labor market during the so-called sacrificial period. If one takes into account the earlier marriage of untrained persons, and the earlier acquisition of family dependents, it is highly dubious that the per capita income of the wage worker is significantly larger than that of the trainee. Even assuming, for the moment, that there is a difference, the amount is by no means sufficient to justify a lifetime of continuing differentials.

What tends to be completely overlooked, in addition, are the psychic and spiritual rewards which are available to the elite trainees by comparison with their age peers in the labor force. There is, first, the much higher prestige enjoyed by the college student and the professional-school student as compared with persons in shops and offices. There is, second, the extremely highly valued privilege of having greater opportunity for self-development. There is, third, all the psychic gain involved in being allowed to delay the assumption of adult responsibilities such as earning a living and supporting a family. There is, fourth, the access to leisure and freedom of a kind not likely to be experienced by the persons already at work.

If these are never taken into account as rewards of the training period it is not because they are not concretely present, but because the emphasis in American concepts of reward is almost exclusively placed on the material returns of positions. The emphases on enjoyment, entertainment, ego enhancement, prestige and esteem are introduced only when the differentials in these which accrue to the skilled positions need to be justified. If these other rewards were taken into account, it would be much more difficult to demonstrate that the training period, as presently operative, is really sacrificial. Indeed, it might turn out to be the case that even at this point in their careers, the elite trainees were being differentially rewarded relative to their age peers in the labor force.

All of the foregoing concerns the quality of the training period under our present system of motivation and rewards. Whatever may turn out to be the factual case about the present system—and the factual case is moot—the more important theoretical question concerns the assumption that the training period under *any* system must be sacrificial.

There seem to be no good theoretical ground for insisting on this assumption. For, while under any system certain costs will be involved in training persons for skilled positions, these costs could easily be assumed by the society-at-large. Under these circumstances, there would be no need to compensate anyone in terms of differential rewards once the skilled positions were staffed. In short, there would be no need or justification for stratifying social positions on *these* grounds.

(4) In order to induce the talented persons to undergo these sacrifices and acquire the training, their future positions must carry an inducement value in the form of differential, i.e., privileged and disproportionate access to the scarce and desired rewards which the society has to offer.

Let us assume, for the purposes of the discussion, that the training period is sacrificial and the talent is rare in every conceivable human society. There is still the basic problem as to whether the allocation of differential rewards in scarce and desired goods and services is the only or the most efficient way of recruiting the appropriate talent to these positions.

For there are a number of alternative motivational schemes whose efficiency and adequacy ought at least to be considered in this context. What can be said, for instance, on behalf of the motivation which De Man called "joy in work," Veblen termed "instinct for workmanship" and which we latterly have come to identify as "intrinsic work satisfaction"? Or, to what extent could the motivation of "social duty" be institutionalized in such a fashion that self interest and social interest come closely to coincide? Or, how much prospective confidence can be placed in the possibilities of institutionalizing "social service" as a widespread motivation for seeking one's appropriate position and fulfilling it conscientiously?

Are not these types of motivations, we may ask, likely to prove most appropriate for precisely the "most functionally important positions"? Especially in a mass industrial society, where the vast majority of positions become standardized and routinized, it is the skilled jobs which are likely to retain most of the quality of "intrinsic job satisfaction" and be most readily identifiable as socially servicable. Is it indeed impossible then to build these motivations into the socialization pattern to which we expose our talented youth?

To deny that such motivations could be institutionalized would be to overclaim our present knowledge. In part, also, such a claim would seem to deprive from an assumption that what has not been institutionalized yet in human affairs is incapable of institutionalization. Admittedly, historical experience affords us evidence we cannot afford to ignore. But such evidence cannot legitimately be used to deny absolutely the possibility of heretofore untried alternatives. Social innovation is as important a feature of human socieities as social stability.

On the basis of these observations, it seems that Davis and Moore have stated the case much too strongly when they insist that a "functionally important position" which requires skills that are scarce, "must command great prestige, high salary, ample leisure, and the like," if the appropriate talents are to be attracted to the position. Here, clearly, the authors are postulating the unavoidability of very specific types of rewards and, by implications, denying the possibility of others.

(5) These scarce and desired goods consist of rights and perquisites attached to, or built into, the positions and can be classified into those things which contribute to (a) sustenance and comfort, (b) humor and diversion, (c) self-respect and ego expansion.

(6) This differential access to the basic rewards of the society has as a consequence the differentiation of the prestige and esteem which various strata acquire. This may be said, along with the rights and perquisites, to constitute institutionalized social inequality, i.e., stratification.

With the classification of the rewards offered by Davis and Moore there need be little argument. Some question must be raised, however, as to whether any reward system, built into a general stratification system, must allocate equal amounts of all three types of reward in order to function effectively, or whether one type of reward may be emphasized to the virtual neglect of others. This raises the further question regarding which types of emphasis is likely to prove most effective as a differential inducer. Nothing in the known facts about human motivation impels us to favor one type of reward over the other, or to insist that all three types of reward must be built into the positions in comparable amounts if the position is to have an inducement value.

It is well known, of course, that socieites differ considerably in the kinds of rewards they emphasize in their efforts to maintain a reasonable balance between responsibility and reward. There are, for instance, numerous socieites in which the conspicuous display of differential economic advantage is considered extremely bad taste. In short, our present knowledge commends to us the possibility of considerable plasticity in the way in which differnt types of reward can be structured into a functioning society. This is to say, it cannot yet be demonstrated that it is *unavoidable* that differential prestige and esteem shall accrue to positions which command differential reward in power and property.

What does seem to be unavoidable is that differential prestige shall be given to those in any society who conform to the normative order as against those who deviate from that order in a way judged immoral and detrimental. On the assumption that the continuity of a society depends on the continuity and stability of its normative order, some such distinction between conformists and deviants seems inescapable.

It also seems to be unavoidable that in any society, no matter how literate its tradition, the older, wiser and more experienced individuals who are charged with the enculturation and socialization of the young must have more power than the young, on the assumption that the task of effective socialization demands such differential power.

But this differentiation in prestige between the conformist and the deviant is by no means the same distinction as that between strata of individuals each of which operates *within* the normative order, and is composed of adults. The *latter* distinction, in the form of differentiated rewards and prestige between social strata is what Davis and Moore, and most sociologists, consider the structure of a stratification system. The *former* distinctions have nothing necessarily to do with the workings of such a system nor with the efficiency of motivation and recruitment of functionally important personnel.

Nor does the differentiation of power between young and old necessarily create differentially valued strata. For no society rates its young as less morally worthy than its older persons, no matter how much differential power the older ones may temporarily enjoy.

(7) Therefore, social inequality among different strata in the amounts of scarce and desired goods, and the amounts of prestige and esteem which they receive, is both positively functional and inevitable in any society.

If the objections which have hertofore been raised are taken as reasonable, then it may be stated that the only items which any society *must* distribute unequally are the power and property necessary for the performance of different tasks. If such differential power and property are viewed by all as commensurate with the differential responsibilities, and if they are culturally defined as *resources* and not as rewards, then, no differentials in prestige and esteem need follow.

Historically, the evidence seems to be that every time power and property are distributed unequally, no matter what the cultural definition, prestige and esteem differentiations have tended to result as well. Historically, however, no systematic effort has ever been made, under propitious circumstances, to develop the tradition that each man is as socially worthy as all other men so long as he performs his appropriate tasks conscientiously. While such a tradition seems utterly utopian, no known facts in psychological or social science have yet demonstrated its impossibility or its dysfunctionality for the continuity of a society. The achievement of a full institutionalization of such a tradition seems far too remote to contemplate. Some successive approximations at such a tradition, however, are not out of the range of prospective social innovation.

What, then, of the "positive functionality" of social stratification? Are there other, negative, functions of institutionalized social inequality which can be identified, if only tentatively? Some such dysfunctions of stratification have already been suggested in the body of this paper. Along with others they may now be stated, in the form of provisional assertions, as follows:

(1) Social stratification systems function to limit the possiblity of discovery of the full range of talent available in a society. This results from the fact of unequal access to appropriate motivation, channels of recruitment and centers of training.

(2) In foreshortening the range of available talent, social stratification systems function to set limits upon the possibility of expanding the productive resources of the society, at least relative to what might be the case under conditions of greater equality of opportunity.

(3) Social stratification systems function to provide the elite with the political power necessary to procure acceptance and dominance of an ideology which rationalizes the *status quo,* whatever it may be, as "logical," "natural" and "morally right." In this manner, social stratification systems function as essentially conservative influences in the societies in which they are found.

(4) Social stratification systems function to distribute favorable self-images unequally throughout a population. To the extent that such favorable self-images are requisite to the development of the creative potential inherent in men, to that extent stratification systems function to limit the development of this creative potential.

(5) To the extent that inequalities in social reward cannot be made fully acceptable to the less privileged in a society, social stratification systems function to encourage hostility, suspicion and distrust among the various segments of a society and thus to limit the possibilities of extensive social integration.

(6) To the extent that the sense of significant membership in a society depends on one's place on the prestige ladder of the society, social stratification systems function to distribute unequally the sense of significant membership in the population.

(7) To the extent that loyalty to a society depends on a sense of significant membership in the society, social stratification systems function to distribute loyalty unequally in the population.

(8) To the extent that participation and apathy depend upon the sense of significant membership in the society, social stratification systems function to distribute the motivation to participate unequally in a population.

Each of the eight foregoing propositions contains implicit hypotheses regarding the consequences of unequal distribution of rewards in a society in accordance with some notion of the functional importance of various positions. These are empirical hypotheses, subject to test. They are offered here only as exemplary of the kinds of consequences of social stratification which are not often taken into account in dealing with the problem. They should also serve to reinforce the doubt that social inequality is a device which is uniformly functional for the role of guaranteeing that the most important tasks in a society will be performed conscientiously by the most competent persons.

The obviously mixed character of the functions of social inequality should come as no surprise to anyone. If sociology is sophisticated in any sense, it is certainly with regard to its awareness of the mixed nature of any social arrangement, when the observer takes into account long as well as short range consequences and latent as well as manifest dimensions.

Summary

In this paper, an effort has been made to raise questions regarding the inevitability and positive functionality of stratification, or institutionalized social inequality in rewards, allocated in accordance with some notion of the greater and lesser functional importance of various positions. The possible alternative meanings of the concept "functional importance" has been shown to be one difficulty. The question of the scarcity or abundance of available talent has been indicated as a principal source of possible variation. The extent to which the period of training for skilled positions may reasonably be viewed as sacrificial has been called into question. The possibility has been suggested that very different types of motivational schemes might conceivably be made to function. The separability of differentials in power and property considered as resources appropriate to a task from such differentials considered as rewards for the performance of a task has also been suggested. It has also been maintained that differentials in prestige and esteem do not necessarily follow upon differentials in power and property when the latter are considered as appropriate resources rather than rewards. Finally, some negative functions, or dysfunctions, of institutionalized social inequality have been tentatively identified, revealing the mixed character of the outcome of social stratification, and casting doubt on the contention that

> Social inequality is thus an unconsciously evolved device by which societies insure that the most important positions are conscientiously filled by the most qualified persons.[8]

Notes

The writer has had the benefit of a most helpful criticism of the main portions of this paper by Professor W. J. Goode of Columbia University. In addition, he has had the opportunity to expose this paper to criticism by the Staff Seminar of the Sociology Section at Princeton. In deference to a possible rejoinder by Professors Moore and Davis, the writer has not revised the paper to meet the criticisms which Moore has already offered personally.

1. *American Sociological Review,* X (April, 1945), pp. 242–249. An earlier article by Kingsley David, entitled, "A Conceptual Analysis of Stratification," *American Sociological Review,* VII (June, 1942), pp. 309–321, is devoted primarily to setting forth a vocabulary for stratification analysis. A still earlier article by Talcott Parsons, "An Analytical Approach to the Theory of Social Stratification," *American Journal of Sociology,* XLV (November, 1940), pp. 849–862, approaches the problem in terms of why "differential ranking is considered a really fundamental phenomenon of social systems and what are the respects in which such ranking is important." The principal line of integration asserted by Parsons is with the fact of the normative orientation of any society. Certain crucial lines of connection are left unexplained, however, in this article, and in the Davis and Moore article of 1945 only some of these lines are made explicit.

2. The "scarcity and demand" qualities of goods and services are never explicitly mentioned by Davis and Moore. But it seems to the writer that the argument makes no sense unless the goods and services are so characterized. For if rewards are to function as differential inducements they must not only be differentially distributed but they must be both scarce and demanded as well. Neither the scarcity of an item by itself nor the fact of its being in demand is sufficient to allow it to function as a differntial inducement in a system of unequal rewards. Leprosy is scarce and oxygen is highly demanded.

3. The arguments to be advanced here are condensed versions of a much longer analysis entitled, *An Essay on Social Stratification.* Perforce, all the reasoning necessary to support some of the contentions cannot be offered within the space limits of this article.

4. Davis and Moore are explicitly aware of the difficulties involved here and suggest two "independent clues" other than survival value. See footnote 3 of their article.

5. Davis and Moore state this point briefly but do not elaborate it.

6. In the United States, for instance, we are only now becoming aware of the amount of productivity we, as a society, lose by allocating inferior opportunities and rewards, and hence, inferior motivation, to our Negro population. The actual amount of loss is difficult to specify precisely. Some rough estimate can be made, however, on the assumption that there is present in the Negro population about the same range of talent that is found in the White population.

7. These are only very rough estimates, of course, and it is certain there that is considerable income variation within the so-called elite group, so that the proposition holds only relatively more or less.

8. Davis and Moore, *op. cit.,* p. 243.

Part II: Related Readings

Blau, Peter M., and Otis Dudley Duncan. 1967. *The American Occupational Structure*. New York: Wiley.

Braun, Denny. 1997. *The Rich Get Richer: The Rise of Income Inequality in the United States and the World*, 2nd ed. Chicago: Nelson Hall.

Domhoff, G. William. 1998. *Who Rules America?* Mountain View, Calif.: Mayfield Publishing.

Gilbert, Dennis L. 1993. *The American Class Structure: A New Synthesis*, 4th ed. Belmont, Calif.: Wadsworth Publishing.

Jackman, Mary R., and Robert W. Jackman. 1983. *Class Awareness in the United States*. Berkeley: University of California Press.

Lipset, Seymour Martin, Reinhard Bendix, and Hans L. Zetterberg, eds. 1959. *Social Mobility in Industrial Society*. Berkeley: University of California Press.

Turner, Bryan S., ed. 1997. *The Early Sociology of Class: Readings on the Sociology of Social Class*. New York: Routledge.

Vanneman, Reeve, and Lynn Weber Cannon. 1987. *The American Perception of Class*. Philadelphia: Temple University Press.

Wrong, Dennis H. 1959. "The Functional Theory of Stratification: Some Neglected Considerations." *American Sociological Review* 24:772–82.

Part III

Neo-Marxian and Neo-Weberian Perspectives on Social Class

In his short piece "Marx and Weber: Problems of Class Structure," Anthony Giddens outlines what he takes to be the basic theoretical differences between Marx and Weber with respect to analyzing the class structure. Giddens argues that Marx's emphasis on understanding class structure in terms of production relations is the best way to understand class divisions, yet states that Weber's emphasis on market relations is significant when understanding class society and the structuration of different class forms. In an excerpt from his book *Marxism and Class Theory: A Bourgeois Critique*, Frank Parkin criticizes the Marxist emphasis on the exploitative nature of class relations and argues that the Weberian notion of social closure is a much more useful way of conceptualizing the basis of social inequality. In the excerpt reprinted here, Parkin elaborates on Weber's conceptualization of social closure. Parkin's piece is an excellent example of neo-Weberian views on social class. Erik Olin Wright presents a neo-Marxian analysis of class in the excerpt from his book *Class Counts*. Using a Marxist exploitation model of class analysis, Wright develops a conceptualization of the middle classes in capitalism. In addition, Wright offers a somewhat different interpretation from Giddens's as to the difference between a Weberian and a Marxist analysis of class.

⇢ 7 ⇠

Marx and Weber:
Problems of Class Structure

Anthony Giddens

Over recent years, there has grown up a tradition of scholarship, particularly among American authors, which treats the writings of Max Weber on issues of class structure, class conflict and capitalism as 'extensions' or 'elaborations' of Marx's views on these matters. Perhaps the origin of this standpoint is to be found in Gerth and Mills's introduction to what was, and probably remains, the most widely used selection of translations from the spectrum of Weber's works. 'Much of Weber's work', they say, is 'informed by a skilful application of Marx's historical method'; and they continue: 'part of Webers' own work may be thus seen as an attempt to "round out" Marx's economic materialism by a political and military materialism.'[1] The intellectual relation between Marx and Weber is a matter of some complexity since, as has just been indicated, Weber's proximate polemical targets were often the leading Marxists of his time, whose versions of Marxism were mainly of a 'mechanical' kind. But there are clear conceptual continuities between Marx and Weber in the latter's use of the terms 'class', 'class conflict' and 'capitalism',[2] and it is important to recognize that such terminological similarities readily may serve to gloss over what are perhaps the most deep-lying divergencies between the two thinkers.

Weber's specific use of 'class' connects both with his characterization of 'capitalism' as a type of socio-economic organization, and more generally as the modern Western form of society and culture, on the one hand, and with the emphases of his methodological writings on the other; all of these decisively separate his views from those of Marx. It is commonly accepted that Weber's famous threefold differentiation of class, status

Reprinted from Anthony Giddens, "Marx and Weber: Problems of Class Analysis" (New York, Basic Books, 1977): 203–207, by permission of the author.

and party is in some part directed polemically against what Weber saw as Marx's tendency to reduce too much of history to the history of class struggles. 'Status groups' *(Stände)* play a major role in history, and are not based directly upon economic relations as classes are; and in recognizing the third mode of organization linked to the promotion of interests, the formation of parties in the modern polity, Weber gives conceptual recognition to his theme that politics is not merely, or even perhaps primarily, an expression of class divisions. But it is not these factors alone that set Weber's analysis off from that of Marx: the more basic differences centre upon the notions of 'class' and 'class conflict' themselves.

Weber, like Marx, accepts that ' "property" and "lack of property" are . . . the basic categories of all class situations';[3] and his typology of 'ownership' and 'acquisition classes' is based upon such a categorization. But most of the weight in Weber's discussion is placed upon the advantages that can be mobilized in market relations by the possession of particular types of property—combined with the stress that the kinds of services that can be offered on the market also provide for the differential mobilization of market advantages among the propertyless. For Weber, 'class' is thus distinctively associated with the growth of *markets,* and 'class interests' refer to the distribution of interests in the competitive encounters of labour and commodity markets. Thus Weber says, for example, that the creditor–debtor relation only becomes the basis of class situations where a 'credit market' comes into existence: 'therewith, "class struggles" begin.'[4] 'Class situation' equals 'market situation'. For Marx, the connection between class and property, or more accurately private property, is quite different, and is bound in a most basic way to the characterization of global types of society. His very definition of capitalism or bourgeois society is in terms of the class relation between capital and wage-labour, expressed as relations of production: this is both the most integral feature of capitalism and of course the medium of its transformation. Weber recognizes that the preconditions of modern capitalism (as distinct from the various prior types of capitalistic activity that have existed) include not just the accumulation of capital itself, but the development of formally 'free' wage-labour, severed from control of its means of production.[5] But while the capital/wage-labour relation is necessary to the formation of modern economic enterprise, it is not its most basic defining feature. The most essential characteristic of modern capitalism is the 'rational', routinized organziation of economic activity within organizations having a stable and disciplined division of labour.

This characterization of capitalism is undoubtedly connected with themes in Weber's methodological writings, and more particularly with his emphasis upon the subjective interpretation of meaning. The subject-matter of history and of sociology is essentially 'meaningful social action' and its objective consequences. The decisive impetus to the emergence of modern capitalistic activity was given by the unintended consequences of conduct oriented to the Puritan ethos. The 'spirit of modern capitalism' is an ideal-typical formulation of the meaningful content of a definite form of economic activity. Weber's methodological position, which ties understanding the meaning of conduct to a version of what has subsequently come to be called 'methodological individualism', precluded him from systematically integrating a treatment of modern capitalistic activity, regarded as meaningful conduct, with the overall institutional character of capitalist society and its dynamics. Weber's discussions of modern capitalism as a generic form of economy and society thus tend to cluster into those concerned with capitalistic action and its 'spirit' on the one hand, and those offering an abstract classification of types of economic organization on the other. The same tendency appears in his analyses of class. There are two general, although brief, discussions of class in *Economy and Society*. One, now familiar as 'Class, status and party', discusses the modes of action that may be associated with economic interests; the other outlines the formal typology of ownership and acquisition classes. But it is not easy to discern how the first discussion is supposed to relate to the typology abstractly detailed in the latter. Weber does mention what he calls 'social class', as differentiated from 'class situation' (i.e. market position), but provides only a cursory and uninformative description of what the term is supposed to refer to.[6]

Weber's concept of class or 'class situation' cannot be accepted as a basis for a theory of class structure, for three reasons, each connected with what has been said above. First, the identification of class situation with market situation, and the general thesis that class divisions and class conflicts are phenomena of market relations, have to be rejected. Class relations, we should insist, as Marx did, are phenomena founded in production. Second, Weber's characterization of modern capitalism as involving above all the 'rational' organization of resources geared to the accumulation of profit is unsatisfactory, if only for the reason that it is not connected to a systematic treatment of the tensions created by the class system integral to capitalist society as a global order. Third, Weber's methodological standpoint, as reflected in his discussion of class, does not provide an adequate medium for connecting 'types of action' on the one hand, with 'supra-individual' institutions on the other.

To disavow the Weberian viewpoint in these terms is not, however, to write off Weber's contributions as worthless. For in emphasizing the importance of market advantages, and the collective interests associated with them, Weber's notion of class helps illuminate areas that are not clearly elucidated in Marx. Class relations, for Marx, are relations of production involved in the extraction of surplus value: but the phrase 'relations of production' covers several types of socio-economic relationships that Marx tends to run diffusely into one another.[7] We may distinguish the following such relationships: 1) those presumed in the operation of the 'task division of labour' in a given technique of production, e.g. between workers engaged in assembly-line production (paratechnical relations); 2) those more broadly involved in the organization of the enterprise, including especially the authority or power relations that pertain within it; 3) those involved in the linkages between productive organizations within commodity and labour markets; and 4) those brought into being through the connections between production and distribution, or the 'consumption' of goods. Weber's discussion of class concentrates upon 3) and indicates the importance, within the societies in which the economy is insulated from direct and overall political control, of the mobilization of advantages stemming from divergent 'market capacities' in class formation. But by identifying class situation and market situation, severing off 1) and 2) to a generalized theory of the rational organization of modern economic life, and 4) to the province of 'status groups', Weber moved away in a basic fashion from the Marxian standpoint.

I have suggested elsewhere how a reconstructed theory of classes and class conflict, which still insists that class divisions are founded in the system of production, and accepts the transformational potential of class conflict, can acknowledge the significance of market relations.[8] The essentials of this position are as follows. 'Class' is a phenomenon of the totality, in the sense in which, in a capitalist society, it expresses a system of exploitative domination cohered in terms of a definite alignment of economy and polity, sanctioned by the state. While this takes different forms in the period of 'classical capitalism' as contrasted with 'neo-' or 'corporate capitalism', it involves in each case the existence of a protective insulation that separates economic from political life—that neutralizes conflicts in industry by declaring them 'non-political'. Private property is the crucial support to this differentiation, guaranteeing definite rights to the mobilization of economic resources, and ensuring the dominance of the 'commodity form'. But in and of itself this is not enough to explicate or analyse class relations as definite structural forms: the generic concept 'class society' covers a variety of different types of class structuration. The structuration of classes as definite social forms, I have suggested, can be examined as in terms of the several aspects of the relations of production distinguished previously. Differential market capacity within the labour market, from this perspective, especially in so far as it is connected with 'closure' in mobility chances both inter- and intra-generationally, is basic to class structuration. But the consequences of the differentiation of market capacities can be either concentrated or fragmented by the influence of the more 'proximate' sources of structuration: the division of labour, and authority system, within economic organizations, and 'distributive groupings' (especially community or neighbourhood segregation). These influences upon class structuration should not be regarded as aggregate factors, but as systematically connected with one another.

Notes

1. H. H. Gerth and C. Wright Mills, *From Max Weber: Essays in Sociology*, New York, 1958, p. 47.
2. cf. Dieter Lindenlaub, *Richtungskämpfe im Verein für Sozialpolitik*, Wiesbaden, 1967.
3. Max Weber, *Economy and Society*, New York, 1968, vol. 2, p. 927.
4. ibid., p. 928.
5. Weber, *General Economic History* [New York, 1961], London, 1966, pp. 208–9.
6. *Economy and Society*, op. cit., vol. 1, p. 305.
7. For a slightly different formulation, cf. *The Class Structure of the Advanced Societies*. London [New York], 1973, p. 86.
9. ibid., p. 99. I hope this will make clear the arguments I set out in *The Class Structure of the Advanced Societies* are not to be characterized as 'Weberian', either in the narrow sense that they employ a similar notion of class to that of Weber, or in the wider connotation that they presuppose acceptance of Weber's philosophical and methodological views. Several critical discussions of the book, especially those emanating from more dogmatic Marxist authors, have seriously—almost wilfully—misrepresented my position in these respects.

✦ 8 ✦

Marxism and Class Theory: A Bourgeois Critique

Frank Parkin

The 'Boundary Problem' in Sociology

The persistent attractions of Marxist class theory have almost certainly been boosted by the less than inspiring alternative offered by academic sociology. In so far as there is any sort of tacitly agreed upon model of class among western social theorists it takes the form of the familiar distinction between manual and non-manual labour. No other criterion for identifying the class boundary seems to enjoy such widespread acceptance among those who conduct investigations into family structure, political attitudes, social imagery, life-styles, educational attainment, and similar enquiries that keep the wheels of empirical sociology endlessly turning. Paradoxically, however, although the manual/non-manual model is felt to be highly serviceable for research purposes, it is not commonly represented as a model of class cleavage and conflict. That is to say, the two main social categories distinguished by sociology for purposes of class analysis are not invested with antagonistic properties comparable to those accorded to proletariat and bourgeoisie in Marxist theory. This would be less cause for comment if proponents of the manual/non-manual model normally construed the social order as a harmonious and integrated whole; but to construe it instead in terms of conflict, dichotomy, and cleavage, as most of these writers now appear

Reprinted from Frank Parkin, *Marxism and Class Theory* (New York: Columbia University Press, 1979), by permission of the publisher. Copyright © 1979 by Columbia University Press.

to do, seems to reveal an awkward contrast between the empirical model of class and the general conception of capitalist society.

The strongest case that could be made out for identifying the line between manual and non-manual labour as the focal point of class conflict would be one that treated capitalist society as the industrial firm writ large. It is only within the framework of 'factory despotism' that the blue-collar/white-collar divide closely corresponds to the line of social confrontation over the distribution of spoils and the prerogatives of command. And this is particularly the case in those industrial settings where even the lowest grades of white-collar staff are cast in the role of managerial subalterns physically and emotionally removed from the shop-floor workers. Within the microcosm of capitalism represented by the typical industrial firm, the sociological model of class has something to recommend it as an alternative to one constructed around the rights of property.

The drawback is, however, that social relations within the capitalist *firm* are a less accurate guide to class relations within capitalist *society* than they might once have been. The reason for this is that the postwar expansion of the public sector has given rise to an ever-increasing assortment of non-manual groups in local government and welfare services that cannot in any real sense be thought of as the tail-end of a broad managerial stratum aligned against a manual workforce. Frequently, in fact there is no manual workforce to confront in the occupational settings within which these white-collar groups are employed.[1] And even where teachers, social workers, nurses, local government clerks, lower civil servants, and the like do form part of an organization that includes janitors, orderlies, cleaners, and other workers by hand, they do not usually stand in the same quasi-managerial relationship to them as does the staff employee to the industrial worker in the capitalist firm.

The usual rationale for treating intermediate and lower white-collar groups as a constituent element of a dominant class is that these groups traditionally have identified themselves with the interests of capital and management rather than with the interests of organized labour. But for various reasons this identification is easier to accomplish in the sphere of private industry and commerce than in the public sector. In the latter, as already pointed out, not only is there usually no subordinate manual group physically present to inspire a sense of white-collar status elevation, but also the charms of management are likely to seem less alluring when the chain of command stretches ever upwards and out of sight into the amorphous and unlovely body of the state. Moreover, public sector employees do not have the same opportunities as those in the commercial sector for transferring their special skills and services to different and competing employers; all improvements in pay and conditions must be negotiated with a monopoly employer, and one who is under close budgetary scrutiny. All this makes for a relationship of some tension between white-collar employees and the state *qua* employer, a condition more akin to that found between manual labour and management than between white-collar employees and management in the private sector. Thus, the validity of the manual/non-manual model as a representation of class conflict relies more heavily upon a view of the commercial employee as the prototypical case of the white-collar worker than really is justified, given the enormous growth of public-sector employment.

What this suggests is that manual and non-manual groups can usefully be thought of as entities socially differentiated from each other in terms of life-chances and opportunities, but not as groups standing in a relationship of exploiter and exploited, of dominance and subordination, in the manner presumably required of a genuine conflict model. Expressed differently, the current sociological model does not fulfil even the minimal Weberian claim that the relations between classes are to be understood as 'aspects of the distribution of power'. Instead of a theoretical framework organized around the central ideas of mutual antagonism and the incompatibility of interests we find one organized around the recorded facts of mere social differentiation. . . .

The 'Boundary Problem' in Marxism

The variety of [Marxist] interpretations on offer make it more than usually difficult to speak of 'the' Marxist theory of class. In some respects the range of differences within this camp has tended to blur the simple contrast between Marxist and bourgeois theories; and this is particularly so given the tendency for Marxists to adopt familiar sociological categories under substitute names. The most striking example of this is the tacit acknowledgment of the role of *authority* in the determination of bourgeois status. This arises from the need to find some theoretical principle by which the managerial stratum, in particular, can be assigned to the same class as the owners of capital. Although allusions may occasionally be made to the fact that managers are sometimes shareholders in the companies that employ them, it is clear that this is a contingent feature of managerial status and could not be regarded as theoretically decisive. Managers with and without private company shares do not appear to be different political and ideological animals.

The exercise of discipline over the workforce, on the other hand, is a necessary feature of the managerial role, not a contingent one; and as such it recommends itself as a major criterion of bourgeois class membership. Indeed, for some Marxists managerial authority has in certain respects superseded property ownership as *the* defining attribute of a capitalist class. According to Carchedi, 'the manager, rather than the capitalist rentier, is the central figure, he, rather than the capitalist rentier, is the non-labourer, the non-producer, the exploiter. He, rather than the capitalist rentier, is capital personified.'[2]

Interestingly, by proclaiming that the supervision and control of subordinates is the new hallmark of bourgeois status, Marxist theorists have come surprisingly close to endorsing Dahrendorf's view of the determinate role of authority in establishing the class boundary.[3] Their strict avoidance of this term in favour of some synonym or circumlocution ('mental labour', 'global function of capital', 'labour of superintendence') is perhaps a tacit admission of this embarrassing affinity with Dahrendorf's position. Although none of these writers would accept Dahrendorf's proposition that authority is a general phenomenon that encompasses property; it is nevertheless the case that their treatment of authority relations, however phrased, takes up far more of their analysis than the discussion of property relations.

To make property the centrepiece of class analysis would bring with it the duty of explaining precisely why the apparatus of managerial authority and control was thought to grow out of the institution of private ownership. Presumably it has come to the attention of western Marxists that societies that have done away with property in its private forms nevertheless have their own interesting little ways of seeing to the 'superintendence of labour'. The view that class and authority relations under capitalism are a unique product of private ownership must rest on a belief that these things are ordered in a very different way under the socialist mode of production. The fact that this mode of production figures not at all in any of the class analyses referred to suggests that Marxists are none too happy about drawing the very comparisons that are so essential to their case. After all, supposing it was discovered that factory despotism, the coercive uses of knowledge, and the privileges of mental labour were present not only in societies where the manager was 'capital personified', but also in societies where he was the party personified? Marxists would then be faced with the unwelcome choice of either having to expand the definition of capitalism to embrace socialist society, or of disowning the cherished concepts of private property and surplus extraction upon which their class theory is grounded. The obvious reluctance to engage in the comparative analysis of class under the two ostensibly different modes of production is therefore understandable enough. As for the credibility of Marxist class theory, it would seem that the advent of socialist society is about the worst thing that could have happened to it.

A further difficulty encountered by this theory is the attempt to arrive at some general principles by which to demarcate the established professions from routine white-collar employees, a distinction required by the evident self-identification of the former with the general interests of the bourgeoisie. In place of any general principles, however, resort is had to an eclectic assortment of descriptive indices demonstrating that 'higher' white-collar groups are in various ways simply better off than 'lower' white-collar groups. Braverman, for example, lists advantages such as higher pay, security of employment, and the privileged market position of the professions.[4] In similar vein, Westergaard and Resler suggest drawing a line of class demarcation beneath professional and managerial groups on the grounds that 'they are not dependent on the markets in which they sell their labour in anything like the way that other earners are'.[5] Their incomes 'are determined by market rules and mechanisms over which, in effect, they themselves have considerable influence in their own corners of the market'.[6]

The one notable thing about this kind of analysis is that despite its avowedly Marxist provenance it is indistinguishable from the approach of modern bourgeois social theory. It is, after all, Weber rather than Marx who provides the intellectual framework for understanding class in terms of market opportunities, life-chances, and symbolic rewards. The focus upon income differences and other market factors is difficult to reconcile with the standard Marxist objection to bourgeois sociology that it mistakenly operates on the level of distribution instead of on the level of productive relations. It might also be said that it is from Weber rather than Marx that the postulated link between class position and bureaucratic authority most clearly derives. The fact that these normally alien concepts of authority relations, life-chances, and market rewards have now been comfortably absorbed by contemporary Marxist theory is a handsome, if unacknowledged, tribute to the virtues of bourgeois sociology. Inside every neo-Marxist there seems to be a Weberian struggling to get out. . . .

Social Closure

By social closure Weber means the process by which social collectivities seek to maximize rewards by restricting access to resources and opportunities to a limited circle of eligibles. This entails the singling out of certain social or physical attributes as the justificatory basis of exclusion. Weber suggests that virtually any group attribute—race, language, social origin, religion—may be seized upon provided it can be used for 'the monopolization of specific, usually economic opportunities'.[7] This monopolization is directed against competitors who share some positive or negative characteristic; its purpose is always the closure of social and economic opportunities to *outsiders*'.[8] The nature of these exclusionary practices, and the completeness of social closure, determine the general character of the distributive system.

Surprisingly, Weber's elaboration of the closure theme is not linked in any immediate way with his other main contributions to stratification theory, despite the fact that processes of exclusion can properly be conceived of as an aspect of the distribution of power, which for Weber is practically synonymous with stratification. As a result, the usefulness of the concept for the study of class and similar forms of structured inequality becomes conditional on the acceptance of certain refinements and enlargements upon the original usage.

An initial step in this direction is to extend the notion of closure to encompass other forms of collective social action designed to maximize claims to rewards and opportunities. Closure strategies would thus include not only those of an exclusionary kind, but also those adopted by the excluded themselves as a direct response to their status as outsiders. It is in any case hardly possible to consider the effectiveness of exclusion practices without due reference to the countervailing actions of socially defined ineligibles. As Weber acknowledges: 'Such group action may provoke a corresponding reaction on the part of those against whom it is directed.'[9] In other words, collective efforts to resist a pattern of dominance governed by exclusion principles can properly be regarded as the other half of the social closure equation. This usage is in fact employed by Weber in his discussion of 'community closure' which, as Neuwirth has shown, bears directly upon those forms of collective action mounted by the excluded—that is, 'negatively privileged status groups'.[10]

The distinguishing feature of exclusionary closure is the attempt by one group to secure for itself a privileged position at the expense of some other group through a process of subordination. That is to say, it is a form of collective social action which, intentionally or otherwise, gives rise to a social category of ineligibles or outsiders. Expressed metaphorically, exclusionary closure represents the use of power in a 'downward' direction because it necessarily entails the creation of a group, class, or stratum of legally defined inferiors. Countervailing action by the 'negatively privileged', on the other hand, represents the use of power in an upward direction in the sense that collective attempts by the excluded to win a greater share of resources always threaten to bite into the privileges of legally defined superiors. It is in other words a form of action having usurpation as its goal. *Exclusion* and *usurpation* may therefore be regarded as the two main generic types of social closure, the latter always being a consequence of, and collective response to, the former.[11]

Strategies of exclusion are the predominant mode of closure in all stratified systems. Where the excluded in their turn also succeed in closing off access to remaining rewards and opportunities, so multiplying the number of substrata, the stratification order approaches the furthest point of contrast to the Marxist model of class polarization. The traditional caste system and the stratification of ethnic communities in the United States provide the clearest illustrations of this closure pattern, though similar processes are easily detectable in societies in which class formation is paramount. Strategies of usurpation vary in scale from those designed to bring about marginal redistribution to those aimed at total expropriation. But whatever their intended scale they nearly always contain a potential challenge to the prevailing system of allocation and to the authorized version of distributive justice.

All this indicates the ease with which the language of closure can be translated into the language of power. Modes of closure can be thought of as different means of mobilizing power for the purpose of engaging in distributive struggle. To conceive of power as a built-in attribute of closure is at the very least to dispense with those fruitless searches for its 'location' inspired by Weber's more familiar but completely unhelpful definition in terms of the ubiquitous struggle between contending wills. Moreover, to speak of power in the light of closure principles is quite consistent with the analysis of class relations. Thus, to anticipate the discussion, the familiar distinction between bourgeoisie and proletariat, in its classic as well as in its modern guise, may be conceived of as an expression of conflict between classes defined not specifically in relation to their place in the productive process but in relation to their prevalent modes of closure, exclusion and usurpation, respectively. . . .

In modern capitalist society the two main exclusionary devices by which the bourgeoisie constructs and maintains itself as a class are, first, those surrounding the institutions of property; and, second, academic or professional qualifications and credentials. Each represents a set of legal arrangements for restricting access to rewards and privileges: property ownership is a form of closure designed to prevent general access to the means of production and its fruits; credentialism is a form of closure designed to control and monitor entry to key positions in the division of labour. The two sets of beneficiaries of these state-enforced exclusionary practices may thus be thought of as the core components of the dominant class under modern capitalism. Before taking up the discussion of common class interests fostered by private property and credentials it may be useful to consider each of the two principal closure strategies separately.

It has already been remarked upon how the concept of property has been devalued in the modern sociology of class as a result of the heavy weighting accorded to the division of labour. This has not always been true of bourgeois sociology. Weber was in full accord with Marx in asserting that ' "Property" and "lack of property" are . . . the basic characteristics of all class situations'.[12] The post-Weberian tendency to analyse social relations as if the propertyless condition had painlessly arrived is perhaps a natural extension of the use of 'western' or 'industrial' to denote societies formerly referred to as capitalist. The post-war impact of functionalist theory certainly contributed to this tendency, since the proclamation of belief in the ultimate victory of achievement values and the merit system of reward naturally cast doubt on the importance of property as an institution. The inheritance of wealth after all requires notably little expenditure of those talents and efforts that are said to be the only keys to the gates of fortune.

The extent to which property has come to be regarded as something of an embarrassing theoretical anomaly is hinted at in the fact that it receives only the most cursory acknowledgment in Davis and Moore's functionalist manifesto, and even then in the shape of an assertion that 'strictly legal and functionless ownership . . . is open to attack' as capitalism develops.[13] To propose that the imposition of death duties and estate taxes constitutes evidence for an assault upon property rights is somewhat like suggesting that the introduction of divorce laws is evidence of state support for the dissolution of the family. Property in this scheme of things can only be understood as a case of cultural lag—one of those quaint institutional remnants from an earlier epoch which survives by the grace of social inertia.

Several generations earlier Durkheim had reasoned along similar lines in declaring that property inheritance was 'bound up with archaic concepts and practices that have no part in our present day ethics'.[14] And although he felt it was not bound to disappear on this account he was willing to predict that inherited wealth would 'lose its importance more and more', and if it survived at all it would only be 'in a weakened form'.[15] Durkheim was not of course opposed to private property as such, only its transmission through the family. 'It is obvious that inheritance, by creating inequalities amongst men from birth, that are unrelated to merit or services, invalidates the whole contractual system at its very roots.'[16] Durkheim wanted society made safe for property by removing those legal practices that could not be squared with conceptions of liberal individualism and which therefore threatened to cause as much moral and social disturbance as the 'forced' division of labour.

There was not much likelihood of property itself declining as an institution because it was part of the order of things invested with a sacred character, understood in that special Durkheimian sense of an awesome relationship rooted deeply in the *conscience collective*. Although the sacred character of property arose originally from its communal status, the source of all things holy, the marked evolutionary trend towards the individualization of property would not be accompanied by any decline in its divinity. Personal rights to property were therefore seen by Durkheim as part of that general line of social development by which the individual emerges as a distinct and separate entity from the shadow of the group. The individual affirms himself as such by claiming exclusive rights to things over and above the rights of the collectivity. There is more than an echo here of Hegel's dictum that 'In his property a person exists for the first time as reason'.[17] As Plamenatz comments:

> 'It makes sense to argue, as Hegel does, that it is partly in the process of coming to own things, and to be recognised as their owners, that human beings learn to behave rationally and responsibly, to lead an ordered life. It is partly in the process of learning to distinguish mine from thine that a child comes to recognise itself as a person, as a bearer of rights and duties, as a member of a community with a place of its own inside it.'[18]

As Plamenatz goes on to say, however plausible as a defence of personal property this may be, as a defence of capitalist property relations it is 'lamentably inadequate'.[19]

The reason for this is that Hegel, like Durkheim, and many contemporary sociologists, never clearly distinguishes between property as rights to personal *possessions* and property as capital. Parsons is only one of many who reduces all forms of property to the status of a possession; this is understood as 'a right or a bundle of rights. In other words it is a set of expectations relative to social behaviour and attitudes.'[20] If property is simply a specific form of possession, or a certain bundle of rights, then everyone in society is a proprietor to some degree. On this reckoning there can be no clear social division between owners and non-owners, only a gradual, descending scale from those with very much to those with very little. This is well in line with Parsons' usual theoretical strategy of asserting the benign quality of any resource by reference to its widespread distribution. The possession of a toothbrush or an oilfield confers similar rights and obligations upon their owners, so that property laws cannot be interpreted as class laws. As Rose and his colleagues have suggested:

> 'the ideological significance of such a universalistic and disinterested legal interpretation of property in modern capitalist society is two-fold. First, as the law protects and recognises *all* private property, and as virtually all members of the society can claim title to *some* such property, it may be claimed that all members of society have some vested interest in the *status quo*. From such a perspective, therefore, it can be argued that, far from representing an irreconcilable conflict of interests, the distribution of property in modern capitalist society gives rise to a commensurability of interests, any differences being variations of degree rather than kind. The office developer, the shareholder, the factory-owner, the householder and even the

second-hand car owner may thus be represented as sharing fundamentally
common interests, if not identities.'[21]

What the sociological definition of property as possessions interestingly fails to ask is why only certain limited forms of possession are legally admissible. It is patently not the case, for example, that workers are
permitted to claim legal possession of their jobs; nor can tenants claim
rights of possession to their homes, nor welfare claimants enforceable
rights to benefits. Possession in all these cases is pre-empted by the conflicting claims of employers, landlords, and the state respectively, which
are accorded legal priority. Although the law may treat the rights of ownership in true universalistic fashion it is silent on the manner by which
only some 'expectations' are successfully converted to the status of property rights and others not. . . .

The case for restoring the notion of property into the centre of class
analysis is that it is the most important single form of social closure common to industrial societies. That is to say, rights of ownership can be
understood not as a special case of authority so much as a specific form
of exclusion. As Durkheim expresses it, 'the right of property is the right
of a given individual to exclude other individual and collective entities
from the usage of a given thing'.[22] Property is defined negatively by 'the
exclusion it involves rather than the prerogatives it confers.[23] Durkheim's
reference to *individual* rights of exclusion clearly indicates that once
again he has possessions in mind, and that, characteristically, he sees no
important distinction between objects of personal ownership, and the
control of resources resulting in the exercise of power.

It is clearly necessary to distinguish property as possessions from property as capital, since only the latter is germane to the analysis of class
systems. Property as capital is, to paraphrase Macpherson, that which
'confers the right to deny men access to the means of life and labour'.[24]
This exclusionary right can obviously be vested in a variety of institutional forms, including the capitalist firm, a nationalized industry, or a
Soviet enterprise. All these are examples of property that confers legal
powers upon a limited few to grant or deny general access to the means
of production and the distribution of its fruits. Although personal possessions and capital both entail rights of exclusion, it is only the exclusionary rights embedded in the latter that have important consequences for
the life-chances and social condition of the excluded. To speak of property in the context of class analysis is, then, to speak of capital only, and
not possessions.

Once property is conceptualized as a form of exclusionary social closure there is no need to become entangled in semantic debates over
whether or not workers in socialist states are 'really' exploited. The rele-

vant question is not whether surplus extraction occurs, but whether the state confers rights upon a limited circle of eligibles to deny access to the 'means of life and labour' to the rest of the community. If such exclusionary powers are legally guaranteed and enforced, an exploitative relationship prevails as a matter of definition. It is not of overriding importance to know whether these exclusionary powers are exercised by the formal owners of property or by their appointed agents, since the social consequences of exclusion are not demonstrably different in the two cases. Carchedi and other neo-Marxists may therefore be quite correct in suggesting that 'the manager is capital personified'; but all the needs to be added is first, that this dictum holds good not only for monopoly capitalism, but for *all,* including socialism, systems in which access to property and its benefices is in the legal gift of a select few; and, second, that it squares far more comfortably with the assumptions of bourgeois, or at least Weberian, sociology than with classical marxist theory.

Of equal importance to the exclusionary rights of property is that set of closure practices sometimes referred to as 'credentialism'—that is, the inflated use of educational certificates as a means of monitoring entry to key positions in the division of labour. Well before the onset of mass higher education, Weber had pointed to the growing use of credentials as a means of effecting exclusionary closure.

'The development of the diploma from universities, and business and engineering colleges, and the universal clamour for the creation of educational certificates in all fields make for the formation of a privileged stratum in bureaus and offices. Such certificates support their holders' claims for intermarriages with notable families . . . , claims to be admitted into the circles that adhere to "codes of honour", claims for a "respectable" remuneration rather than remuneration for work well done, claims for assured advancement and old-age insurance, and, above all, claims to monopolize social and economically advantageous positions. When we hear from all sides the demand for an introduction of regular curricula and special examinations, the reason behind it is, of course, not a suddenly awakened "thirst for education" but the desire for restricting the supply of these positions and their monopolization by the owners of educational certificates. Today the "examination" is the universal means of this monopolization, and therefore examinations irresistibly advance.'[25]

The use of credentials for closure purposes, in the manner elaborated by Weber, has accompanied the attempt by an ever-increasing number of white collar occupations to attain the status of professions. Professionalization itself may be understood as a strategy designed, amongst other things, to limit and control the supply of entrants to an occupation in order to safeguard or enhance its market value. Much of the literature on the professions has tended to stress their differences from workaday occupations, usually accepting the professions' own evaluation of their singularity in creating rigorous codes of technical competence and ethical standards. It is perfectly possible to accept that the monopolization of skills and services does enable the professions to exercise close control over the moral and technical standards of their members, whilst also endorsing Weber's judgement that 'normally this concern for efficient performance recedes behind the interest in limiting the supply of candidates for the benefices and honours of a given occupation.'[26]

It would seem to be the professions' anxiety to control the supply side of labour that accounts, in part at least, for the qualifications epidemic referred to by Dore as the 'diploma disease'.[27] This is the universal tendency among professions to raise the minimum standards of entry as increasing numbers of potential candidates attain the formerly scarce qualifications. The growing reliance upon credentials as a precondition of professional candidature is commonly justified by reference to the greater complexity of the tasks to be performed and the consequent need for more stringent tests of individual capacity. Yet Berg's careful analysis of these claims was able to turn up no evidence to show that variations in the level of formal education were matched by variations in the quality of work performance.[28] Nor was there anything to suggest that professional tasks were in fact becoming more complex such as to justify a more rigorous intellectual screening of potential entrants. Berg's conclusion, in line with Weber's, is that credentials are accorded their present importance largely because they simplify and legitimate the exclusionary process. It is on these grounds, among others, that Jencks suggests that 'the use of credentials or tests scores to exclude "have not" groups from desirable jobs can be viewed in the same light as any other arbitrary form of discrimination'.[29]

Formal qualifications and certificates would appear to be a handy device for ensuring that those who possess 'cultural capital' are given the best opportunity to transmit the benefits of professional status to their own children. Credentials are usually supplied on the basis of tests designed to measure certain class-related qualities and attributes rather than those practical skills and aptitudes that may not so easily be passed on through the family line. It is illuminating in this respect to contrast the white-collar professions with the sporting and entertaining professions. What is especially remarkable about the latter is how relatively few of the children of successful footballers, boxers, baseball and tennis stars, or the celebrities of stage and screen have succeeded in reproducing their parents' elevated status. One reason for this would seem to be that the skills called for in these pursuits are of a kind that must be acquired and cultivated by the individual in the actual course of performance, and which are thus not easily transferred from parent to child. That is, there seems to be no equivalent to cultural capital that can be socially transmitted to the children of those gifted in the performing arts that could give them a head start in the fiercely competitive world of professional sport and show business. Presumably, if the rewards of professional sport could be more or less guaranteed along conventional career or bureaucratic lines serious proposals would eventually be put forward to limit entry to those candidates able to pass qualifying examinations in the theory of sporting science. This would have the desired effect of giving a competitive edge to those endowed with examination abilities over those merely excelling in the activity itself.[30]

The reason why professional sports, and the entertainment professions in general, are likely to be resistant to the 'diploma disease' offers a further instructive comment upon the nature of the white-collar professions. The supreme advantage of occupational closure based upon credentials is that all those in possession of a given qualification are deemed competent to provide the relevant skills and services for the rest of their professional lives. There is no question of retesting abilities at a later stage in the professional career. The professional bodies' careful insistence that members of the lay public are not competent to sit in judgement on professional standards effectively means that a final certificate is a meal ticket for life. In the sporting and entertainment professions, by contrast, the skills and abilities of the performers are kept under continuous open review by the public; those who consume the services are themselves the ultimate arbiters of an individual's competence and hence his market value, as expressed via their aggregate purchasing power. There can be no resort to the umbrella protection of a professional licence when sporting prowess and the ability to entertain are felt to be in decline in the eyes of those who pass collective judgement.

Against this exacting yardstick, then, credentialism stands out as a doubly effective device for protecting the learned professions from the hazards of the marketplace. Not merely does it serve the convenient purpose of monitoring and restricting the supply of labour, but also effectively masks all but the most extreme variations in the level of ability of professional members, thereby shielding the least competent from ruinous economic punishment. The small irony is that credentialist strategies aimed at neutralizing the competitive effects of the market confer most benefit upon that class that is most prone to trumpet the virtues of a free market economy and the sins of collectivism.

The use of systematic restrictions upon occupational entry has not of course been wholly confined to the white-collar professions. Certain skilled manual trades have adopted similar techniques designed to regulate supply, as in the case of the apprenticeship system or certain forms of the closed shop. Some unskilled occupations such as dock work and market-portering have also sought to restrict entry to the kinsmen of those already employed, though this does not normally guarantee control over the actual volume of labour supply. The crucial difference between these attempts at occupational exclusion by manual trades and those adopted by the professions is that the latter generally seek to establish a *legal monopoly* over the provision of services through licensure by the state. Whereas the learned professions have been remarkably successful in winning for themselves the status of what Weber calls 'legally privileged groups', it has been far less common for the manual trades to secure the blessing of the state for their exclusionary tactics. Indeed, the resort to 'restrictive practices' on the part of organized labour is commonly condemned as a breach of industrial morality that should be curbed rather than sanctified by law. Presumably the fact that governments have usually been reluctant to legislate formally against such practices is not unrelated to the awkwardness that might arise in drawing legal distinctions between these practices and the exclusionary devices of the professions, including the profession of law itself.

A further point of difference between professional closure and restrictive practices by trade unions is that the main purpose behind the latter activity has been the attempt to redress in some small part the disadvantages accruing to labour in its uneven contest with capital. Closure by skilled workers has been a strategy embarked upon in the course of struggle against a superior and highly organized opponent, and not primarily with the conscious intent of reducing the material opportunities of other members of the labour force. Credentialism, on the other hand, cannot be seen as a response to exploitation by powerful employers; the learned or free professions were never directly subordinate to an employing class during the period when they were effecting social closure. Their conflict, concealed beneath the rhetoric of professional ethics was, if anything, with the lay public. It was the struggle to establish a monopoly of certain forms of knowledge and practice and to win legal protection from lay interference. The aim was to ensure that the professional-client relationship was one in which the organized few confronted the disorganized many. Under modern conditions, where many professionals are indirectly in the service of the state and occasionally in conflict with the government of the day over pay and conditions, a somewhat better case could perhaps be made for likening the position of professions to that of craft unions, in so far as both could be said to employ closure for purposes of bargaining with a more powerful agency. But however acrimonious relations may become between professional bodies and the state, it is worth noting that the state rarely if ever threatens to take sanctions against professions in the way that would most seriously damage their interests—namely, by rescinding their legal monopoly.

On all these grounds it is necessary to regard credentialism as a form of exclusionary social closure comparable in its importance for class formation to the institution of property. Both entail the use of exclusionary rules that confer benefits and privileges on the few through denying access to the many, rules that are enshrined in law and upheld by the coercive authority of the state. It follows from this that the dominant class under modern capitalism can be thought of as comprising those who possess or control productive capital and those who possess a legal monopoly of professional services. These groups represent the core body of the dominant or exploiting class by virtue of their exclusionary powers which necessarily have the effect of creating a reciprocal class of social inferiors and subordinates. . . .

Class Reproduction

There is a definite tension between the commitment to closure by way of property and credentials on the part of one generation and the desire to pass on benefits to subsequent generations of kith and kin. It is not in the least necessary to deny that most members of the exclusionary class will strive to put their own advantages to the service of their children, while asserting at the same time that bourgeois forms of closure are not exactly tailor-made for self-recruiting purposes. In fact exclusionary institutions formed under capitalism do not seem to be designed first and foremost to solve the problem of class reproduction through the family line. The kinship link can only be preserved as a result of *adaptation* by the bourgeois family to the demands of institutions designed to serve a different purpose; it does not come about as a natural consequence of the closure rules themselves. In systems based on aristocratic, caste, or racial exclusion, families of the dominant group can expect to pass on their privileged status to their own descendants as a direct result of the closure rules in operation, however socially lethargic those families might be. The bourgeois family, by contrast, cannot rest comfortably on the assumption of automatic class succession; it must make definite social exertions of its own or face the very real prospect of generational decline. In other words, although the typical bourgeois family will certainly be better equipped than most to cope with the closure system on its children's behalf, it must still approach the task more in the manner of a challenge with serious risks attached than as a foregone conclusion. Even when it is successful it must face the prospect of sharing bourgeois status with uncomfortably large numbers of parvenus. What kind of system is this to provoke such anxieties in the breasts of those supposedly in command?

The answer must be that it is a system designed to promote a class formation biased more in the direction of sponsorship and careful selection of successors than of hereditary transmission. Although *both* aims might be held desirable, the first takes ideological precedence over the second, so that succession along kinship lines must be accomplished in conformity with the application of criteria that are ostensibly indifferent to the claims of blood. There is nothing especially bizarre about an arrangement whereby a dominant class relinquishes its children's patrimony in order to ensure that the calibre of its replacements is of the highest possible order. It would only appear strange to those unable to conceive that the attachment to doctrine could ever take precedence over the claims of kinship. As Orwell noted in his discussion of communist party oligarchies:

> 'The essence of oligarchical rule is not father-to-son inheritance, but the persistence of a certain world-view and a certain way of life, imposed by the dead upon the living. A ruling group is a ruling group so long as it can nominate its successors. The Party is not concerned with perpetuating its blood with perpetuating itself.'[31]

There are also powerful forces in capitalist society that are more dedicated to the perpetuation of bourgeois values than bourgeois blood. Ideological commitment to the rights of property and the value of credentials may be just as fierce as any faith in Leninist party principles. Each represents a set of ideals that can be held quite irrespective of the consequences upon the family fortunes of their advocates. The party militant's belief in a system of political selection and exclusion that could tell against his own ideologically wayward children has its counterpart in the liberal's belief in the validity of meritocratic criteria that would find against his not too clever offspring. It was perhaps examples of this kind that Weber had in mind when referring to patterns of closure distinguished by a 'rational commitment to values.' The same idea is also more than hinted at in Marx's well-known assertion that the bourgeoisie always puts the interests of the whole class above the interests of any of its individual members. These priorities are not, presumably, reversed whenever the individual members in question happen to be someone's children.

To suggest that predominant forms of closure under modern capitalism are in some tension with the common desire to transmit privileges to one's own is to point up politically significant differences of interpretation of bourgeois ideology. The classical liberal doctrine of individualism contains a powerful rejection of those principles and practices that evaluate men on the basis of group or collectivist criteria. The political driving force of individualist doctrines arose in part from the opposition of the emergent middle classes to aristocratic pretensions and exclusiveness centred around the notion of descent. The emphasis upon lineage was an obvious hindrance to those who had raised themselves into the ranks of property by way of industry and commerce, but who lacked the pedigree necessary to enter the charmed circles inhabited by those of political power and social honour. Although non-landed wealth could occasionally be cleansed through marriage into the nobility, the new rising class sought to make property respectable in its own right by divorcing it from its associations with particular status groups. Property in all its forms was to become the hallmark of moral worth without reference back, as it were, to the quality of proprietorial blood. In the individualist credo, property thus assumed the same characteristic as money in the marketplace, where the ability to pay overrides all questions as to the actual source of the buyer's cash. . . .

One reason for pressing the distinction between collectivist and individualist criteria underlying all forms of exclusion is to suggest that subordinate classes or strata are likely to differ in their political character according to which of the two sets of criteria is predominant. Looked at in ideal-typical terms, purely collectivist types of exclusion, such as those based on race, religion, ethnicity, and so on, would produce a subordinate group of a communal character—that is, one defined in terms of a total all-encompassing negative status. Blacks under *apartheid* or minority groups herded into religious and racial ghettoes are the familiar modern examples. The polar archetypal case would be that of exclusion based solely on individualist criteria, giving rise to a subordinate group marked by intense social fragmentation and inchoateness. The example here is furnished by the model of a pure meritocracy in which class is virtually replaced by a condition of discrete segmental statuses never quite reaching the point of coalescence. In non-fictional societies, of course, individualist and collectivist criteria are usually applied in some combination or other, so producing stratified systems located at various points between these two extremes. This can be depicted in simplified form as follows:

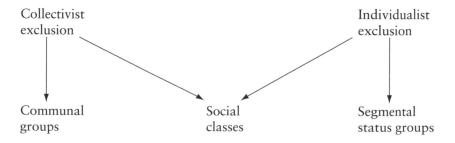

Collectivist exclusion → Communal groups

Individualist exclusion → Segmental status groups

Collectivist exclusion and Individualist exclusion → Social classes

Thus, of the three major types of subordination, classes are presented as a combination of both types of exclusionary criteria. Schematically, a subordinate class could be located towards either of the opposite poles according to the relative weighting of the two sets of criteria. The proletariat of early and mid-nineteenth century Europe, for example, would approximate to the communal pole by virtue of its wholesale exclusion from civil society arising from the treatment of its members as a *de facto* collectivity. The badge of proletarian status carried with it the kinds of stigmata commonly associated with subordinate racial and ethnic groups. It was a total condition which permitted little leeway for the cultivation of those small part-time identities that bring temporary release from the humilities of servile status. Correspondingly, of course, the proletarian condition under communal exclusion offered fertile ground for movements and ideologies which raised large questions about the nature of the political order and its legitimacy, and not merely about the fact of unequal shares.

It is the very hallmark of the communal condition that subordination is experienced through a myriad of direct personal degradations and affronts to human dignity, encouraged by the submersion of the individual into the stereotype of his 'membership' group. It is largely as a result of this that the politics of communal exclusion so frequently stresses the need for subordinate groups to create an alternative moral identity to that fashioned for them by their oppressors. Although the condition of the early proletariat was never completely of a communal kind, it was not so different from that of a despised ethnic group, if only because the visible signs and trappings of status were as unmistakably clear as racial features. Certainly the mixture of horror, fear, and revulsion felt by the upper classes for the great unwashed was not a far remove from the sentiments usually held by dominant racial or ethnic groups towards those whom they simultaneously exploit and despise.

To speak of a gradual shift in the nature of exclusionary rules, from collectivism to individualism, is thus to point to those tendencies making for the progressive erosion of the communal components of proletarian status, otherwise referred to as working-class incorporation into civil society. Although under advanced capitalism labour remains an exploited commodity, the status of the worker does not derive to anything like the same extent from his immersion in a total collective identity and its accompanying rituals of personal degradation. Mills' portrayal of the pattern of 'status cycles' by which the modern urban worker is able to find escape in class anonymity during leisure periods and vacations may be somewhat overdrawn;[32] but there is a real sense in which the absence of clearly visible and unambiguous marks of inferior status has made the enforcement of an all-pervasive deference system almost impossible to sustain outside the immediate work situation. It would now take an unusually sharp eye to detect the social class of Saturday morning shoppers in the High Street, whereas to any earlier generation it would have been the most elementary task. More to the point, even assuming that a lynx-eyed bourgeois could accurately spot a worker in mufti, what real hope could he now entertain of having any claim to deference actually honoured? A system of deference can only operate effectively when the status of strangers can accurately be judged, and the information required for this is difficult to come by without the aid of a collectivist stereotype. In this respect the personal dignity of the modern worker has been enhanced by the evolution towards individualist exclusion, even though his subordination to capital remains a central fact of life.

As class subordination becomes increasingly less communal in character, the political ideals and programmes that flourish among its members tend to become less inspired by visions of a new moral order and the promise of emancipation, and rather more preoccupied with the issues of distributive justice. Those who deplore the apparent flickering of those energies and passions that produced nineteenth-century socialism might care to reflect on the possibility that this has less to do with the iniquities of working-class leadership than with the system of modern exploitation, in which the engines of political resentment are not so lavishly fuelled by the personal degradations arising from wholesale collectivist exclusion. . . .

Conclusion

By way of concluding this part of the discussion, it might be appropriate to offer some general remarks on the explanatory status of the closure model. This model, like any other, recommends the use of a particular sociological vocabulary and an attendant battery of concepts that contain barely disguised moral assumptions about the nature of class society. It is not strictly speaking a 'theory' of class but a way of conceptualizing it that differs from that proposed by other variants of bourgeois sociology or by Marxism. Most of what we conventionally call theories of class are in fact conceptual methods of this kind. They are, for the most part, take-it-or-leave-it moral classifications, not sets of propositions that stand or fall under the impact of evidence. What conceivable social facts could destroy either the Marxist conception of class as an exploitative relationship, or the liberal conception of class as an exchange relationship? Since conceptual models are ways of presenting social reality, it follows that the preference for one presentation over another entails a personal judgement of some kind about the moral standing of class society.

On this score, the closure model is almost bound to appear defective by liberal and Marxist theorists alike. Liberal theory endorses a contractual view of class, in which the notion of mutual interest and harmony is the essential ingredient. Marxism, on the other hand, assumes not merely the absence of harmony and common class interests, but, more importantly, the presence of irresolvable antagonisms that drive the system to ultimate breakdown. The neo-Weberian position advanced here is that the relation between classes is neither one of harmony and mutual benefit, nor of irresolvable and fatal contradiction. Rather, the relationship is understood as one of mutual antagonism and permanent *tension;* that is, a condition of unrelieved distributive struggle that is not necessarily impossible to 'contain'. Class conflict may be without cease, but it is not inevitably fought to a conclusion. The competing notions of harmony, contradiction, and tension could thus be thought of as the three broad possible ways of conceptualizing the relation between classes, and on which all class models are grounded.

Since class models are not subject to direct empirical assault, the case for advancing the cause of one in preference to another rests partly on the claim that it draws attention to a set of problems and issues that are otherwise obscured. Thus, one of the attractions of the closure model is that it highlights the fact of communal cleavage and its relationship to class, and seeks to analyse both within the same conceptual framework. More generally, it proposes that intra-class relations be treated as conflict phenomena of the same general order as inter-class relations, and not as mere disturbances or complications within a 'pure' class model. Hence the extension of the concept of exploitation to cover both sets of phenomena. There is, in addition, a recommendation that social classes be defined by reference to their mode of collective action rather than to their place in the productive process or the division of labour. The reason for this is that incumbency of position in a formally defined structure does not normally correspond to class alignment where it really counts—at the level of organized political sentiment and conduct. This serious lack of fit between all positional or systemic definitions of class and the actual behaviour of classes in the course of distributive struggle, is not due to any lack of the categories employed. It arises from the initial theoretical decision to discount the significance and effect of variations in the cultural and social make-up of the groups assigned to the categories in question. Models constructed upon such formal, systemic definitions require of their advocates much ingenuity in accounting for the continuous and wholesale discrepancies between class position and class behaviour. A good deal of the intellectual energy of western Marxism has been dissipated in wrestling with this very problem which is of its own conceptual making.

Notes

1. The hospital setting provides, perhaps, the most important exception. Industrial conflicts between medical staff and the manual workers' unions over issues such as 'pay beds' are unusual in having clear-cut ideological, rather than bread-and-butter, causes.

2. Carchedi 1975:48. For Braverman, too, managers and executives are 'part of the class that personifies capital . . .' (1974:405).

3. Dahrendorf 1959.

4. Braverman 1974: Chapter 18.

5. Westergaard and Resler 1975:92.

6. Westergaard and Resler 1975:346.

7. Weber (eds Roth and Wittich) 1968:342.

8. Weber (eds Roth and Wittich) 1968:342.

9. Weber (eds Roth and Wittich) 1968:342.

10. Neuwirth 1969.

11. These arguments were first tentatively sketched out in my 'Strategies of Social Closure in Class Formation' (Parkin 1974). In that publication the two types of closure were referred to as *exclusion* and *solidarism*. This latter term does not, however, satisfactorily describe a mode of collective action standing in direct opposition to exclusion, since solidaristic behaviour can itself be used for blatantly exclusionary ends. That is to say, solidarism does not properly refer to the purposes for which power is employed. The term *usurpation* more adequately captures the notion of collective action designed to improve the lot of a subordinate group at the expense of a dominant group. Solidarism is simply one means among others to this end.

12. Weber (eds Gerth and Mills) 1948:182.

13. Davis and Moore 1945:247.

14. Durkheim 1957:174.

15. Durkheim 1957:175 and 217.

16. Durkheim 1957:213.

17. Plamenatz 1975:120.

18. Plamenatz 1975:121.

19. Plamenatz 1975:121.

20. Parsons 1951:119. The entry in the index under 'Property' invites the reader to 'see Possessions'.

21. Rose *et al.* 1976:703.

22. Durkheim 1957:142.

23. Durkheim 1957:142.

24. Macpherson 1973.
25. Weber (eds Gerth and Mills) 1948:241–42.
26. Weber (eds Roth and Wittich) 1968:344.
27. Dore 1976.
28. Berg 1973.
29. Jencks 1972:192.
30. It transpires that the idea is not so far-fetched after all. The Council for National Academic Awards has recently approved the syllabus for a BA Degree in Sports Studies. Undergraduates will be instructed in 'the variables influencing performance in sport; a science and its sports application; scientific methods, statistics and computing; and wide practical experience in a number of sports.' *Daily Telegraph,* Monday, 28 August 1978, p. 3.
31. Orwell 1949:215.
32. Mills 1956:257–58.

References

Berg, I. (1973) *Education and Jobs: The Great Training Robbery.* Harmondsworth: Penguin Books.
Braverman, H. (1974) *Labor and Monopoly Capital.* New York: Monthly Review Press.
Carchedi, G. (1975) On the Economic Identification of the New Middle Class. *Economy and Society* 4 (1).
Dahrendorf, R. (1959) *Class and Class Conflict in Industrial Society.* London: Routledge.
Davis, K. and Moore, W. E. (1945) Some Principles of Stratification. *American Sociological Review* X (2).
Dore, R. (1976) *The Diploma Disease.* London: Allen and Unwin.
Durkheim, E. (1957) *Professional Ethics and Civic Morals.* London: Routledge.
Jencks, C. (1972) *Inequality.* New York: Basic Books.
Macpherson, C. B. (1973) A Political Theory of Property. In, *Democratic Theory: Essays in Retrieval.* Oxford University Press.
Mills, C. W. (1956) *White Collar.* New York: Oxford University Press.
Neuwirth, G. (1969) A Weberian Outline of a Theory of Community: Its Application to the 'Dark Ghetto.' *British Journal of Sociology* 20 (2).
Orwell, G. (1949) *Nineteen Eighty-Four.* London: Secker and Warburg.
Parkin, F. (ed.) (1974) *The Social Analysis of Class Structure.* London: Tavistock.
Parsons, T. (1951) *The Social System.* London: Routledge.
Plamenatz, J. (1975) *Karl Marx's Philosophy of Man.* Oxford: Clarendon Press.
Rose, D., Saunders, P., Newby, H., and Bell, C. (1976) Ideologies of Property: A Case Study. *Sociological Review* 24 (4).
Weber, M. (1945) *From Max Weber.* Gerth, H. H. and Mills, C. W. (eds) London: Routledge.
———. (1968) *Economy and Society.* Roth, G. and Wittich, C. (eds) New York: Bedminster Press.
Westergaard, J. and Resler, H. (1975) *Class in a Capitalist Society.* London: Heinemann.

☆ 9 ☆

Class Analysis

Erik Olin Wright

Within the Marxist tradition of class analysis, class divisions are defined primarily in terms of the linkage between property relations and exploitation. Slave masters and slaves constitute classes because a particular property relation (property rights in people) generates exploitation (the appropriation of the fruits of labor of the slave by the slave master). Homeowners and the homeless would not constitute "classes" even though they are distinguished by property rights in housing since this division does not constitute a basis for the exploitation of the homeless by homeowners.[1]

Exploitation is a loaded theoretical term, since it suggests a moral condemnation of particular relations and practices, not simply an analytical description. To describe a social relationship as exploitative is to condemn it as both harmful and unjust to the exploited. Yet, while this moral dimension of exploitation is important, the core of the concept revolves around a particular type of *antagonistic interdependence of material interests* of actors within economic relations, rather than the injustice of those relations as such. As I will use the term, class exploitation is defined by three principal criteria:

(a) *The material welfare of one group of people causally depends on the material deprivations of another.*

(b) *The causal relation in (a) involves the asymmetrical exclusion of the exploited from access to certain productive resources.* Typically this exclusion is backed by force in the form of property rights, but in special cases it may not be.[2]

Reprinted from Erik Olin Wright, *Class Counts: Comparative Studies in Class Analysis* (New York: Cambridge University Press, 1997), by permission of the publisher.

(c) *The causal mechanism which translates exclusion (b) into differential welfare (a) involves the appropriation of the fruits of labor of the exploited by those who control the relevant productive resources.*[3]

This is a fairly complex set of conditions. Condition (a) establishes the antagonism of material interests. Condition (b) establishes that the antagonism is rooted in the way people are situated within the social organization of production. The expression "asymmetrical" in this criterion is meant to exclude "fair competition" from the domain of possible exploitations. Condition (c) establishes the specific mechanism by which the interdependent, antagonistic material interests are generated. The welfare of the exploiter depends upon the *effort* of the exploited, not merely the deprivations of the exploited.[4]

If only the first two of these condtions are met we have what can be called "nonexploitative economic oppression," but not "exploitation." In nonexploitative economic oppression there is no transfer of the fruits of labor from the oppressed to the oppressor; the welfare of the oppressor depends simply on the exclusion of the oppressed from access to certain resources, but not on their effort. In both instances, the inequalities in question are rooted in ownership and control over productive resources.

The crucial difference between exploitation and nonexploitative oppression is that in an exploitative relation, the exploiter *needs* the exploited since the exploiter depends upon the effort of the exploited. In the case of nonexploitative oppression, the oppressors would be happy if the oppressed simply disappeared. Life would have been much easier for the European settlers in North America if the continent had been uninhabited by people.[5] Genocide is thus always a potential strategy for nonexploitative oppressors. It is not an option in a situation of economic exploitation because exploiters require the labor of the exploited for their material well-being. It is no accident that culturally we have the abhorrent saying, "the only good Indian is a dead Indian," but not the saying "the only good worker is a dead worker" or "the only good slave is a dead slave." It makes sense to say "the only good worker is an obedient and conscientious worker," but not "the only good worker is a dead worker." The contrast between North America and South Africa in the treatment of indigenous peoples reflects this difference poignantly: in North America, where the indigenous people were oppressed (by virtue of being coercively displaced from the land) but not exploited, genocide was the basic policy of social control in the face of resistance; in South Africa, where the European settler population heavily depended upon African labor for its own prosperity, this was not an option.

Exploitation, therefore, does not merely define a set of *statuses* of social actors, but a pattern of on-going *interactions* structured by a set of social relations, relations which mutually bind the exploiter and the exploited together. This dependency of the exploiter on the exploited gives the exploited a certain from of power, since human beings always retain at least some minimal control over their own expenditure of effort. Social control of labor which relies exclusively on repression is costly and, except under special circumstances, often fails to generate optimal levels of diligence and effort on the part of the exploited. As a result, there is generally systematic pressure on exploiters to moderate their domination and in one way or another to try to elicit some degree of consent from the exploited, at least in the sense of gaining some level of minimal cooperation from them. Paradoxically perhaps, exploitation is thus a constraining force on the practices of the exploiter. This contraint constitutes a basis of power for the exploited.

People who are oppressed but not exploited also may have some power, but it is generally more precarious. At a minimum oppressed people have the power that comes from the human capacity for physical resistance. However, since their oppressors are not economically constrained to seek some kind of cooperation from them, this resistance is likely very quickly to escalate into quite bloody and violent confrontations. It is for this reason that the resistance of Native Americans to displacement from the land led to massacres of Native Americans by white settlers. The pressure on nonexploitative oppressors to seek accommodation is very weak; the outcomes of conflict therefore tend to become simply a matter of the balance of brute force between enemies. When the oppressed are also exploited, even if the exploiter feels no moral compunction, there will be economic constraints on the exploiter's treatment of the exploited.

Describing the material interests of actors generated by exploitation as antagonistic does not prejudge the moral question of the justice or injustice of the inequalities generated by these antogonisms. One can believe, for example, that it is morally justified to prevent poor people in third world countries from freely coming into the United States and still recognize that there is an objective antagonism of material interests between US citizens and the excluded would-be third world migrants. Similarly, to recognize the capital–labor conflict as involving antagonistic material interests rooted in the appropriation of labor effort does not necessarily imply that capitalist profits are unjust; it simply means that they are generated in a context of inherent conflict.

Nevertheless, it would be disingenuous to claim that the use of the term "exploitation" to designate this form of antagonistic interdependency of material interests is a strictly scientific, technical choice. Describing the appropriation of labor effort as "exploitation" rather than simply a "transfer" adds a sharp moral judgment to the analytical claim. Without at least a thin notion of the moral status of the appropriation, it would be impossible, for example, to distinguish such things as legitimate taxation from exploitation. Taxation involves coercive appropriation, and in many instances there is arguably a conflict of material interests between the taxing authorities and the taxpayer as a private individual. Even under deeply democratic and egalitarian conditions, many people would not voluntarily pay taxes since they would prefer to enhance their personal material interests by free-riding on other people's tax payments. Right-wing libertarians in fact do regard taxation as a form of exploitation because it is a violation of the sanctity of private property rights and thus an unjust, coercive appropriation. The motto "taxation is theft" is equivalent to "taxation is exploitation." The claim that the capitalist appropriation of labor effort from workers is "exploitation," therefore, implies something more than simply an antagonism of material interests between workers and capitalists; it implies that this appropriation is unjust.

While I feel that a good moral case can be made for the kind of radical egalitarianism that provides a grounding for treating capitalist appropriation as unjust, it would take us too far afield here to explore the philosophical justifications for this claim.[6] In any case, for purposes of sociological class analysis, the crucial issue is the recognition of the antagonism of material interests that are linked to class relations by virtue of the appropriation of labor effort, and on this basis I will refer to this as "exploitation."

In capitalist society, the central form of exploitation is based on property rights in the means of production. These property rights generate three basic classes: *capitalists* (exploiters), who own the means of production and hire workers; *workers* (exploited), who do not own the means of production and sell their labor power to capitalists; and *petty bourgeois* (neither exploiter nor exploited), who own and use the means of production without hiring others.[7] The Marxist account of how the capital–labor relation generates exploitation is a familiar one: propertyless workers, in order to acquire their means of livelihood, must sell their labor power to people who own the means of production.[8] In this exchange relation, they agree to work for a specified length of time in exchange for a wage which they use to buy their means of subsistence. Because of the power relation between capitalists and workers, capitalists are able to force workers to produce more than is needed to provide them with this subsistence. As a result, workers produce a surplus which is owned by the capitalist and takes the form of profits. Profits, the amount of the social product that is left over after the costs of producing and reproducing all of the imputs (both labor power inputs and physical inputs) have been deducted, constitute an appropriation of the fruits of labor of workers.

Describing this relation as exploitative is a claim about the basis for the inherent conflict between workers and capitlaists in the employment relation. It points to the crucial fact that the conflict between capitalists and workers is not simply over the *level of wages,* but over the *amount of work effort* performed for those wages. Capitalists always want workers to expend more effort than workers willingly want to do. As Bowles and Gintis (1990) have argued, "the whistle while you work" level of effort of workers is always suboptimal for capitalists, and thus capitalists have to adopt various strategies of surveillance and control to increase labor effort. While the intensity of overt conflict generated by these relations will vary over time and place, and class compromises may occur in which high levels of cooperation between labor and management take place, nevertheless, this underlying antagonism of material interests remains so long as the relationship remains exploitative.

For some theoretical and empirical purposes, this simple image of the class structure may be sufficient. For example, if the main purpose of an analysis is to explore the basic differences between the class structures of feudalism and capitalism, then an analysis which revolved entirely around the relationship between capitalists and workers might be adequate. However, for many of the things we want to study with class analysis, we need a more nuanced set of categories. In particular, we need concepts which allow for two kinds of analyses: first, the analysis of the variation across time and place in the class structures of concrete capitalist societies, and second, the analysis of the ways individual lives are affected by their location within the class structure. The first of these is needed if we are to explore macro-variations in a fine-grained way; the second is needed if we are to use class effectively in micro-analysis.[9]

Both of these tasks involve elaborating a concept of class structure in capitalist societies that moves beyond the core polarization between capitalists and workers. More specifically, this involves solving two general problems in class structural analysis: first, the problem of locating the "middle class" within the class structure, and second, locating people not in the paid labor force in the class structure.

The Problem of the "Middle Class" among Employees

If we limit the analysis of class structure in capitalism to the ownership of, and exclusion from, the means of production, we end up with a class structure in which there are only three locations—the capitalist class, the working class and the petty bourgeoisie (those who own means of production but do not hire workers)—and in which around 85–90% of the population in most developed capitalist countries falls into a single class. While this may in some sense reflect a profound truth about capitalism— that the large majority of the population are separated from the means of production and must sell their labor power on the labor market in order to survive—it does not provide us with an adequate conceptual framework for explaining many of the things we want class to help explain. In particular, if we want class structure to help explain class consciousness, class formation and class conflict, then we need some way of understanding the class-relevant divisions within the employee population.

In ordinary language terms, this is the problem of the "middle class"— people who do not own their own means of production, who sell their labor power on a labor market, and yet do not seem part of the "working class." The question, then, is on what basis can we differentiate class locations among people who share a common location of nonownership within capitalist property relations? In the analyses here, I will divide the class of employees along two dimensions: first, their relationship to authority within production, and second, their possession of skills or expertise.[10]

Authority

There are two rationales for treating authority as a dimension of class relations among employees. The first concerns the role of *domination* within capitalist property relations. In order to insure the performance of adequate effort on the part of workers, capitalist production always involves an apparatus of domination involving surveillance, positive and negative sanctions and varying forms of hierarchy. Capitalists do not simply *own* the means of production and *hire* workers; they also *dominate* workers within production.

In these terms, managers and supervisors can be viewed as exercising delegated capitalist class powers in so far as they engage in the practices of domination within production. In this sense they can be considered *simultaneously* in the capitalist class *and* the working class: they are like capitalists in that they dominate workers; they are like workers in that they are controlled by capitalists and exploited within production. They thus occupy what I have called *contradictory locations within class relations*. The term "contradictory" is used in this expression rather than simply "dual" since the class interests embedded in managerial jobs combine the inherently antagonistic interests of capital and labor. The higher one moves in the authority hierarchy, the greater will be the weight of capitalist interests within this class location. Thus upper managers, and especially Chief Executive Officers in large corporations will be very closely tied to the capitalist class, while the class character of lower level supervisor jobs will be much closer to that of the working class.

The second rationale for treating the authority dimension as a criterion for differentiating class locations among employees centers on the relationship between their earnings and the appropriation of surplus. The strategic position of managers within the organization of production enables them to make significant claims on a portion of the social surplus (defined in the counterfactual manner discussed above) in the form of relatively high earnings.[11] In effect this means that the wages and salaries of managerial labor power are above the costs of producing and reproducing their labor power (including whatever skills they might have).

The specific mechanism through which this appropriation takes place can be referred to as a "loyalty rent." It is important for the profitability of capitalist firms that managers wield their power in an effective and responsible way. The difficulty is that a high level of surveillance and threats is generally not an effective strategy for eliciting this kind of behavior, both because managerial performance is generally rather hard to monitor and because repressive controls tend to undermine initiative rather than stimulate creative behavior. What is needed, then, is a way of generating some level of real commitment on the part of managers to the goals of the organization. This is accomplished by relatively high earnings linked to careers and promotion ladders within authority hierarchies. These higher earnings involve a redistribution of part of the social surplus to managers in order to build their loyalty to the organization. Of course, negative sanctions are still present in the background: managers are sometimes fired, they are disciplined for poor work by failing to get promotions or raises, etc. But these coercive forms of control gain their efficacy from their link to the strong inducements of earnings that, especially for higher level managers, are significantly above the costs of producing the skills of managers.[12] Managers thus not only occupy contradictory locations within class relations by virtue of domination, they occupy what might be termed a *privileged appropriation location within exploitation relations*. Both of these differentiate them from the working class.

Skills and Expertise

The second axis of class differentiation among employees centers on the possession of skills or expertise. Like managers, employees who possess high levels of skills/expertise are potentially in a privileged appropriation location within exploitation relations. There are two primary mechanisms through which this can happen. First, skills and expertise are frequently scarce in labor markets, not simply because they are in short supply, but also because there are systematic obstacles in the way of increasing the supply of those skills to meet the requirements of employing organizations. One important form of these obstacles is credentials, but rare talents could also constitute the basis for sustained restrictions on the supply of a particular form of labor power.[13] The result of such restrictions on supply is that owners of the scarce skills are able to receive a wage above the costs of producing and reproducing their labor power. This "skill rent" is a way by which employees can appropriate part of the social surplus.

Second, the control over knowledge and skills frequently renders also the labor effort of skilled workers difficult to monitor and control. The effective control over knowledge by such employees means that employers must rely to some extent on loyalty enhancing mechanisms in order to achieve desired levels of cooperation and effort from employees with high levels of skills and expertise, just as they have to do in the case of managers. Employees with high levels of expertise, therefore, are able to appropriate surplus both because of their strategic location within the organization of production (as controllers of knowledge), and because of their strategic location in the organization of labor markets (as controllers of a scarce form of labor power).

Understood in this way, the possession of skills and expertise defines a distinctive location within class relations because of a specific kind of power they confer on employees. It may also be the case that expertise, skills and knowledge are associated with various kinds of "symbolic capital" and distinctive life-styles, as Bourdieu (1984) and others have noted. While these cultural correlates of class may be of considerable explanatory importance for a variety of sociological questions, they do not constitute the essential rationale for treating skills and expertise as a dimension of class location within a materialist class analysis (except in so far as symbolic capital plays a role in acquiring skills and credentials). That rationale rests on the claim that experts, like managers, occupy a privileged appropriation location within exploitation relations that differentiates them from ordinary workers.

Throughout this book I will frequently use "skills and expertise" as a couplet. The term "skill" by itself sometimes is taken to refer simply to manual skills, rather than the more general idea of enhanced or complex labor power, contrasted to "raw" or undeveloped labor power. This enhancement can take many forms, both physical and cognitive. It may provide great flexibility to engage in a variety of work settings, or it may be highly specialized and vulnerable to obsolescence. Enhanced labor power is often legally certified in the form of official credentials, but in some circumstances skills and expertise may function effectively without such certification. The important theoretical idea is that skills and expertise designate an asset embodied in the labor power of people which enhances their power in labor markets and labor processes.

A Map of Middle-Class Class Locations

Adding position within authority hierarchies and possession of scarce skills and expertise to the fundamental dimension of capitalist property relations generates the map of class locations presented in Figure 1. With appropriate modifications depending upon our specific empirical objectives, this is the basic schema that underlies the investigations of this book. It is important to stress that this is a map of class *locations*. The cells in the typology are not "classes" as such; they are locations within class relations. Some of these are contradictory locations within class relations, others are privileged appropriation locations within exploitation relations and still others are polarized locations within capitalist property relations. By convention the polarized locations—"capitalists" and "workers" in capitalism—are often called "classes," but the more precise terminology would be to describe these as the fundamental locations within the capitalist class structure. The typology is thus not a proposal for a six-class model of the class structure of capitalism, but rather a model of a class structure which differentiates six locations within class relations.

In some of the empirical analyses we will discuss, we will combine some of the locations in this typology, typically to generate a four cate-

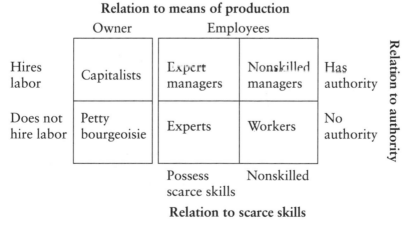

Figure 1   Basic class typology

gory typology consisting of capitalists, petty bourgeois, "middle-class" locations (contradictory locations and privileged appropriation locations among employees) and workers. In other analyses we will modify the typology by adding intermediary categories along each of the dimensions. On the relation to means of production dimension this involves distinguishing between proper capitalists, small employers who only have a few employees, and the petty bourgeoisie (self-employed people with no employees). On the authority dimension this means differentiating between proper managers—people who are involved in organizational decision making—and mere supervisors, who have power over subordinates but are not involved in policy-making decisions. And, on the skill dimension this involves distinguishing between occupations which typically require advanced academic degrees, and other skilled occupations which require lower levels of specialized training. The result will be the twelve-location class-structure matrix presented in Figure 2.

This way of specifying the distinctiveness of the class location of managers and experts is similar in certain respects to Goldthorpe's (1982) treatment of the concept of the "service class." Goldthorpe draws a distinction between two kinds of employment relations: one based on a labor contract, characteristic of the working classes; and one based on what he terms a "service relationship," characteristic of managers and experts. In the latter, employees enter a career structure, not simply a job, and their rewards are in significant ways prospective, rather than simply payments for labor performed. Such a service relation, Goldthorpe argues, is "likely to be found where it is required of employees that they

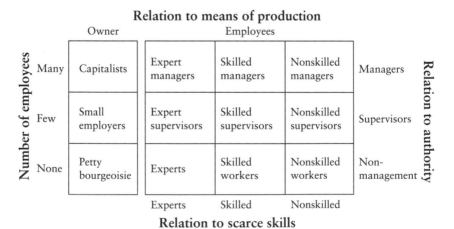

Figure 2   Elaborated class typology

exercise *delegated authority or specialized knowledge and expertise* in the interests of their employing organization. In the nature of the case . . . their performance will depend upon the degree of moral commitment that they feel toward the organization rather than on the efficacy of external sanctions" (Goldthorpe and Erikson 1993: 42). This characterization is closely related to the idea that, because of their strategic power within organizations, the cooperation of middle-class employees is achieved in part through the payment of loyalty rents embodied in their earnings. The main difference between Goldthorpe's conceptual analysis and the one adopted here is, first, that Goldthorpe does not link his analysis of service-class jobs to the problem of exploitation and antagonistic interests, and second, that he treats the authority dimension of managerial positions simply in terms of heightened responsibilities, not domination. Nevertheless, Goldthorpe's conceptualization of class structure taps many of the same relational properties of managerial and expert positions as the conceptualization adopted here.

People Not in the Paid Labor Force

Many people in capitalist societies—probably the majority—do not fill jobs in the paid labor force. The most obvious case is children. How should babies be located in the class structure? But there are many other categories as well: retirees, permanently disabled people, students, people on welfare, the unemployed and full-time homemakers.[14] Each of the categories of people poses special problems for class structure analysis.

As a first approximation we can divide this heterogeneous set of situations into two broad categories: people who are tied to the class structure through family relations, and people who are not. To be in a "location" within class structure is to have one's material interests shaped by one's relationship to the process of exploitation. One way such linkages to exploitation are generated by class structures is through *jobs*. This is the kind of class location we have been exploring so far. I will refer to these as *direct class locations*. But there are other mechanisms by which people's lives are linked to the process of exploitation. Of particular importance are the ways in which family structures and kinship relations link an individual's material interests to the process of exploitation. Being born into a wealthy capitalist family links the child to the material interests of the capitalist class via family relations. It makes sense, then, to say that this child is "in" the capitalist class. If that child, as a young adult, works in a factory but stands to inherit millions of dollars of capitalist wealth and can rely on family resources for various needs, then that person would simultaneously be in two class locations: the capitalist class by virtue of family ties and the working class by virtue of the job.

I will refer to these situations as *mediated class locations*. Family ties are probably the most important basis for mediated class locations, but membership in certain kinds of communities or the relationship to the state may also provide such linkages. In each case the question one asks is "how do the social relations in which a person's life is embedded link that person to the various mechanisms of class exploitation and thus shape that person's material interests?" Many people, of course, have both direct and mediated class locations. This is of particular importance in developed capitalist economies for households in which both spouses are in the labor force, for this creates the possibility that husbands and wives will have different direct class locations, and thus each of them will have different direct and mediated locations.

There are, however, people for whom family ties provide at most extremely tenuous linkages to the class structure. Most notably, this is the situation of many people in the so-called "underclass." This expression is used in a variety of ways in contemporary policy discussions. Sometimes it is meant to be a pejorative term rather like the old Marxist concept of "lumpenproletariat"; at other times it is used more descriptively to designate a segment of the poor whose conditions of life are especially desperate and whose prospects for improvement are particularly dismal. In terms of the analysis of this chapter, one way of giving this concept a more precise theoretical status is to link it to the concepts of exploitation and oppression: an "underclass" can be defined as a category of social agents who are economically oppressed but not consistently exploited within a given class system.[15]

Different kinds of class structures will generate different forms of an "underclass." In many parts of the world today and throughout much of human history, the pivotal resource which defines the underclass is land. Landlords, agrarian capitalists, peasants and exploited agrarian producers all have access to land; people who are excluded from such access constitute the underclass of agrarian societies. In these terms, many Native Americans were transformed into an underclass in the nineteenth century when they were pushed off of the land onto the reservations.

In contemporary advanced capitalism, the key resource which defines the predicament of the underclass is labor power itself. This might seem like an odd statement since in capitalism, at least since the abolition of slavery, everyone supposedly owns one "unit" of labor power, him or herself. The point is that some people do not in fact own *productively saleable* labor power. The situation is similar to a capitalist owning outmoded machines. While the capitalist physically controls these pieces of machinery, they cease to be "capital"—a capitalistically productive asset—if they cannot be deployed within a capitalist production process profitably. In the case of labor power, a person can physically control his or her own laboring capacity, but that capacity can cease to have economic value in capitalism if it cannot be deployed productively. This is the essential condition of people in the "underclass." They are oppressed because they are denied access to various kinds of productive resources, above all the necessary means to acquire the skills needed to make their labor power saleable. As a result, they are not consistently exploited.[16]

Understood in this way, the underclass consists of human beings who are largely expendable *from the point of view of the logic of capitalism*. Like Native Americans who became a landless underclass in the nineteenth century, repression rather than incorporation is the central mode of social control directed toward them. Capitalism does not need the labor power of unemployed inner city youth. The material interests of the wealthy and privileged segments of American society would be better served if these people simply disappeared. However, unlike in the nineteenth century, the moral and political forces are such that direct genocide is no longer a viable strategy. The alternative, then, is to build prisons and to cordon off the zones of cities in which the underclass lives.

Marxist versus Weberian Class Analysis

As a set of empirical categories, the class structure matrix in Figures 1 and 2 could be deployed within either a Weberian or Marxist framework. The control over economic resources is central to both Marxist and Weberian class analysis, and both frameworks could be massaged to allow for the array of categories I am using. Indeed, a good argument could be made that the proposed class structure concept incorporates significant Weberian elements, since the explicit inclusion of skills as a criterion for class division and the importance accorded income privileges for both managers and credentialed experts are hallmarks of Weberian class analysis. In a real sense, therefore, the empirical categories used here can be seen as a hybrid of the categories conventionally found in Marxist and Weberian class analysis.[17] In what sense, therefore, does this class structure analysis remain "Marxist"?

To answer this question we need to compare the theoretical foundations of the concept of class in the Marxist and Weberian traditions.[18] The contrast between Marx and Weber has been one of the grand themes in the history of Sociology as a discipline. Most graduate school programs have a sociological theory course within which Marx versus Weber figures as a central motif. However, in terms of class analysis, posing Marx and Weber as polar opposites is a bit misleading because in many ways Weber is speaking in his most Marxian voice when he talks about class. The concept of class within these two streams of thought share a number of important features:

- Both Marxist and Weberian approaches differ from what might be called simple gradational notions of class in which classes are differentiated strictly on the basis of inequalities in the material conditions of life.[19] This conceptualization of class underwrites the common inventory of classes found in popular discourse and the mass media: upper class, upper middle class, middle class, lower middle class, lower class, underclass. Both Marxist and Weberian class analysis define classes *relationally,* i.e. a given class location is defined by virtue of the social relations which link it to other class locations.
- Both traditions identify the concept of class with the relationship between people and economically relevant assets or resources. Marxists call this relation to the means of production; Weberians refer to "market capacities." But they are both really talking about very similar empirical phenomena.
- Both traditions see the causal relevance of class as operating, at least in part, via the ways in which these relations shape the material interests of actors. Ownership of the means of production and ownership of one's own labor power are explanatory of social action because these property rights shape the strategic alternatives people face in pursuing their material well-being. What people *have* imposes constraints on what they can *do* to get what they *want.* To be sure, Marxists tend to put more weight on the objective character of these "material interests" by highlighting the fact that these constraints are imposed on individuals, whereas Weberians tend to focus on the subjective conditions, by emphasizing the relative contingency in what people want. Nevertheless, it is still the case that at their core, both class concepts involve the causal connection between (a) social relations to resources and (b) material interests via (c) the way resources shape strategies for acquiring income.

How then do they differ? The pivotal difference is captured by the contrast between the favorite buzz-words of each theoretical tradition: *life chances* for Weberians, and *exploitation* for Marxists. The reason why production is more central to Marxist than to Weberian class analysis is because of its salience for the problem of exploitation; the reason why Weberians give greater emphasis to the market is because it so directly shapes life chances.

The intuition behind the idea of life chances is straightforward. "In our terminology," Weber (in Gerth and Mills 1958:181–2) writes:

"classes" are not communities; they merely represent possible, and frequent, bases for communal action. We may speak of a "class" when (1) a number of people have in common a specific causal component of their life chances, in so far as (2) this component is represented exclusively by economic interests in the possession of goods and opportunities for income, and (3) is represented under conditions of the commodity or labor markets. [These points refer to "class situation," which we may express more briefly as the typical chance for a supply of goods, external living conditions and life experiences, in so far as this chance is determined by the amount and kind of power, or lack of such, to dispose of goods or skills for the sake of income in a given economic order. The term "class" refers to any group of people that is found in the same class situation] . . . But always this is the generic connotation of the concept of class: that the kind of chance in the *market* is the decisive moment which presents a common condition for the individual's fate. "Class situation" is, in this sense, ultimately "market situation."

In short, the kind and quantity of resources you own affects your opportunities for income in market exchanges. "Opportunity" is a description of the feasible set individuals face, the trade-offs they encounter in deciding what to do. Owning means of production gives a person different alternatives from owning credentials, and both of these are different from simply owning unskilled labor power. Furthermore, in a market economy, access to market-derived income affects the broader array of life experiences and opportunities for oneself and one's children. The study of the life chances of children based on parents' market capacity is thus an integral part of the Weberian agenda of class analysis.

Within a Weberian perspective, therefore, the salient issue in the linkage of people to different kinds of economic resources is the way this confers on them different kinds of economic opportunities and disadvantages and thereby shapes their material interests. One way of representing this idea in a simple way is by examining the income–leisure trade-offs faced by people in different classes as pictured in Figure 3. In this figure, everyone faces some trade-off between leisure and income: less leisure yields more income.[20] However, for the propertied class it is possible to have high income with no work (thus the expressions "the leisure class" or the "idle rich"), whereas for both the middle class and the working class in this stylized drawing, zero work corresponds to zero income. The middle class has "greater" opportunities (life chances) in the market than workers because the slope they face (i.e. the wage rate) is steeper. Some workers in fact might actually have a higher standard of living than some people in the middle class, but the trade-offs they face are nevertheless less desirable. These common trade-offs, then, are the basis for a potential commonality of interests among members of a class, and thus constitute the basis for potential common action.

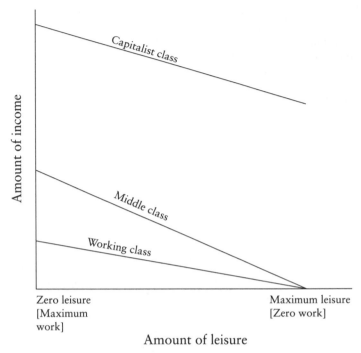

Figure 3 *Leisure vs. consumption trade-offs faced by people in different economic classes*

Within a Marxist framework, the feature of the relationship of people to economic resources which is at the core of class analysis is "exploitation." Both "exploitation" and "life chances" identify inequalities in material well-being that are generated by inequalities in access to resources of various sorts. Thus both of these concepts point to conflicts of interest over the *distribution* of the assets themselves. What exploitation adds to this is a claim that conflicts of interest between classes are generated not simply by what people *have,* but also by what people *do* with what they have.[21] The concept of exploitation, therefore, points our attention to conflicts within production, not simply conflicts in the market.

This contrast between the Marxist and Weberian traditions of class analysis is summarized in Figure 4. Weberian class analysis revolves around a single causal nexus that works through market exchanges. Marxist class analysis includes the Weberian causal processes, but adds to them a causal structure within production itself as well as an account of the interactions of production and exchange. Part of our analysis of the class location of managers, for example, concerns the "loyalty rent"

I. Simple gradational class analysis

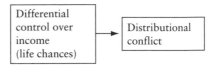

II. Weberian class analysis

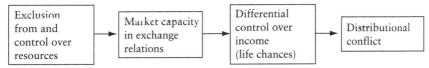

III. Marxist class analysis

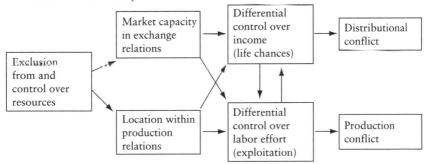

Figure 4 *Three models of class analysis*

which managers receive by virtue of their position within the authority structure of production. This reflects the way in which location within the relations of production and not simply within market relations affects the "life chances" of managers. The analysis of such things as the way transfer payments of the welfare state affect the market capacity of workers illustrates how market capacity has an impact on the extraction of labor effort within production. The Marxist concept of class directs our attention both theoretically and empirically towards these interactions.

A Weberian might reply that there is nothing in the Weberian idea of market-based life chances that would *prevent* the analysis of the extraction of labor effort within production. A good and subtle Weberian class analyst could certainly link the analysis of market capacities within exchange relations to power relations within the labor process, and thus explore the causal structures at the center of Marxist class analysis. In systematically joining production and exchange in this way, however, the

Weberian concept would in effect become Marxianized. Frank Parkin (1979: 25), in a famous gibe, said, "Inside every neo-Marxist there seems to be a Weberian struggling to get out." One could just as easily say that inside every left-wing Weberian there is a Marxist struggling to stay hidden.

There are three main reasons why one might want to ground the concept of class explicitly in exploitation rather than simply market-based life chances. First, the exploitation-centered class concept affirms the fact that production and exchange are intrinsically linked, not merely contingently related. The material interests of capitalists and workers are *inherently* shaped by the interaction of these two facets of the social relations that bind them together. This provides us with the way of understanding the class location of managers as determined not simply by their position within the market for managerial labor power, but also by their position within the relations of domination in production. More broadly, the exploitation-based class concept points our attention to the fact that class relations are relations of power, not merely privilege.

Second, theorizing the interests linked to classes as grounded in inherently antagonistic and interdependent practices facilitates the analysis of social conflict. Explanations of conflict always require at least two elements: an account of the opposing *interests* at stake in the conflict and an account of the *capacity* of the actors to pursue those interests. A simple opposition of interests is not enough to explain active conflict between groups. Exploitation is a powerful concept precisely because it brings together an account of opposing interests with an account of the rudimentary capacity for resistance. Exploiters not only have a positive interest in limiting the life chances of the exploited, but also are *dependent* upon the exploited for the realization of their own interests. This dependency of the exploiter on the exploited gives the exploited an inherent capacity to resist. Exploitation, therefore, does not simply predict an opposition of interests, but a tendency for this antagonism of interests to generate manifest conflicts between classes. This understanding of the inherent power of exploited classes is marginalized when class is defined strictly in terms of market relations.

Finally, the exploitation-centered class analysis implies that classes can exist in nonmarket societies, whereas Weberian class analysis explicitly restricts the relevance of class to markets. For Marxist class analysis, the relationship between slave master and slave or lord and serf are instances of class relations because they all involve exploitation linked to property rights in the forces of production.[22] The relationship between bureaucratic exploiters and producers in command economies can also be considered a form of class relations since the capacity of the state bureaucratic elite to appropriate surplus rests on their effective control over the society's productive resources (Wright 1994: ch. 6). For Weberian class analysis these are not class relations, but rather examples of castes or estates or some other form of inequality of power, since the differences in "life chances" of the slave and slave master, the lord and serf, the bureaucratic appropriator and producer, are not the result of their meeting within a market. The Weberian restriction of the concept of class to market societies, therefore, directs our attention away from the underlying commonality of these relations across different kinds of social systems.

There is, of course, no metatheoretical rule of sociology which says that every sociologist must choose between these two ways of grounding class analysis. It certainly might be possible to construct an eclectic hybrid between Marxist and Weberian class analysis by seeing exploitation as defining the central cleavages within a class structure and differential market capacities as defining salient *strata within classes*. Strata within the capitalist class would be defined by differential capacity to appropriate surplus; strata within the working class would be determined by differences in incomes and working conditions generated by different market capacities. In such a hybrid class analysis, what I have been calling the "middle class" might be more appropriately described as privileged strata within the working class.

Nevertheless, throughout this book I will interpret the class-structure matrix we will be using within a neo-Marxist class analysis framework. In the end, the decision to do this rather than adopt a more eclectic stance comes at least in part from political commitments, not simply dispassionate scientific principles. This does not mean that Marxist class analysis is pure ideology or that it is rigidly dictated by radical egalitarian values. My choice of analytical framework is also based on my beliefs in the theoretical coherence of this approach—which I have argued for in this chapter—and in its capacity to illuminate empirical problems, which I hope to demonstrate in the rest of this book. But this choice remains crucially bound up with commitments to the socialist tradition and its aspirations for an emancipatory, egalitarian alternative to capitalism.

Readers who are highly skeptical of the Marxist tradition for whatever reasons might feel that there is no point in struggling through the masses of numbers, graphs and equations in the rest of this book. If the conceptual justifications for the categories are unredeemably flawed, it might be thought, the empirical results generated with those categories will be worthless. This would be, I think, a mistake. The empirical categories themselves can be interpreted in a Weberian or hybrid manner. Indeed, as a practical set of operational categories, the class structure matrix used in this book does not dramatically differ from the class typology used by Goldthorpe (1980) and Erikson and Goldthorpe (1993). As is usually the case in sociology, the empirical categories of analysis are *under*determined by the theoretical frameworks within which they are generated or interpreted. This means that readers who are resolutely unconvinced about the virtues of understanding classes in terms of exploitation can still engage the empirical analyses of this book as investigations of classes differentially situated with respect to life chances in the market.

Notes

1. If homeowners exchanged housing in vacant rooms for domestic service, then the property rights in housing might become the basis for a class relation. The sheer fact of homeownership and homelessness, however, does not itself constitute a form of exploitation and thus is not a class division. It is only when this property right is translated into a power relation between actors within which labor is appropriated that it becomes exploitative.

2. An example of an exclusion from productive resources which is not backed by force but which, nevertheless, could be the basis for exploitation, is the unequal distribution of talents. While one could stretch the notion of "coercive" exclusion to cover talents (since the untalented are coercively prohibited from owning the talented as slaves), in the actual functioning of capitalist societies, the relevant exclusion is not primarily guaranteed by force.

3. The expression "appropriation of the fruits of labor" refers to the appropriation of that which labor produces. It does *not* imply that the value of those products is exclusively determined by labor effort, as claimed in the labor theory of value. All that is being claimed here is that a surplus is appropriated—a surplus beyond what is needed to reproduce all of the inputs of production—and that this surplus is produced through labor effort, but not that the appropriate metric for the surplus is labor time. For a discussion of this way of understanding the appropriation of the fruits of labor, see Cohen (1988: 209–238).

4. There are situations in which conditions (a) and (c) are present, but not (b). For example, in what is sometimes called a "tributary mode of production," a centralized, authoritarian state apparatus appropriates surplus from peasants through taxation without directly being involved in production at all. The peasants are surely being exploited in this situation, but the state elite is not a fully-fledged "class" insofar as their social location and power is not determined by their location within the social relations of production. One could, perhaps, stretch the meaning of condition (b) somewhat by treating the direct appropriation of the peasants' product by the state elite as a form of "exclusion" of peasants from productive resources (since the surplus itself is a productive resource). But the core mechanism involved does not center on the social relations *of production,* but the direct control of violence by the state, and thus the state elite is not a "class" in the standard sense.

5. This is not to deny that in certain specific instances the settlers benefited from the knowledge of Native Americans, but simply to affirm the point that the

displacement of the indigenous people from the land was a costly and troublesome process.

6. For an insightful discussion of radical egalitarian values that provides a basis for regarding capitalist appropriations as exploitative, see Cohen (1988: ch. 11).

7. As Roemer (1982) argues, it is possible that some petty bourgeois might be exploited or even be exploiters through uneven exchange in the market. A petty bourgeois working with highly capital intensive means of production, for example, may be able to appropriate the fruits of labor of others through exchange.

8. To be somewhat more precise, in order to acquire the means of subsistence, at least some members of a propertyless family (defined as the unit of shared consumption) must sell labor power to employers. In some times and places, this has meant that the male "breadwinner" entered the labor market while the female "housewife" stayed home. In contemporary advanced capitalism, generally all adult members of households sell their labor power.

9. For an extended discussion of the limitations of the overly abstract polarized concept of class structure, see Wright (1989a: 271–278).

10. The conceptual discussion here differs in a number of ways from the way I approached these questions in my earlier book, *Classes* (Wright 1985). In that book I argued that the rationale for considering authority and skills to be dimensions of the class structure was that the control of organizational assets (i.e. authority) and skill assets were the basis for distinctive forms of exploitation. For reasons which I elaborated in a subsequent essay (Wright 1989a: ch. 8) this no longer seems a satisfactory way of specifying the class character of the "middle class." While the formulation presented here lacks the symmetry of the earlier strategy of analysis, I believe it is conceptually sounder.

11. In earlier work I argued that by virtue of this appropriation of surplus by managers they should be seen as exploiters. The problem with this formulation is that managers also contribute to the surplus through their own laboring activity, and thus their surplus income may simply reflect a capacity to appropriate part of the surplus which they contribute to production. Instead of being "exploiters," therefore, many managers may simply be less exploited than other employees. Because of this ambiguity, therefore, it is better simply to see managers as occupying a *privileged* position with respect to the process of exploitation which enables them to appropriate part of the social surplus in the form of higher incomes.

12. This rent component of the earnings of managers has been recognized in "efficiency wage" theory which acknowledges that the market-clearing wage may be suboptimal from the point of view of the goals of the employer. Because of the difficulty in enforcing labor contracts, employers have to pay employees more than the wages predicted by theories of competitive equilibria in order to gain compliance. While this mechanism may generate some small "employment rents" for all employees, it is especially salient for those employees who occupy strategic jobs requiring responsible, diligent performance of duties. For the mainstream economics discussion of efficiency wages, see Akerloff and Yellen (1986). For

arguments that extend efficiency wage theory to Marxist arguments about the "extraction" of labor effort from workers, see Bowles and Gintis (1990).

13. Credentials would not constitute a restriction on the supply of a particular kind of skill if there were no obstacles for individuals acquiring the credentials. A variety of such obstacles exist: restrictions on the number of slots in the training programs, restrictions in credit markets to get loans to obtain the training; inequality in the distribution of "cultural capital" (including such things as manners, accent, appearance, etc.) and "social capital" (especially such things as access to networks and information); and, of course, inequalities in genetic endowments.

14. The claim that the people in these categories do not participate directly in production is simple enough for the unemployed, retirees and children, but it is problematic for housewives, since housewives obviously work and produce things in the home. This has led some theorists (e.g. Delphy, 1984) to argue that the work of housewives should be treated as domestic labor performed within a domestic mode of production in which housewives occupy a distinctive class location, the domestic worker. Others have argued that household production is a subsidiary part of the capitalist mode of production. It has even been argued (Fraad, Resnick and Wolff, 1994) that household production is a special form of feudal production in which housewives are feudally exploited by their husbands since the husbands directly "appropriate" use-values from their wives. All of these views in one way or another attempt to treat the gender and kinship relations within a family as if they were a form of class relations. This amalgamation of class and gender undercuts the explanatory specificity of both class and gender and does not, I believe, enhance our capacity to explain the processes in question. In any case, since the analysis in this book is restricted to people in the paid labor force, we will bracket these issues.

15. Although he does not explicitly elaborate the term "underclass" in terms of a theory of exploitation and economic oppression, the definition proposed here is consistent with the more structural aspects of way the term is used by William Julius Wilson (1982, 1987) in his analysis of the interconnection between race and class in American society. Wilson argues that as legal barriers to racial equality have disappeared and as class differentiation within the black population has increased, the central determining structure of the lives of many African-Americans is no longer race as such, but class. More specifically, he argues that there has been a substantial growth of an urban underclass of people without marketable skills and with very weak attachments to the labor force, living in crumbling central cities isolated from the mainstream of American life and institutions.

16. It is perhaps controversial to amalgamate the exclusion of the contemporary urban underclass from human capital and other job resources with the exclusion of Native Americans from the land. In the latter case there was a zero-sum character to access to the resource in question and massive coercion was used to enforce the exclusion, whereas in the case of education, skills and even good jobs, it is not so obvious that the resources in question are a fixed quantity and that access is being denied through force. Thus the factual inequalities of

access to these resources may not in fact be instances of coercively enforced exclusions which benefit certain groups of people at the expense of others. The plight of the underclass might still be a matter of serious moral concern, but it would not count as an instance of nonexploitative oppression analogous to the condition of Native Americans.

17. It should not be so surprising to see Marxist and Weberian elements conjoined in class analysis. After all, Weber's class analysis was deeply indebted to the Marxist legacy which was part of the general intellectual discourse of his time. In spite of the fact that Weber constantly distanced himself from Marxism, particularly because of its tendencies toward economic determinism which were especially pronounced in his day, when Weber talks of classes he is speaking in a rather Marxian voice.

18. For discussions of the contrast between Marxist and Weberian class analysis, see for example, Parkin (1979), Burris (1987), Giddens (1973), Wright (1979: ch. 1).

19. The contrast between "gradational" and "relational" concepts of class was first introduced into sociology by Ossowski (1963). For a more extended discussion of gradational concepts of class, see Wright (1979: ch. 1).

20. For simplicity, the leisure–consumption trade-off is pictured here as a linear relation. For the working class and the middle class the slope of the line thus represents a linear wage rate. Of course, in the real world, because of such things as overtime on the one hand, and substandard wages for part-time work on the other, the relation would not be linear. The slope of the capitalist class curve in the figure is given as roughly the same as that of the middle class. If we consider all capitalists, not simply those with great entrepreneurial talent, there is no reason to assume *a priori* that their imputed hourly wage (i.e. the part of their earnings that is derived from labor time rather than from their property) would be greater than that of the middle class (skilled employees and managers). In any event, for our present purposes the main point about the capitalist curve is that it does not intersect the x-axis.

21. The conceptual distinction between life chances and exploitation being argued for here runs against the arguments of John Roemer (1985), who insists that exploitation is strictly a way of talking about the injustice of the effects of what people have (assets) on what people get (income). In this sense, he collapses the problem of exploitation into the problem of life chances and thus dissolves the distinction between Marxist and Weberian class analysis. The notion of the extraction of labor effort disappears from his analysis of exploitation.

22. The classic Marxist description of feudalism is a society in which the lords appropriate surplus products directly from the serfs through the use of what is generally called "extra-economic coercion." This coercion either takes the form of forcing the peasant to work part of the week on the land of the lord, or exacting some portion of the produce of the peasant. An alternative characterization is to say that in feudalism the lord and the serf are joint owners of the labor power of the serf. This gives the lord property rights in the laboring capacity of serfs. Slavery, in these terms, is simply the limiting case in which the slave has lost all property rights in his or her own labor power. This joint ownership of the

serf's labor power is reflected in the laws which tie serfs to the land and which prevent the flight of serfs to the city. Such flight is simply a form of theft: the fleeing serf, like the fleeing slave, has stolen property from the lord. The use of extra-economic coercion, then, is simply the means of enforcing these property rights, no different from the use of extra-economic coercion to prevent workers from taking over a factory. For an extended discussion of this way of understanding feudalism, see Wright (1985: 77–78).

References

Akerloff, G.A., and J.L. Yellen (eds.). 1986. *Efficiency Wage Models of the Labor Market.* Cambridge: Cambridge University Press.

Bowles, Samuel, and Herb Gintis. 1990. "Contested Exchange: New Microfoundations for the Political Economy of Capitalism," *Politics and Society* 18, 2: 165–222.

Burris, Val. 1987. "The Neo-Marxist Synthesis of Marx and Weber on Class," in N. Wiley (ed.) *The Marx-Weber Debate.* Newbury Park, Calif.: Sage Publications.

Cohenn, G.A. 1988. *Karl Marx's Theory of History: A Defense.* Princeton: Princeton University Press.

Delphy, Christine. 1984. *Close to Home: A Materialist Analysis of Women's Oppression.* London: Hutchinson.

Erikson, Robert, and John H. Goldthorpe. 1993. *The Constant Flux.* Oxford: Oxford University Press.

Fraad, Harriet, Stephen Resnick, and Richard Wolff. 1994. *Bringing it All Back Home: Class Gender and Power in the Modern Household.* London: Pluto Press.

Gerth, Hans, and C. Wright Mills. 1958. *From Max Weber.* New York: Oxford University Press.

Giddens, Anthony. 1973. *The Class Structure of the Advanced Societies.* New York: Harper and Row.

Goldthorpe, John. 1980. *Social Mobility and Class Structure in Modern Britain.* Oxford: Oxford University Press.

Ossowski, Stanislaw. 1963. *Class Structure in the Social Consciousness.* London: Routledge & Kegan Paul.

Parkin, Frank. 1979. *Marxism and Class Theory: A Bourgeois Critique.* New York: Columbia University Press.

Roemer, John. 1982. *A General Theory of Exploitation and Class.* Cambridge, Mass.: Harvard University Press.

Wilson, William Julius. 1982. *The Declining Significance of Race.* Chicago: University of Chicago Press.

———. 1987. *The Truly Disadvantaged.* Chicago: University of Chicago Press.

Wright, Erik Olin. 1979. *Class Structure and Income Determination.* New York: Academic Press.

———. 1985. *Classes.* London: New Left Books.

———. 1989a. "Rethinking, Once Again, the Concept of Class Structure," pp. 269–348, in Erik Olin Wright, Uwe Becker, Johanna Brenner, Michael Burawoy, Val Burris, Gugliemo Carchedi, Gordon Marshall, Peter Meiksins, David Rose, Arthur Stinchcombe, Philip Van Parjis, 1989, *The Debate on Classes*. London: Verso.

———. 1994. *Interrogating Inequality*. London: Verso.

Part III: Related Readings

Anderson, Charles H. 1974. *The Political Economy of Social Class*. Englewood Cliffs, N.J.: Prentice-Hall.

Carchedi, Guglielmo. 1987. *Class Analysis and Social Research*. New York: Basil Blackwell.

Cottrell, Allin. 1984. *Social Classes in Marxist Theory*. London: Routledge and Kegan Paul.

Dahrendorf, Ralf. 1965. *Class and Class Conflict in Industrial Society*. Stanford, Calif.: Stanford University Press.

Giddens, Anthony. 1973. *The Class Structure of the Advanced Societies*. New York: Harper and Row.

Hall, John R. 1997. *Reworking Class*. Ithaca, N.Y.: Cornell University Press.

Ossowski, Stanislaw. 1963. *Class Structure in the Social Consciousness*. London: Routledge and Kegan Paul.

Wright, Erik Olin. 1989. *The Debate on Classes*. London: Verso.

Part IV

Nonclass Forms of Inequality: Statements on Gender and Racial Stratification

In the brief excerpt from *The Origins of the Family, Private Property and the State,* Friedrich Engels outlines the materialist basis for women's subordination to men. He pays particular attention to the form of the family in relation to the mode of production, for it is the form of the family that leads to the oppression of women. Engels was probably the first to analyze seriously and specifically women's oppression within the capitalist family. In the excerpt reprinted here, he lays out how with the development of capitalism women's roles became subservient to men's roles. For Engels, the domination of women by men was a functional requirement for the furthering of private property.

Almost a century later Juliet Mitchell built on Engel's materialist conception of women's oppression and developed a model from which to understand the position of women in any society. In the excerpt from her book *Women's Estate,* Mitchell develops what she calls a Marxist answer to feminist questions. Mitchell is critical of feminists who see women as the most fundamentally oppressed group in capitalist society and argues for an analysis that understands the concrete situation of women in contemporary capitalist society. In order to do this, Mitchell argues that four structures need to be examined: production, or the economic position of women in terms of their class location, and three structures within the domestic sphere—reproduction, sexuality, and the socialization of children. Mitchell argues that to understand the concrete nature of women's inequality in society, one must understand the combination of these four structures; each one must be analyzed separately, but it is the unity of the structures that explains women's position in society. In essence, Mitchell develops a model from which to understand the "unity" of the class posi-

tion of women and their position in the family to arrive at a better understanding of both historical and contemporary gender inequality. In a
more recent essay, David Lockwood responds to feminist critiques of
stratification theory that argue the focus on class and status inequality
has ignored gender inequality. Lockwood argues that stratification theory, with its focus on class and status, has not been misconceived. Gender, for Lockwood, cannot be conceptualized in the same fashion as
either class or status, although this does not mean that gender does not
have status implication.

In the brief excerpt from *Souls of Black Folk,* published in 1903,
W. E. B. Du Bois outlines the specificity of race in the American context.
He points out that African Americans experience two worlds, the world
of white America and the world of being a racial minority. Du Bois's
account is one of the earliest pieces to suggest that the experience of race
intersects with that of class and status. Gunnar Myrdal argues in "Facets
of the Negro Problem," an excerpt from his famous book *An American
Dilemma,* that the economic and political history of the United States has
resulted in "the Negro Problem." Myrdal analyzes race in the United
States, and the specific situation of African Americans, as consequences
of the inadequacies of white moral values. In the excerpt reprinted here,
Myrdal conceptualizes African Americans as a caste with internal class
divisions. Myrdal's approach was severely criticized by Oliver Cox in his
book *Class, Caste, and Race.* In the excerpt reprinted here, Cox outlines
succinctly his view of race relations as a specific form of class conflict in
capitalist society. Elaborating on the Marxist approach to class, Cox located racial inequality within the general framework of capitalist development.

In the final selection in this part, Patricia Hill Collins calls for a recon-
ceptualization of race, class, and gender as categories of analysis. Collins
critiques models that view various types of inequality and oppression as
additive, and outlines what she takes to be a more satisfying mode of
analysis for understanding multiple forms of inequality and oppression.
She argues that race, class, and gender are interconnected systems that
shape basic relationships of domination and subordination. Collins's
piece represents new directions in the study of social inequality that call
for understanding the connections between race, class, and gender, while
understanding each form of inequality in its own right. In many ways,
Collins's position is similar to Mitchell's, although she adds race as a
crucial variable.

↷ 10 ↶

The Patriarchal Family

Friedrich Engels

T he pairing family, itself too weak and unstable to make an independent household necessary, or even desirable, did not by any means dissolve the communistic household transmitted from earlier times. But the communistic household implies the supremacy of women in the house, just as the exclusive recognition of a natural mother, because of the impossibility of determining the natural father with certainty, signifies high esteem for the women, that is, for the mothers. That woman was the slave of man at the commencement of society is one of the most absurd notions that have come down to us from the period of Enlightenment of the eighteenth century. Woman occupied not only a free but also a highly respected position among all savages and all barbarians of the lower and middle stages and partly even of the upper stage. Let Arthur Wright, missionary for many years among the Seneca Iroquois, testify what her place still was in the pairing family: "As to their family system, when occupying the old long houses [communistic households embracing several families] . . . it is probable that some one clan [gens] predominated, the women taking husbands from other clans [gentes]. . . . Usually the female portion ruled the house; the stores were in common; but woe to the luckless husband or lover who was too shiftless to do his share of the providing. No matter how many children or whatever goods he might have in the house, he might at any time be ordered to pack up his blanket and budge; and after such orders it would not be healthful for him to attempt to disobey. The house would be too hot for him; and he had to retreat to his own clan [gens]; or, as was often done,

Reprinted from Friedrich Engels, *The Origin of the Family, Private Property, and the State*, in Robert C. Tucker, ed., *The Marx-Engels Reader*, 2nd ed., (New York: W. W. Norton, 1978): 735–736, 757–758, by permission of the publisher.

go and start a new matrimonial alliance in some other. The women were the great power among the clans [gentes], as everywhere else. They did not hesitate, when occasion required, to knock off the horns, as it was technically called, from the head of the chief and send him back to the ranks of the warriors." . . .

As wealth increased, it, on the one hand, gave the man a more important status in the family than the woman, and, on the other hand, created a stimulus to utilise this strengthened position in order to overthrow the traditional order of inheritance in favour of his children. But this was impossible as long as descent according to mother right prevailed. This had, therefore, to be overthrown, and it was overthrown; and it was not so difficult to do this as it appears to us now. For this revolution—one of the most decisive ever experienced by mankind—need not have disturbed one single living member of a gens. All the members could remain what they were previously. The simple decision sufficed that in future the descendants of the male members should remain in the gens, but that those of the females were to be excluded from the gens and transferred to that of their father. The reckoning of descent through the female line and the right of inheritance through the mother were hereby overthrown and male lineage and right of inheritance from the father instituted. We know nothing as to how and when this revolution was effected among the civilised peoples. It falls entirely within prehistoric times. That it was actually *effected* is more than proved by the abundant traces of mother right which have been collected, especially by Bachofen. How easily it is accomplished can be seen from a whole number of Indian tribes, among whom it has only recently taken place and is still proceeding, partly under the influence of increasing weath and changed methods of life (transplantation from the forests to the prairies), and partly under the moral influence of civilisation and the missionaries. Of eight Missouri tribes, six have male and two still retain the female lineage and female inheritance line. Among the Shawnees, Miamis and Delawares it has become the custom to transfer the children to the father's gens by giving them one of the gentile names obtaining therein, in order that they may inherit from him. "Innate human causuistry to seek to change things by changing their names! And to find loopholes for breaking through tradition within tradition itself, wherever a direct interest provided a sufficient motive!" (Marx) As a consequence, hopeless confusion arose; and matters could only be straightened out, and partly were straightened out, by the transition to father right. "This appears altogether to be the most natural transition." (Marx) As for what the experts on comparative law have to tell us regarding the ways and means by which this transition was effected among the civilised peoples of the Old World—almost mere hypotheses, of course—see M. Kovalevsky, *Outline of the Origin and Evolution of the Family and Property,* Stockholm, 1890.

The overthrow of mother right was the *world-historic defeat of the female sex.* The man seized the reins in the house also, the woman was degraded, enthralled, the slave of the man's lust, a mere instrument for breeding children. This lowered position of women, especially manifest among the Greeks of the Heroic and still more of the Classical Age, has become gradually embellished and dissembled and, in part, clothed in a milder form, but by no means abolished. . . .

Slavery was the first form of exploitation, peculiar to the world of antiquity; it was followed by serfdom in the Middle Ages, and by wage labour in modern times. These are the three great forms of servitude, characteristic of the three great epochs of civilisation; open, and, latterly, disguised slavery, are its steady companions.

The stage of commodity production, with which civilisation began, is marked economically by the introduction of 1) metal money and thus, of money capital, interest and usury; 2) the merchants acting as middlemen between producers; 3) private ownership of land and mortgage; 4) slave labour as the prevailing form of production. The form of the family corresponding to civilisation and under it becoming the definitely prevailing form is monogamy, the supremacy of the man over the woman, and the individual family as the economic unit of society. The cohesive force of civilised socity is the state, which in all typical periods is exclusively the state of the ruling class, and in all cases remains essentially a machine for keeping down the oppressed, exploited class. Other marks of civilisation are: on the one hand fixation of the contrast between town and country as the basis of the entire division of social labour; on the other hand, the introduction of wills, by which the property holder is able to dispose of his property even after his death. This institution, which was a direct blow at the old gentile constitution, was unknown in Athens until the time of Solon; in Rome it was introduced very early, but we do not know when. Among the Germans it was introduced by the priests in order that the good honest German might without hindrance bequeath his property to the Church.

With this constitution as its foundation civilisation has accomplished things with which the old gentile society was totally unable to cope. But it accomplished them by playing on the most sordid instincts and passions of man, and by developing them at the expense of all his other faculties. Naked greed has been the moving spirit of civilisation from the first day of its existence to the present time; wealth, more wealth and wealth again; wealth, not of society, but of this shabby individual was its sole and determining aim. If, in the pursuit of this aim, the increasing development of science and repeated periods of the fullest blooming of art fell into its lap, it was only because without them the ample present-day achievements in the accumulation of wealth would have been impossible.

Since the exploitation of one class by another is the basis of civilisation, its whole development moves in a continuous contradiction. Every advance in production is at the same time a retrogression in the condition of the oppressed class, that is, of the great majority. What is a boon for the one is necessarily a bane for the other; each new emancipation of one class always means a new oppression of another class. The most striking proof of this is furnished by the introduction of machinery, the effects of which are well known today. And while among barbarians, as we have seen, hardly any distinction could be made between rights and duties, civilisation makes the difference and antithesis between these two plain even to the dullest mind by assigning to one class pretty nearly all the rights and to the other class pretty nearly all the duties.

But this is not as it ought to be. What is good for the ruling class should be good for the whole of the society with which the ruling class identifies itself. Therefore, the more civilisation advances, the more it is compelled to cover the ills it necessarily creates with the cloak of love, to embellish them, or to deny their existence; in short, to introduce conventional hypocrisy—unknown both in previous forms of society and even in the earliest stages of civilisation—that culminates in the declaration: The exploiting class exploits the oppressed class solely and exclusively in the interest of the exploited class itself; and if the latter fails to appreciate this, and even becomes rebellious, it thereby shows the basest ingratitude to its benefactors, the exploiters.

⇥ 11 ⇤

The Position of Women

Juliet Mitchell

Radical feminism attempts to solve the problem of analysing the oppression of women by making it *the* problem. The largest, first and foremost. While such a theory remains descriptive of the experience, it *does* nevertheless stress the magnitude of the problem. What we need is a theory that is at once large enough and yet is capable of being specific. We have to see *why* women have always been oppressed, and *how* they are oppressed now, and how differently elsewhere. As radical feminists demand, we must dedicate ourselves to a theory of the oppression of all women and yet, at the same time, not lose sight of the historical specificity in the general statement. We should ask the feminist questions, but try to come up with some Marxist answers.

The situation of women is different from that of any other oppressed social group: they are half of the human species. In some ways they are exploited and oppressed like, and along with, other exploited classes or oppressed groups—the working-class, Blacks, etc. . . . Until there is a revolution in production, the labour situation will prescribe women's situation within the world of men. But women are offered a universe of their own: the family. Women are exploited at work, and relegated to the home: the two positions compound their oppression. Their subservience in production is obscured by their assumed dominance in their own world—the family. What is the family? And what are the actual functions that a woman fulfils within it? Like woman herself, the family appears as a natural object, but is actually a cultural creation. There is nothing inevitable about the form or role of the family, any more than there is about the character or role of women. It is the function of ideology to present these given social types as aspects of Nature itself. Both can be exalted, paradoxically, as ideals. The 'true' woman and the 'true' family are images of peace and plenty: in actuality they may both be sites of violence and despair. The apparently natural condition can be made to appear more attractive than the arduous advance of human beings towards culture. But what Marx wrote about the bourgeois myths of the Golden Ancient World describes precisely women's realm.

> . . . in one way the child-like world of the ancients appears to be superior; and this is so, insofar as we seek for closed shape, form and established limitation. The ancients provide a narrow satisfaction, whereas the modern world leaves us unsatisfied, or, where it appears to be satisfied with itself, is *vulgar* and *mean*.[1]

The ideology of 'woman' presents her as an undifferentiated whole—'a woman', alike the world over, eternally the same. Likewise the 'concept' of the family is of a unit that endures across time and space, there have always been families. . . . Within its supposed permanent structure, eternal woman finds her place. So the notion goes. . . . Any analysis of woman, and of the family, must uncoil this ideological concept of their permanence and of their unification into an monolithic whole, mother and child, a woman's place . . . her natural destiny. Theoretical analysis and revolutionary action must destructure and destroy the inevitability of this combination.

Past socialist theory has failed to differentiate woman's condition into its separate structures, which together form a complex—not a simple—unity. To do this will mean rejecting the idea that woman's condition can be deduced derivatively from the economy (Engles), or equated symbolically with society (early Marx). Rather, it must be seen as a *specific* structure, which is a unity of different elements. The variations of woman's condition throughout history will be the result of different combinations of these elements—we will thus have not a linear narrative of economic development (De Beauvoir) for the elements will be combined in different ways at different times. In a complex totality each independent sector has its own autonomous reality though each is ultimately, but only ultimately, determined by the economic factor. This complex totality means that no contradiction in society is ever simple. As each sector can move at a different pace, the synthesis of the different time-scales in the total structure means that sometimes contradictions cancel each other out, and sometimes they reinforce one another. Because the unity of woman's condition at any time is in this way the product of several structures, moving at different paces, it is always 'overdetermined'.[2]

The key structures of woman's situation can be listed as follows: Production, Reproduction, Sexuality and the Socialization of Children. The concrete combination of these produce the 'complex unity' of her position; but each separate structure may have reached a different 'moment' at any given historical time. Each then must be examined separately in order to see what the present unity is, and how it might be changed. The notes that follow do not pretend to give a historical account of each sector. They are only concerned with some general reflections on the different roles of women and some of their interconnections.

1. Production

The biological differentiation of the sexes into male and female and the division of labour that is based on this have *seemed*, throughout history, an interlocked necessity. Anatomically smaller and weaker, woman's physiology and her psychobiological metabolism appear to render her a less useful member of a work-force. It is always stressed how, particularly in the early stages of social development, man's physical superiority gave him the means of conquest over nature which was denied to women. Once woman was accorded the menial tasks involved in maintenance while man undertook conquest and creation, she became an aspect of the things preserved: private property and children. Marx, Engels, Bebel, De Beauvoir—the major socialist writers on the subject—link the confirmation and continuation of woman's oppression after the establishment of her physical inferiority for hard manual work with the advent of private property. But woman's physical weakness has never prevented her from performing work as such (quite apart from bringing up children)—only specific types of work, in specific societies. In Primitive, Ancient, Oriental, Medieval and Capitalist societies, the *volume* of work performed by women has always been considerable (it has usually been much more than this). It is only its form that is in question. Domestic labour, even today, is enormous if quantified in terms of productive labour.[3] It has been calculated in Sweden, that 2,340 million hours a year are spent by women in housework compared with 1,290 million hours in industry. The Chase Manhattan Bank estimated a woman's overall working week averaged 99.6 hours. In any case women's physique alone has never permanently or even predominantly relegated them to menial domestic chores. In many peasant societies, women have worked in the fields as much as, or more than, men.

Physical Weakness and Coercion

The assumption behind most socialist analyses is that the crucial factor starting the whole development of feminine subordination was women's lesser capacity for demanding physical work. But, in fact, this is a major oversimplification. Even in these terms, historically it has been woman's lesser capacity for violence as well as for work, that has determined her subordination. In most societies woman has not only been less able than man to perform arduous kinds of work, she has also been less able to fight. Man not only has the strength to assert himself against nature, but also against his fellows. *Social coercion* has interplayed with the straightforward division of labour, based on biological capacity, to a much greater extent than is generally admitted. Women have been *forced* to do 'women's work'. Of course, this force may not be actualized as direct aggression. In primitive societies women's lesser physical suitability for the hunt is assumed to be evident. In agricultural societies where women's inferiority is socially instituted, they are given the arduous task of tilling and cultivation. For this coercion is necessary. In developed civilizations, and more complex societies, woman's physical deficiencies again become relevant. Women are thought to be of no use either for war or in the construction of cities. But with early industrialization, coercion once more becomes important. As Marx wrote: 'insofar as machinery dispenses with muscular power, it becomes a means of employing labourers of slight muscular strength, and those whose bodily development is incomplete, but whose limbs are all the more supple. The labour of women and children was, therefore, the first thing sought for by capitalists who used machinery'.[4]

René Dumont points out that in many zones of tropical Africa today men are often idle, while women are forced to work all day. 'The African woman experiences a three-fold servitude: through forced marriage; through her dowry and polygamy, which increases the leisure time of men and simultaneously their social prestige; and finally through the very unequal division of labour'[5] (This exploitation has no 'natural' source whatever. Women may perform their 'heavy' duties in contemporary African peasant societies, not for fear of physical reprisal by their men, but because these duties are 'customary' and built into the role structures of the society. A further point is that coercion implies a different relationship from coercer to coerced than does exploitation. It is political rather than economic. In describing coercion Marx said that the master treated the slave or serf as the 'inorganic and natural condition of its own reproduction'. That is to say, labour itself becomes like other natural things—cattle or soil:

> The original conditions of production appear as natural prerequisites, *natural conditions of the existence of the producer,* just as his living body, however reproduced and developed by him, is not originally established by himself, but appears as his *prerequisite.*[6]

This is pre-eminently woman's condition. For far from woman's *physical* weakness removing her from productive work, her *social* weakness has in these cases evidently made her the major slave of it.

This truth, elementary though it may seem, has nevertheless been constantly ignored by socialist writers on the subject, with the result that there is an unfounded optimism in their predictions of the future. For, if it is just the biological incapacity for the hardest physical work which has determined the subordination of women, then the prospect of an advanced machine technology, abolishing the need for strenuous physical exertion, would seem to promise, therefore, the liberation of women. For a moment industrialization itself thus seems to herald women's liberation. Engels, for instance, wrote:

> The first premise for the emancipation of women is the re-introduction of the entire female sex into public industry. . . . And this has become possible only as a result of modern large-scale industry, which not only permits of the participation of women in production in large numbers, but actually calls for it and, moreover strives to convert private domestic work also into a public industry.[7]

What Marx said of early industrialism is no less, but also *no more* true of an automated society:

> . . . it is obvious that the fact of the collective working group being composed of individuals of both sexes and all ages, must necessarily, *under suitable conditions,* become a source of human development; although in its spontaneously developed, brutal, capitalist form, where the labourer exists for the process of production, and not the process of production for the labourer, that fact is a pestiferous source of corruption and slavery.[8]

Industrial labour and automated technology both promise the preconditions for women's liberation alongside man's—but no more than the preconditions. It is only too obvious that the advent of industrialization has not so far freed women in this sense, either in the West or in the East. De Beauvoir hoped that automation would make a decisive, qualitative difference by abolishing altogether the physical differential between the sexes. But any reliance on this in itself accords an independent role to technique which history does not justify. Under capitalism, automation could possibly lead to an ever-growing structural unemployment which would expel women (along with immigrants)—the latest and least integrated recruits to the labour force and ideologically the most expendable for a bourgeois society—from production after only a brief interlude in it. Technology is mediated by the total structure, and it is this which will determine woman's future in work relations. It is the relationship between the social forces and technology that Firestone's 'ecological' revolution ultimately ignores.

Physical deficiency is not now, any more than in the past, a sufficient explanation of woman's relegation to inferior status. Coercion has been ameliorated to an ideology shared by both sexes. Commenting on the results of her questionnaire of working women, Viola Klein notes: 'There is no trace of feminine egalitarianism—militant or otherwise—in any of the women's answers to the questionnaire; nor is it even implicitly assumed that women have a "Right to Work".'⁹ Denied, or refusing, a role in *production,* woman does not even create the preconditions of her liberation. But even her presence in the work force does not erode her oppression in the family.

2. The Reproduction of Children

Women's absence from the critical sector of production historically, of course, has been caused not just by their assumed physical weakness in a context of coercion—but also by their role in reproduction. Maternity necessitates withdrawals from work, but this is not a decisive phenomenon. It is rather women's role in reproduction which has become, in capitalist society at least, the spiritual 'complement' of men's role in production. Bearing children, bringing them up, and maintaining the home—these form the core of woman's natural vocation, in this ideology. This belief has attained great force because of the seeming universality of the family as a human institution. There is little doubt that Marxist analyses have underplayed the fundamental problems posed here. The complete failure to give any operative content to the slogan of 'abolition' of the family is striking evidence of this (as well as of the vacuity of the notion).

The biological function of maternity is a universal, atemporal fact, and as such has seemed to escape the categories of Marxist historical analysis. However, from it is made to follow the so-called stability and omnipresence of the family, if in very different forms.¹⁰ Once this is accepted, women's social subordination—however emphasized as an honourable, but different role (cf. the equal-but-'separate' ideologies of Southern racists)—can be seen to follow inevitably as an *insurmountable* bio-historical fact. The causal chain then goes: maternity, family, absence from production and public life, sexual inequality.

The lynch-pin in this line of argument is the idea of the family. The notion that 'family' and 'society' are virtually co-extensive or that an advanced society not founded on the nuclear family is now inconceivable, despite revolutionary posturings to the contrary, is still widespread. It can only be seriously discussed by asking just what the family is—or rather what women's role in the family is. Once this is done, the problem appears in quite a new light. For it is obvious that woman's role in the family—primitive, feudal or bourgeois—partakes of three quite different structures: reproduction, sexuality, and the socialization of children. These are historically, not intrinsically, related to each other in the present modern family. We can easily see that they needn't be. For instance, biological parentage is not necessarily identical with social parentage (adoption). Thus it is essential to discuss not the family as an unanalysed entity, but the separate *structures* which today compose it but which tomorrow may be decomposed into a new pattern.

As I have said, reproduction is seen as an apparently constant atemporal phenomenon—part of biology rather than history. In fact this is an illusion. What is true is that the 'mode of reproduction' does not vary with the 'mode of production'; it can remain effectively the same through a number of different modes of production. For it has been defined till now by its uncontrollable, natural character and to this extent has been an unmodified biological fact. As long as reproduction remained a natural phenomenon, of course, women were effectively doomed to social exploitation. In any sense, they were not 'masters' of a large part of their lives. They had no choice as to whether or how often they gave birth to children (apart from precarious methods of contraception or repeated dangerous abortions); their existence was essentially subject to biological processes outside their control.

Contraception

Contraception which was finally invented as a rational technique only in the nineteenth century was thus an innovation of world-historic importance. It is only just now beginning to show what immense consequences it could have, in the form of the Pill. For what it means is that at last the mode of reproduction potentially could be transformed. Once childbearing becomes totally voluntary (how much so is it in the West, even today?) its significance is fundamentally different. It need no longer be the sole or ultimate vocation of woman; it becomes one option among others.

History is the development of man's transformation of nature, and thereby of himself—of human nature—in different modes of production. Today there are the technical possibilities for the transformation and 'humanization' of the most natural part of human culture. This is what a change in the mode of reproduction could mean.

We are far from this state of affairs yet. In Italy the sale of contraceptives remains illegal. In many countries it is difficult to get reliable means.

The oral contraceptive is still the privilege of a moneyed minority in a few western countries. Even here the progress has been realized in a typically conservative and exploitative form. It is made only for women, who are thus 'guinea-pigs' in a venture which involves both sexes.

The fact of overwhelming importance is that easily available contraception threatens to dissociate sexual from reproductive experience—which all contemporary ideology tries to make inseparable, as the *raison d'être* of the family.

Reproduction and Production

At present, reproduction in our society is often a kind of sad mimicry of production. Work in a capitalist society is an alienation of labour in the making of a social product which is confiscated by capital. But it can still sometimes be a real act of creation, purposive and responsible, even in the conditions of the worst exploitation. Maternity is often a caricature of this. The biological product—the child—is treated as if it were a solid product. Parenthood becomes a kind of substitute for work, an activity in which the child is seen as an object created by the mother, in the same way as a commodity is created by a worker. Naturally, the child does not literally escape, but the mother's alienation can be much worse than that of the worker whose product is appropriated by the boss. The child as an autonomous person, inevitably threatens the activity which claims to create it continually merely as a *possession* of the parent. Possessions are felt as extensions of the self. The child as a possession is supremely this. Anything the child does is therefore a threat to the mother herself, who has renounced her autonomy through this misconception of her reproductive role. There are few more precarious ventures on which to base a life.

Furthermore even if the woman has emotional control over her child, legally and economically both she and it are subject to the father. The social cult of maternity is matched by the real socio-economic powerlessness of the mother. The psychological and practical benefits men receive from this are obvious. The converse of woman's quest for creation in the child is man's retreat from his work into the family: 'When we come home, we lay aside our mask and drop our tools, and are no longer lawyers, sailors, soldiers, statesmen, clergymen, but only men. We fall again into our most human relations, which, after all, are the whole of what belongs to us as we are ourselves.'[11]

Unlike her non-productive status, her capacity for maternity *is* a definition of woman. But it is only a physiological definition. Yet so long as it is allowed to remain a substitute for action and creativity, and the home an area of relaxation for men, woman will remain confined to the species, to her universal and natural condition.

3. Sexuality

Sexuality has traditionally been the most tabooed dimension of women's situation. The meaning of sexual freedom and its connection with women's freedom is a subject which few socialist writers have cared to broach. 'Socialist morality' in the Soviet Union for a long time debarred serious discussion of the subject within the world communist movement. Marx himself—in this respect somewhat less liberal than Engels—early in his life expressed traditional views on the matter:

> . . . the sanctification of the sexual instinct through exclusivity, the checking of instinct by laws, the moral beauty which makes nature's commandment ideal in the form of an emotional bond—(this is) the spiritual essence of marriage.[12]

Yet it is obvious that throughout history women have been appropriated as sexual objects, as much as progenitors or producers. Indeed, the sexual relationship can be assimilated to the statute of possession much more easily and completely than the productive or reproductive relationship. Contemporary sexual vocabulary bears eloquent witness to this—it is a comprehensive lexicon of reification—'bird, fruit, chick . . .' Later Marx was well aware of this: '*Marriage* . . . is incontestably a form of *exclusive private property*.'[13] But neither he nor his successors ever tried seriously to envisage the implications of this for socialism, or even for a structural analysis of women's conditions. Communism, Marx stressed in the same passage, would not mean mere 'communalization' of women as common property. Beyond this, he never ventured.

Some historical considerations are in order here. For if socialists have said nothing, the gap has been filled by liberal ideologues. Fairly recently, in his book, *Eros Denied*, Wayland Young argues that western civilization has been uniquely repressive sexually, and, in a plea for greater sexual freedom today, compares it at some length with oriental and ancient societies. It is striking, however, that his book makes no reference whatever to women's status in these different societies, or to the different forms of marriage-contract prevalent in them. This makes the whole argument a purely formal exercise—an obverse of socialist discussions of women's position which ignore the problem of sexual freedom and its meanings. For while it is true that certain oriental or ancient (and indeed primitive) cultures were much less puritanical than western societies, it is absurd to regard this as a kind of 'transposable value' which can be abstracted from its social structure. In effect, in many of these societies sexual openness was accompanied by a form of polygamous exploitation which made it, in practice, an expression simply of masculine domination. Since art was the province of man, too, this freedom finds a natural and often powerful expression in art—which is often quoted as if it were evidence of the total quality of human relationships in the society. Nothing could be more misleading. What is necessary, rather than this naïve, hortatory core of historical example, is some account of the co-variation between the degrees of sexual liberty and openness, and the position and dignity of women in different societies.

Sexuality and the Position of Women: Some Historical Examples

Some points are immediately obvious. The actual history is much more dialectical than any liberal account presents it. Unlimited juridical polygamy—whatever the sexualization of the culture which accompanies it—is clearly a total derogation of woman's autonomy, and constitutes an extreme form of oppression. Ancient China is a perfect illustration of this. A sensual culture and a society in which the father as head of the household wielded an extraordinary despotism. The Chinese paterfamilias was 'a liturgical (semi-official) policeman of his kin group'.[14] In the West, however, the advent of monogamy was in no sense an *absolute* improvement. It certainly did not create a one-to-one quality—far from it. Engels commented accurately:

> Monogamy does not by any means make its appearance in history as the reconciliation of man and woman, still less as the highest form of such a reconciliation. On the contrary, it appears as the subjugation of one sex by the other, as the proclamation of a conflict between the sexes entirely unknown hitherto in prehistoric times.[15]

But in the Christian era, monogamy took on a very specific form in the West. It was allied with an unprecedented regime of general sexual repression. In its Pauline version, this had a markedly anti-feminine bias, inherited from Judaism. With time this became diluted—feudal society, despite its subsequent reputation for asceticism, practised formal monogamy with considerable actual acceptance of polygamous behaviour, at least within the ruling class. But here again the extent of sexual freedom was only an index of masculine domination. In England, the truly major change occurred in the sixteenth century with the rise of militant puritanism and the increase of market relations in the economy. Lawrence Stone observes:

> In practice, if not in theory, the early sixteenth century nobility was a polygamous society, and some contrived to live with a succession of women despite the official prohibition on divorce. . . . But impressed by Calvinist criticisms of the double standard, in the late sixteenth century public opinion began to object to the open maintenance of a mistress.[16]

Capitalism and the attendant demands of the newly emergent bourgeoisie accorded women a new status as wife and mother. Her legal rights improved; there was vigorous controversy over her social position: wife-beating was condemned. 'In a woman the bourgeois man is looking for a counterpart, not an equal.'[17] At the social periphery woman did occasionally achieve an equality which was more than her feminine function in a market society. In the extreme non-conformist sects women often had completely equal rights: the Quaker leader Fox argued that the Redemption restored Prelapsarian equality and Quaker women thereby gained a real autonomy. But once most of the sects were institutionalized, the need for family discipline was re-emphasized and woman's obedience with it. As one historian, Keith Thomas, says, the Puritans 'had done something to raise women's status, but not really very much'.[18] The patriarchal system was retained and maintained by the new economic mode of production—capitalism. The transition to complete effective monogamy accompanied the transition to modern bourgeois society as we know it today. Like the capitalist market system itself, it represented a historic advance, at great historic cost. The formal, juridical equality of capitalist society and capitalist rationality now applied as much to the marital as to the labour contract. In both cases, nominal parity masks real exploitation and inequality. But in both cases the formal equality is itself a certain progress, which can help to make possible a further advance.

Sexuality and the Position of Women: Today

The situation today is defined by a new contradiction. Once formal conjugal equality (monogamy) is established, sexual freedom as such—which under polygamous conditions was usually a form of exploitation—becomes, conversely, a possible force for liberation. It then means, simply, the freedom of both sexes to transcend the limits of present sexual institutions.

Historically, then, there has been a dialectical movement in which sexual expression was 'sacrificed' in an epoch of more-or-less puritan repression, which nevertheless produced a greater parity of sexual roles and in turn creates the precondition for a genuine sexual liberation, in the dual sense of equality *and* freedom—whose unity defines socialism.

Love and Marriage

This movement can be verified within the history of the 'sentiments'. The cult of *love* only emerges in the twelfth century in opposition to legal marital forms and with a heightened valorization of women (courtly love). It thereafter gradually became diffused, and assimilated to marriage as such, producing that absurdity—a *free* choice for *life*. What is striking here is that monogamy as an institution in the West, anticipated the idea of love by many centuries. The two have subsequently been officially harmonized, but the tension between them has never been abolished. There is a formal contradiction between the voluntary contractual character of 'marriage' and the spontaneous uncontrollable character of 'love'—the passion that is celebrated precisely for its involuntary force. The notion that it occurs only once in every life and can therefore be integrated into a voluntary contract, becomes decreasingly plausible in the light of everyday experience—once sexual repression as a psycho-ideological system becomes at all relaxed.

Obviously, the main breach in the traditional value-pattern has, so far, been the increase in premarital sexual experience. This is now virtually legitimized in contemporary society. But its implications are explosive for the ideological conception of marriage that dominates this society: that it is an exclusive and permanent bond. An American anthology, *The Family and the Sexual Revolution,* reveals this very clearly:

> As far as extra-marital relations are concerned, the anti-sexualists are still fighting a strong, if losing, battle. The very heart of the Judaeo-Christian sex ethic is that men and women shall remain virginal until marriage and that they shall be completely faithful after marriage. In regard to premarital chastity, this ethic seems clearly on the way out, and in many segments of the populace is more and more becoming a dead letter.[19]

The current wave of sexual liberalization, in the present context, *could* become conducive to the greater general freedom of women. Equally, it could presage new forms of oppression. The puritan-bourgeois creation of 'counterpart' (not equal) has produced the *precondition* for emancipation. But it gave statutory legal equality to the sexes at the cost of greatly intensified repression. Subsequently—like private property itself—it has become a brake on the further development of a free sexuality. Capitalist market relations have historically been a precondition of socialism; bourgeois marital relations (contrary to the denunciation of the *Communist Manifesto*) may equally be a precondition of women's liberation.

4. Socialization of Children

Woman's biological 'destiny' as mother becomes a cultural vocation in her role as socializer of children. In bringing up children, woman achieves her main social definition. Her suitability for socialization springs from her physiological condition: her ability to produce milk and occasional relative inability to undertake strenuous work loads. It should be said at the outset that suitability is not inevitability. Several anthropologists make this clear. Lévi-Strauss writes:

> In every human group, women give birth to children and take care of them, and men rather have as their speciality hunting and warlike activities. Even there, though, we have ambiguous cases: of course, men never gave birth to babies, but in many societies . . . they are made to act as if they did.[20]

Evans-Pritchard's description of the Nuer tribe depicts just such a situation. Margaret Mead comments on the element of wish-fulfilment in the assumption of a *natural* correlation of feminity and nurturance:

> We have assumed that because it is convenient for a mother to wish to care for her child, this is a trait with which women have been more generously endowed by a careful teleological process of evolution. We have assumed that because men have hunted, an activity requiring enterprise, bravery and initiative, they have been endowed with these useful attitudes as part of their sex-temperament.[21]

However, the cultural allocation of roles in bringing up children—and the limits of its variability—is not the essential problem for consideration. What is much more important is to analyse the nature of the socialization process itself and its requirements.

The sociologist, Talcott Parsons, in his detailed analysis claims that it is essential for the child to have two 'parents,' one who plays an 'expressive' role, and one who plays an 'instrumental' role.[22] The nuclear family revolves around the two axes of generational hierarchy (parents and children), and of the two parental roles (mother-expressive and father-instrumental). The role division derives from the mother's ability and the father's inability to breast-feed. In all groups, Parsons and his colleagues assert, even in those primitive tribes where the father appears to nurture the child (such as those discussed by Evans-Pritchard and Mead), the male plays the instrumental role *in relation* to the wife-mother. At one stage the mother plays an instrumental and expressive role *vis-à-vis* her infant: this is in the very first years when she is the source of approval and disapproval as well as of love and care. However, after this, the father, or male substitute (in matrilineal societies the mother's brother) takes over. In a modern industrial society two types of role are clearly important: the adult role in the family of procreation, and the adult occupational role in outside work. The function of the family as such reflects the function of the women within it; it is primarily expressive. The person playing the integrated-adaptive-expressive role cannot be off all the time on in-strumental-occupational errands—hence there is a built-in inhibition of the woman's work outside the home. Parsons's analysis makes clear the exact role of the maternal socializer in contemporary American society.[23] It fails to go on to state that other aspects and modes of socialization are conceivable. What is valuable in Parsons's work is simply his insistence on the central importance of socialization as a process which is constitutive of any society (no Marxist has provided a comparable analysis). His general conclusion is that:

> It seems to be without serious qualification the opinion of competent personality psychologists that, though personalities differ greatly in their degrees of rigidity, certain broad fundamental patterns of 'character' are laid down in childhood (so far as they are not genetically inherited) and are not radically changed by adult experience. The exact degree to which this is the case or the exact age levels at which plasticity becomes greatly diminished, are not at issue here. The important thing is the fact of childhood character formation and its relative stability after that.[24]

Infancy

This seems indisputable: one of the great revolutions of modern psychology has been the discovery of the decisive specific weight of infancy in the course of an individual life—a psychic time disproportionately greater than the chronological time. Freud began the revolution with his work on infantile sexuality; Melanie Klein radicalized it with her work on the first year of the infant's life. The result is that today we know far more than ever before how delicate and precarious a process the passage from birth to childhood is for everyone. It would seem that the fate of the adult personality can be largely decided in the initial months of life. The preconditions for the later stability and integration demand an extraordinary degree of care and intelligence on the part of the adult who is socializing the child, as well as a persistence through time of the same person.

These undoubted advances in the scientific understanding of childhood have been widely used as an argument to reassert women's quintessential maternal function, at a time when the traditional family has seemed increasingly eroded. The psychologist, Bowlby, studying evacuee children in the Second World War, declared: 'essential for mental health is that the infant and young child should experience a warm, intimate, and continuous relationship with his mother,'[25] setting a trend which has become cumulative since. The emphasis of familial ideology has shifted from a cult of the biological ordeal of maternity (the pain which makes the child precious, etc.) to a celebration of mother-care as a social act. This can reach ludicrous extremes:

> For the mother, breast-feeding becomes a complement to the act of creation. It gives her a heightened sense of fulfilment and allows her to participate in a relationship as close to perfection as any that a woman can hope to achieve. . . . The simple fact of giving birth, however, does not of itself fulfil this need and longing. . . . Motherliness is a way of life. It enables a woman to express her total self with the tender feelings, the protective attitudes, the encompassing love of the motherly woman.[26]

The tautologies, the mystifications, the sheer absurdities point to the gap between reality and ideology.

Family Patterns

This ideology corresponds in dislocated form to a real change in the pattern of the family. As the family has become smaller, each child has become more important; the actual *act* of reproduction occupies less and less time, and the socializing and nurturance process increase commensurately in significance. Contemporary society is obsessed by the physical, moral and sexual problems of childhood and adolescence. Ultimate responsibility for these is placed on the mother. Thus the mother's reproductive role has retreated as her socializing role has increased. In the 1890s in England a mother spent fifteen years in a state of pregnancy and lactation: in the 1960s she spent an average of four years. Compulsory schooling from the age of five, of course, reduces the maternal function very greatly after the initial vulnerable years.

The present situation is then one in which the qualitative importance of socialization during the early years of the child's life has acquired a much greater significance than in the past—while the quantitative amount of a mother's life spent either in gestation or child-rearing has greatly diminished. It follows that socialization cannot simply be elevated to the woman's new maternal vocation. Used as a mystique, it becomes an instrument of oppression. Moreover, there is no inherent reason why the biological and social mother should coincide. The process of socialization is, in itself, invariable—but the person of the socializer can vary. Observers of collective methods of child-rearing in the kibbutzim in Israel note that the child who is reared by a trained nurse (though normally maternally breast-fed) does not suffer the back-wash of typical parental anxieties and thus may positively gain by the system. This possibility should not be fetishized in its turn (Jean Baby, speaking of the post-four-year-old child, goes so far as to say that 'complete separation appears indispensable to guarantee the liberty of the child as well as the mother'.[27]) But what it does reveal is the viability of plural forms of socialization—neither necessarily tied to the nuclear family, not to the biological parent, or rather to *one* of the biological parents—the mother.

Conclusion

The lesson of these reflections is that the liberation of women can only be achieved if *all four* structures in which they are integrated are transformed—Production, Reproduction, Sexuality and Socialization. A modification of any of them can be offset by a reinforcement of another (as increased socialization has made up for decreased reproduction). This means that a mere permutation of the form of exploitation is achieved. The history of the last sixty years provides ample evidence of this. In the early twentieth century, militant feminism in England and the U.S.A. surpassed the labour movement in its violence. The vote—a political right—was eventually won. None the less, though a simple completion of the formal legal equality of bourgeois society, it left the socio-economic situation of women virtually unchanged. The wider legacy of the suffrage was practically nil: the suffragettes, by and large, proved unable to move beyond their own initial demands, and many of their leading figures later became extreme reactionaries. The Russian Revolution produced a quite different experience. In the Soviet Union in the 1920s, advanced social legislation aimed at liberating women above all in the field of sexuality; divorce was made free and automatic for either partner, thus effectively liquidating marriage; illegitimacy was abolished, abortion was free, etc. The social and demographic effects of these laws in a backward, semi-literate society bent on rapid industrialization (needing, therefore, a high birthrate) were—predictably—catastrophic.[28] Stalinism soon produced a restoration of traditional iron norms. Inheritance was reinstated, divorce made inaccessible, abortion illegal, etc.

> The State cannot exist without the family. Marriage is a positive value for the Socialist Soviet State only if the partners see in it a lifelong union. So-called free love is a bourgeois invention and has nothing in common with the principles of conduct of a Soviet citizen. Moreover, marriage receives its full value for the State only if there is progeny, and the consorts experience the highest happiness of parenthood.
>
> From the official journal of the Commissariat of Justice in 1939.[29]

Women still retained the right and obligation to work, but because these gains had not been integrated into the earlier attempts to free sexuality and abolish the family no general liberation has occurred.

In China, today there is still another experience. At this stage of the revolution all the emphasis is being placed on liberating women in *production*. This has produced an impressive social promotion of women. But it seems to have been accompanied by a tremendous repression of sexuality and a rigorous puritanism (rampant in civic life). This corresponds not only to the need to mobilize women massively in economic life, but to a deep cultural reaction against the brutality, corruption and prostitution prevalent in Imperial and Kuo Ming Tang China (a phenomenon unlike anything in Czarist Russia). Because the exploitation of women was so great in the *ancien régime* women's participation at village level in the Chinese Revolution was uniquely high. As for reproduction, the Russian cult of maternity in the 1930s and 1940s has not been repeated for demographic reasons: indeed, China may be one of the first countries in the world to provide free State authorized contraception on a universal scale to the population. Again, however, given the low level of industrialization and fear produced by imperialist encirclement, no all-round advance could be expected.

Probably it is only in the highly developed societies of the West that an authentic liberation of women can be envisaged today. But for this to occur, there must be a transformation of *all* the structures into which they are integrated, and all the contradictions must coalesce, to explode—a *unité de rupture*. A revolutionary movement must base its analysis on the uneven development of each structure, and attack the weakest link in the combination. This may then become the point of departure for a general transformation. What is the situation of the different structures today? What is the concrete situation of the women in each of the positions in which they are inserted?

Notes

1. Karl Marx: *Pre-Capitalist Economic Formations,* ed. Hobsbawm, Lawrence & Wishart, 1964, p. 85.

2. See Louis Althusser: 'Contradiction and Overdetermination', in *For Marx,* Allen Lane, London, 1970. To describe the movement of this complexity, as I have mentioned above, Althusser uses the Freudian term 'overdetermination'. The phrase *'unité de rupture'* (mentioned below) refers to the moment when the contradictions so reinforce one another as to coalesce into the conditions for a revolutionary change.

3. Apologists who make out that housework, though time-consuming, is light and relatively enjoyable, are refusing to acknowledge the dull and degrading routine it entails. Lenin commented crisply: 'You all know that even when women have full rights, they still remain factually downtrodden because all housework is left to them. In most cases housework is the most unproductive,

the most barbarous and the most arduous work a woman can do. It is exceptionally petty and does not include anything that would in any way promote the development of the woman.' (*Collected Works,* vol. XXX, p. 43.)

4. Karl Marx: *Capital,* I, p. 394.

5. René Dumont: *L'Afrique Noire est Mal Partie,* 1962, p. 210.

6. Karl Marx: *Precapitalist Economic Formations,* op. cit., p. 87.

7. Friedrich Engels: op. cit., II, pp. 233, 311.

8. Karl Marx: *Capital,* I, p. 394.

9. Viola Klein: 'Working Wives', *Institute of Personnel Management Occasional Paper,* no. 15, 1960, p. 13.

10. Philippe Ariès in *Centuries of Childhood,* 1962, shows that though the family may in some form always have existed it was often submerged under more forceful structures. In fact according to Ariès it has only acquired its present significance with the advent of industrialization.

11. J. A. Froude: *Nemesis of Faith,* 1849, p. 103.

12. Karl Marx: 'Chapitre de Mariage', *Oeuvres Complètes,* ed. Molitor *Oeuvres Philosophiques,* I, p. 25.

13. Karl Marx: *Private Property and Communism,* op. cit., p. 153.

14. Karl Wittfogel: *Oriental Despotism,* 1957, p. 116.

15. Friedrich Engels: op. cit., II, p. 224.

16. Lawrence Stone: *The Crisis of the Aristocracy,* 1965, pp. 663–4.

17. Simone de Beauvoir: *La Marche Longue,* 1957, trans. *The Long March,* 1958, p. 141.

18. Keith Thomas: *Women and the Civil War Sects,* Past and Present, no. 13, 1958, p. 43.

19. Albert Ellis: 'The Folklore of Sex', in *The Family and the Sexual Revolution,* ed. E. M. Schur, 1966, p. 35.

20. Claude Lévi-Strauss: 'The Family', in *Man, Culture and Society,* ed. H. L. Shapiro, 1956, p. 274.

21. Margaret Mead: 'Sex and Temperament', in *The Family and The Sexual Revolution,* op. cit., pp. 207–8.

22. Talcott Parsons and Robert F. Bales: *Family, Socialization and Interaction Process,* 1956, p. 47. 'The area of instrumental function concerns relations of the systems to its situation outside the system . . . and 'instrumentally' establishing the desired relations to *external* goal-objects. The expressive area concerns the 'internal' affairs of the system, the maintenance of integrative relations between the members, and regulation of the patterns and tension levels of its component units.'

23. One of Parsons' main theoretical innovations in his contention that what the child strives to internalize will vary with the content of the reciprocal role relationships in which he is a participant. R. D. Laing, in *Family and Individual Structure,* 1966, contends that a child may internalize an entire system—i.e. 'the family'.

24. Talcott Parsons: *The Social System,* 1952, p. 227. There is no doubt that the Women's Liberation Movement, with its practical and theoretical stress on the importance of child-care, has accorded the subject the seriousness it needs.

See, for instance, 'Women's Liberation: Notes on Child-Care' produced by the Women's Centre, 36 West 22nd St., New York.

25. John Bowlby, cit. Bruno, Bettelheim: 'Does Communal Education Work? The Case of the Kibbutz', in *The Family and the Sexual Revolution,* op. cit., p. 295. These evacuee war children were probably suffering from more than mother-loss, e.g., bombings and air-raids?

26. Betty Ann Countrywoman: *Redbook,* June, 1960, cit. Betty Friedan: *The Feminine Mystique,* Penguin, 1965, p. 51.

27. Jean Baby: *Un Monde Meilleur,* Maspero, 1964, p. 99.

28. For a fuller account of this see Chapter IVA of Kate Millet's *Sexual Politics,* op. cit.

29. *Sotsialisticheskaya Zakonnost,* 1939, no. 2, cit. N. Timasheff: 'The Attempt to Abolish the Family in Russia', in *The Family,* ed. N. W. Bell and E. F. Vogel, 1960, p. 59.

⇥ 12 ⇤

Class, Status, and Gender

David Lockwood

Since the study of social stratification deservedly occupies the central place in macrosociology, it is perhaps not surprising that its explanatory purpose should have become the target of feminist critiques which concur in the view that traditional approaches to social stratification have been misconceived because they have failed to take into account the fact that the structure of social inequality has at least as much to do with gender, as with class or status, relationships. It is with the validity of this thesis, and its implications, that the present chapter is exclusively concerned.[1] But before attending to it directly, it is necessary to distinguish three separate kinds of enquiry that are generally subsumed under the heading of social stratification analysis. Only then will it be possible to identify the precise respects in which a recognition of the significance of gender relations and sexual inequality calls for changes in accepted modes of thinking about the subject.

The Aims of Stratification Analysis

Weber's observation (1968) that societies can be distinguished according to their degree of class or status formation provides the most convenient summary of the range of facts that social stratification theory is called upon to explain.[2] A vast amount of historical and comparative evidence supports the conclusion that 'communal' and 'corporate' social interactions of a class or status kind constitute more or less systematic properties

---

Reprinted from David Lockwood, "Class, Status, and Gender," in Rosemary Crompton and Michael Mann, eds., *Gender and Stratification* (Oxford: Blackwell Publishers, 1986): 11–22, by permission of the author.

of total societies. For example, the fact that the Ruhr insurrection of 1920 approximated a situation of class war is as indisputable as the fact that the caste system in Tanjore in 1962 still represented a highly developed form of status-group consolidation (Eliasberg 1974; Beteille 1965). The first form of enquiry, then, concerns the extent to which class or status systems are the predominant modes of social action at the societal level.[3] This is why the study of social stratification is of such pre-eminent importance in sociology. Since class and status formation are modes of social interaction which are not only empirically identifiable as variable configurations of total societies, but analytically distinguishable from the 'economy' and the 'polity', it is understandable why, within the division of labor of the social sciences (including Marxist theory), 'social stratification' should have come to be regarded as the distinctive subject-matter of macrosociology. Furthermore, since status-group consolidation and class polarization can be taken as limiting cases of social order and conflict, it is once again not hard to understand why the study of social stratification should be regarded as the specific sociological contribution to the analysis of social (as opposed to system) integration.

Theories of social stratification, then, presuppose as their explanatory object the inter- and intra-societal variability of class and status formation. From this viewpoint, the most important question regarding claims about the significance of sexual inequality is whether societies can be differentiated according to the predominance of systems of gender relations, that is, structures of social action comparable to those within the range of class polarization and status-group consolidation. If they cannot, the thesis that the aims of 'sex-blind' stratification theory are misconceived because they neglect gender relationships must be rejected. In that case also, the further question arises of exactly what kinds of social interactions a gender-informed study of social stratification does in fact seek to explain.

A closely-related kind of enquiry subsumed under the study of social stratification attempts to generalize about the determinants of class and status formation.[4] This is often referred to as the analysis of class (though seldom, status) 'structure' or 'structuration'. Weber's judgement—that economic and technological change favours class stratification and pushes status stratification into the background—is prototypical of this endeavour, which has by now become highly complicated in terms of the independent variables under consideration (consider explanations of why there is no socialism in the United States? as an hors d'oeuvre and with why has the Western working class not been revolutionary? as the entrée). But since the extent of class and status formation is one major measure of social integration, it should come as no surprise that explanations of its variability encompass the widest set of factors. At the struc-

194 ← David Lockwood

tural level, these are what are conventionally (and even in some 'advanced' formulations) thought of as the economic, political and ideological. At the situational level, they refer to the basic elements of the schema of social action: the determinants of actors' ends, their choice of means and their conditions of action, which naturally include the unintended consequences of their interactions. Additionally, and not least, there are factors having to do with a society's history or what is now sometimes called the 'social formation'. To seek to add to this embarrassment of riches the factor of gender is something that could hardly be objected to. But that would mean no more than claiming that class and status formation is significantly affected by the variability of the structure of gender relations. It would not mean that the latter is a 'stratification' phenomenon in its own right: that is, a structure of social relations quite distinct from class and status interactions. The acceptance of this limitation would seem to be implicit in much of the feminist critique of conventional stratification analysis. But it would not be accepted by those who adhere to the idea of patriarchy. For them, gender relations are not part of the explanation of something else; they are the thing that deserves and requires explanation.

Since the determination and explanation of the variability of class and status formation have been the central concerns of the study of social stratification, the documentation of the inequality of opportunities and outcomes—according to socially (though not necessarily sociologically) relevant categories—has occupied a subordinate place. This relegation is justifiable on several grounds. First, because the interest in the distribution of unequal rewards, life-chances, or whatever, is primarily one of social policy, of how different social arrangements could procure 'better' outcomes and opportunities. This is clearly revealed by the 'theoretical' object of such investigations, namely, a set of outcomes that is intelligible only in the statistical sense that it conforms to, or deviates from, some 'ideal', random, or category-neutral, distribution. *Inter alia,* gender-based inequalities will naturally be such an object of interest and are well attested to (see for example Reid and Wormald 1982). What is called the 'sexual division of labour' is one facet of this. But the second reason why this sort of empirical regularity is peripheral to the study of social stratification proper is that the outcomes in question are explicable only in terms of the same factors that can also account for the extent of class or status formation: explaining 'outcomes' is, so to speak, a by-product of stratification analysis. Thirdly, and most importantly, in themselves such 'outcomes' are not necessarily immediately relevant to the explanation of class or status formation. For example, there is now a great mass of evidence that refutes the obstinate idea (never entertained by a De Tocqueville or a Trotsky) that economic deprivation is a necessary or even a sufficient condition of radical, if not revolutionary, class action. Moreover, many of the outcomes that fascinate sociologists are not outcomes whose effects are so immediately tangible to the individuals concerned. For example, it is doubtful that publicizing the precisely documented fact that relative mobility opportunities are highly unequal would arouse a deep and widespread sense of social grievance (see Goldthorpe *et al.* 1980: p. 266). Although such knowledge is an indispensable indication of the persistence and location of status-group stratification, it throws no light on the social actions by which these boundaries are maintained. Matters are not dissimilar when, for example, it comes to interpreting the meaning of conventional measures of working-class radicalism (a good example of how such misinterpretation can arise is provided by Geary 1981). It is then no more than sociological common sense to assert that, whether outcomes are taken either as conditions or as manifestations of class or status-group formation, their significance inheres entirely in the ways in which they are understood and evaluated by those who, through their actions, maintain or change these forms of social relationships.

From these considerations it follows that arguments indicting conventional stratification analysis on the ground that sexual inequalities of opportunity or outcome have escaped its attention are of small weight. The fact that something should be of concern to the Equal Opportunities Commission does not thereby guarantee its sociological relevance.

Has Stratification Analysis Neglected Gender?

Having outlined the three fairly distinct kinds of enquiry subsumed under the heading of stratification analysis, it is now possible to define more precisely the nature of the objection that this field of study is deficient because it has ignored the importance of gender relations. The least significant possible thesis is that the statistical study of the distribution of opportunities or outcomes has been insufficiently concerned with documenting gender (as opposed to a whole range of other) inequalities. Ignoring the questions of how far this is the case, and whether this sort of study fulfils mainly a social-policy or political function, it is fairly clear that the mere accumulation of such data is of sociological relevance only to the extent that it provides certain (though not the most interesting) 'raw materials' which can presumably be explained by theories of the structural determinants of class and status formation. It is not, therefore, the kind of study that deserves extended comment here; but it does lead on to another possible line of criticism, which is that stratification theorists have paid far too little attention to the importance of gender relations as determinants of class and status formation. This is much more serious, and probably the most crucial objection; also, one that is, *prima facie* least disputable.[5]

But it is distinct from the last, and much more ambitious, possible claim that, as structures of social interaction, gender relations are somehow comparable to the kinds of societal configurations that have been thought of traditionally as lying between the limits of class polarization and status-group consolidation. It is of course necessary to be cautious in formulating the problem in this way because, for any particular society at any given time, it may be difficult to establish the exact extent to which it is, in Weber's terms, 'class' or 'status' formed, that is, by reference to the predominant modes of social interaction. Nevertheless, since it has not been found useful to conceptualize the possible range of social formation in other than these broad terms, it seems appropriate to begin by asking whether, judged by the forms of their communal and corporate interactions, men and women constitute anything analogous to 'classes' and 'status groups'.

The objection to even beginning to pursue such thoughts are commonplace. Outside of the pages of *Lysistrata,* the war between the sexes does not eventuate in society-wide 'class struggle'; and even in those instances where there is some slight approximation to such a conflict, the basis of it has been far from enduring or systematic.[6] Again, the cases in which men and women can be said to make up anything approaching identifiable status groups, whose boundaries are maintained by conventional, legal or religious sanctions, are far too exceptional to require a revision of the traditional approach to this subject.[7] Both of these objections rest on the simple fact that gender relations are usually heterosexual (though often homosociable) and are therefore cross-cut by class and status relations.[8] This prevents men and women having economic interests that could lead them to organize collectively against each other in any 'class' action. Furthermore, since some degree of endogamy and commensality is what marks one status group from another, any comparable form of gender interaction is also ruled out. Taken together, these are powerful objections to the claim that gender relations are macrosocial phenomena of the same order as classes and status groups. It is, of course, always possible to argue that gender relationships partake of some kind of ubiquitous, class- or status-oriented interaction at the situational, as opposed to the societal, level: so that they are, so to speak, of only 'subterranean' importance. But a retreat to this position would be identical in its implications to that apparently accepted by those Marxist theoreticians who, faced with the fact that the Western working class has failed to be revolutionary, have sought to redefine 'class struggle' in order to encompass almost all forms of everyday social conflict.[9] In both cases, the price to be paid is much the same: the dissolution of any distinction between gender or class action and social action *per se.*

These considerations also have a bearing on the view that gender relations are somehow similar to ethnic relations.[10] This affinity is no doubt discoverable in the visibility of both types of actors and the saliency of ascriptive properties in governing their relationships with others. But beyond this surface resemblance, the argument does not have much force, particularly as it refers to questions of group formation. Ethnic divisions, far more frequently than those of class, do provide the basis of acute communal conflicts, especially when ethnicity is associated with 'differential incorporation' (Kuper and Smith 1971), or the unequal distribution of citizenship rights. Such conflicts are naturally even more intense when the political domination of one ethnic group by another is accompanied by its economic exploitation and public derogation. Ethnic discrimination and the communal strife to which it often gives rise are therefore best understood as forms of status- rather than class-based stratification and antagonism. This conclusion is supported by the fact that the lack of coincidence of ethnic and class boundaries does not prevent the eruption of communal conflicts which are class-indiscriminate in their scope (Kuper 1974: ch. 7, 8). In general, the consciousness of ethnic belonging is far more widespread, continuous and intense than class consciousness. And in these respects it is certainly similar to gender consciousness. But for reasons already adduced, gender differences (unless they are also associated with highly visible forms of differential incorporation) are unlikely to eventuate in anything at all comparable to ethnic solidarity and conflict. In this century, the struggle for the enfranchisement of women has provided the only significant example of mass mobilization of this kind, and once that single status interest was achieved the movement collapsed.[11]

Marxist Class Theory, Patriarchy, and Gender

The foregoing observations may now be tested by examining the only two major lines of thought that might possibly lead to different conclusions. One is the attempt to accommodate gender relations to Marxist class theory. The other is the idea that gender relations constitute a distinct form of stratification, namely patriarchy.

Since the most recent phase of feminism originated in left-wing movement in the United States (and was motivated partly by the sexism and relative status deprivation that women experienced at that level of the 'class struggle') is is not accidental that attempts to formulate the place of women in the class structure should have become a major concern of

Marxist theoreticians. It is also natural that the present orientation of this school of thought should have led to the conceptualization of sexual divisions in terms that have less to do with actual social relationships, or patterns of social interaction, than with the determination of the 'place' of female labour within the class structure and of its 'functions for capital'. The 'woman question' in Marxism then, is partly just another aspect of the 'boundary debate', i.e., the analysis of 'objective' class positions and class interests, which it is assumed provides a correct understanding of the potentialities of class action. A major question from this perspective is whether or not female domestic labour is part of the working class or proletariat, and, less orthodoxly, whether it is in some sense a class which is exploited domestically, rather than capitalistically. But the 'woman question' (unlike some other issues arising from the 'boundary' debate) is also closely related to the Marxist economic theory of system contradiction via such questions as whether or not domestic labour is a source of surplus value, and whether or not women constitute a 'reserve army of labour'.

To a large extent then, discussion of women's place(s) in the class structure has been dominated by conceptual debates whose energy derives more from their political significance for the protagonists than from the explanatory power of the vying arguments. Certainly the sociological value of such work has yet to be shown. Mere observers of these debates are unlikely to be excited by such belated recent discoveries, as that the whole domestic labour debate throws no light on the fact that it is usually women who do housework, or that the 'reserve army of labour' thesis appears to be vitiated by the fact of sexually-segregated job markets. Nor will they be impressed with the explanatory power of a theory whose main counterfactual appears to be that the withdrawal of women from housework would mean the collapse of capitalism. And if internal critics can level powerful charges of 'functionalism' and 'reductionism' against the basic terms of the debate, it is still not clear what in the way of a more discriminating and positive analysis these condign criticisms lead to.[12]

The domestic labour debate has shown signs of diminishing returns for some time. But from the beginning, it represented a conceptual investment whose profitability was highly questionable, simply because of the 'essentialist' activity in which it engaged and which focused on such questions as what sort of labour *is* domestic labour? Is it really labour that contributes to surplus value? Are women domestic workers really exploited by capital or by their husbands? And so on. In this respect it shares the same features as the 'boundary debate' and the debate on productive and unproductive labour. Marxism has always had difficulties in formulating a stable and coherent theory of action which could relate the analysis of objective class position and of system contradictions to class formation. This is another reason for scepticism about the explanatory power of the theories that are likely to issue from the current domestic labour debate. It is not clear what this debate seeks to explain, although, like all Marxist theory, it is ultimately oriented to an understanding of the development of the class struggle. Nevertheless, its starting point (and perhaps its finishing point) is the analysis of class 'structure' or 'structuration'; it is not concerned primarily with explaining forms of class action or class conflict (except in the sense, already noted above, in which Marxism now views these as endemic in class relations, whether at the economic, political or ideological level).

In this respect, it differs fundamentally from the kind of analysis that has accreted around the concept of 'patriarchy', which, despite the 'essentialist' tendency it shares with Marxist debates, does refer to patterns of behaviour or forms of social interaction, that is, gender raltions. The two approaches also differ in that whereas the orthodox Marxist position holds that women do not constitute a class,[13] while patriarchy is seen as a structure of social relations in which men are privileged systematically and women disprivileged in such a variety of social contexts that it makes sense to think of gender relations as a form of 'stratification', and hence one may suppose of 'gender situations', 'gender interests' and 'gender conflicts'.

The arguments against current uses of the concept of patriarchy have been well rehearsed (see especially Elshtein 1981: pp. 204–28; Beechey 1979). One important objection is that, since patriarchy refers to a quite specific historical form of household relationship and societal ideology, its application to modern societies is quite misleading, and results in the concept losing any possible explanatory value and acquiring instead a merely liturgical character. While matters of terminology are never crucial, it is plain that the highly generalized meaning that patriarchy has acquired tends to preclude serious historical and comparative study of 'gender stratification'. This is partly because all concepts of invariant societal properties tend to regress towards forms of explanation that derive from some kind of 'positivistic' or 'idealistic' action schema.

This is certainly evident in discussions of patriarchy. Those who regard the ubiquity of this phenomenon are more impressive than its historical and social variability have sought to account for its pervasiveness by a whole range of reductionist, extra-sociological explanations, be they biological, cultural, or psychoanalytical, or simply in terms of men's (presumably innate) drive to dominate women. Whatever in other respects might be seen to be the merits of these various theories and their respective redemptory promises, it is clear that they afford no basis for a systematic, comparative, study of gender relations and inequalities. And yet, even among those who eschew the search for origins and who are more interested in bringing women back into the detailed study of societies past and present, it is still commonly assumed that the oppression of women by men is a global feature of social life manifesting itself in every institutional sphere, and therefore in need only of particularization.[14] Thereby, the historical and sociological objective is once again misconceived. It is by now well recognized that if patriarchy is to be a useful concept it must take account of the variability in gender relations. But this discovery of sociological essentials merely echoes what, for example, Mills (1963: p. 344) argued for thirty years ago: 'some sort of classification of women according to their condition'. This hardly exists, and the documentation of 'instances' of patriarchal domination, however detailed this may be, is no substitute for the prior work of decomposing the idea of patriarchal domination itself. For, *contra* Mills, what is needed is not an empirical classification of types of women (such as that provided, for example, by Parsons' categories of 'wife', 'mother', 'good companion', 'career' woman and 'glamour' girl) but rather an analytical differentiation of gender relations; and, naturally, hypotheses about determinants of the variability of these components.[15] No amount of illustration of the institutionally imbricated nature of patriarchal domination will guarantee this result.

Moreover, it is doubtful that further conceptual and empirical investigation of the structure of gender relations would lead to the conclusion that patriarchy constitutes a type of social formation that has been improperly ignored by conventional stratification analysis. Certain theories in which men and women, or husbands and housewives, appear as the subject of a new ground of the class war, are highly factitious. Nevertheless, despite the more extravagant claims of some of its adherents, the idea of patriarchy does represent a challenge to accepted notions of status stratification and indeed poses a rather interesting problem. This is that, although the status situations of men and women differ in certain significant respects, and fairly systematically so in a variety of institutional contexts, it is at the same time true that men and women are not, in any meaningful sense of the term, status groups. Why this should be the case merits further discussion.

Status Groups and Gender

It is convenient to begin with Weber, who defines status situation first negatively as that of 'men whose fate is not determined by the chance of using goods or services for themselves on the market', and then positively, so as to include 'every typical component of the life situation of men that is determined by a specific social estimation of honour' (1968).

While the life-chances of populations of modern Western societies are status-determined—in the strict sense of the term—mainly by the institutional complex of citizenship, it may be thought that, in so far as opportunities to acquire, dispose of, and benefit from, marketable skills are limited by estimations of social worth then this liability is far more evident in the 'fate' of women than in that of men. Weber's second criterion is that status stratification goes hand in hand with the 'monopolization of ideal goods and opportunities' and that 'material monopolies provide the most effective motives for the exclusiveness of a status group.' Among the latter, the most relevant in the present context is the right to pursue certain types of occupations. Thirdly, such monopolization is guaranteed by conventional, or legal, or religious, sanctions.[16] By these criteria also it can be argued that women occupy a fairly distinctive status situation because their life-chances, including their chances of entering employment, and specific kinds of employment, are determined substantially by customary and ideological (if not juridical) constraints; and, furthermore, because these outcomes may be interpreted in significant measure as the result of men's deliberate attempts to monopolize positions of occupational authority and to secure domestic benefits.[17] On these grounds then, it is reasonable to think of the sexual divisions of labour and of other aspects of sexual inequality as being status-determined, that is, as outcomes of the differentiation of status situations specific to men and women. Yet at the same time, it is fairly clear that in itself, sex or gender is a relatively insignificant basis of status-group formation. As Shils (1967) puts it, 'the deference accorded to a woman or to women as a category or to a man or to men as a category is at the margin of macrosocial deference.'

Part of the explanation of this is to be found in the fact that the status a woman inherits or acquires from particular men (or that which she achieves on her own account), is, or appears to be, far more significant than the status she shares with women in general *vis-à-vis* men in general. But there is another, no less important, reason why men and women do not form separate status groups, and this has to do with the fact (so much emphasized by proponents of the idea of patriarchy) that the subjection of women to men tends to occur in every institutional context.

Simply because the relations between the sexes have no specific institutional expression outside of the nuclear family, they are at once the locus of an ever-present potential for discrimination and an unstable basis of status-group formation. For all practical purposes, sexual identity is as unmistakable as the gender connotations attaching to it are unavoidable. Only a few other properties of persons, such as skin colour and age, are of equally direct and pervasive social significance. Many ethnic identifying marks, such as apparel and hair-style are optional, and some ethnic

groups are not outwardly distinct at all. But the sheer visibility of maleness and femaleness means that the relations between the sexes are
charged with (among other sentiments) moral expectations that derive
from estimations of the relative social worth of men and women in general. Naturally, the extent to which such predispositions are expressed in
acts of deference and derogation will vary, according to the formality or
informality of the relationship, on its degree of anonymity and so on. But
the second, elementary point in need of emphasis is that the relationships
in which women customarily defer to men and men derogate women are
predominantly dyadic. These relationships may be private, personal or
domestic; they may be public, anonymous and ephemeral; or they may
be interspersed among bureaucratically organized activities. But in all
instances, they are most commonly status interactions involving a particular man and a particular woman, and not groups of men and women.
It is precisely the highly particularized and limited scope of such relations
that has called forth the feminist slogan 'the personal is political.' At
the same time the latter recognizes, at least tacitly, that the structure of
macrosocial deference has very little to do with the relations between the
sexes.

In contemporary Western societies, whose stratification systems are
based on class relations and the relations of a common legal status of
citizenship, the status hierarchy is, by any historical comparison, relatively unpronounced, its boundaries identifiable principally through patterns of social inclusion and exclusion, of intermarriage and informal
association. While for some purposes it is convenient to assume that non-
legal status is a function of position in the occupational hierarchy, this
formulation is elliptical in that it fails to reveal that the status order is a
system of social action. Shils (1982), who has been foremost in giving
due recognition to this fact, has also shown that status is determined
fundamentally by proximity to the creative and charismatic 'centre' of
society, so that the positions and activities that have highest status are
those that are imbued with the greatest 'authority' (in the original sense
of that word). Now as always, position in the hierarchy of authority of
corporate groups, whether these be armies, churches, parties, business
enterprises, or whatever, is what is decisive for status ranking (and for
that matter, other rewards as well, including income to a large extent).
Status-defining ceremonies and rituals, as well as the interest in publicly
recognized status as an end in itself, become more noticeable at the higher
reaches of corporate groups; and the equivalence of these variously based
high statuses is established by meticulously graded, national honours. All
this is more or less well understood, recognized or acquiesced in by those
who inhabit the middle and even the lower reaches of the status order,
and whose own modes of status-group demarcation are modelled on
those of their respective, immediate superiors from whom they seek rec-

ognition. Indeed, the stability of the status system as a whole depends on the existence of intersecting status groups throughout its various levels; this is the social mechanism by which conceptions of authority and creativity are transmitted from the centre to the periphery.

Such considerations might appear far removed from a question such as whether conventional stratification analysis has erred in assuming that the social status of women is determined by the occupational position of their fathers and husbands. But this is not so. A recent and keen debate on whether the occupations of women should be taken into account in defining the status of family units has focused on the extent and significance of 'cross-class' marriages (see Goldthorpe 1983; and replies by Britten and Heath 1983; Erikson 1984; Goldthorpe 1984; Heath and Britten 1984; Stanworth 1984). But these matters serve simply to bring into prominence the fact that it is the position of an occupation within some hierarchy of authority that is decisive for its status and not the sex of the person who happens to be in it. This does not mean that the sex (or any other ascriptive property) of the incumbents of these positions has no status implications whatsoever, but merely that these effects are marginal in the sense that they do not disturb the familiar rank order of broad occupational strata.[18] At any rate, there is no evidence to suggest, and no reason to believe, that a 'sex-neutral' distribution of persons among occupations would fundamentally alter their relative social standing.[19] In societies where kinship relations are no longer a principal mode of social organization and a major type of corporate group, sexual differentiation lacks a status-conferring institutional basis. This is a basic reason why men and women do not, and cannot, form status groups; and there is no ground for believing that this would not still hold even if heterosexual, monogamous marriage were not the norm.

In the end therefore, the idea of patriarchy serves to draw attention to some of the ways in which the sexual division of labour is reproduced by what has been called the 'subterranean' status relations between men and women. This is an important subject, a part of the study of the distribution of social inequalities. At the same time, patriarchy has not proved to be a concept that entails any radical revision of conventional stratification theory, whose purpose is to explain variations in the degree of class and status formation. It is possible that gender relations may prove to be a more important part of such explanations than has been recognized hitherto. But this again does not mean that the purpose of stratification theory has been misconceived.

Notes

1. In writing this essay I have benefited from discussions with Joan Busfield, Leonore Davidoff, Mary McIntosh and Alison Scott. That they would accept my

conclusions is an altogether different matter. For their comments on the paper presented to the Symposium, I am grateful to John H. Goldthorpe, Gordon Marshall and David Morgan.

2. Weber (1968: P. 307) 'Depending on the prevailing mode of stratification, we shall speak of a "status society" or a "class society".'

3. A formidable task in its own right, and one which impatient theorists of stratification disregard at their peril. Since the Ruhr has been mentioned, see, for example, Geary (1981).

4. The two activities are naturally associated closely. Yet they remain distinct in that the description and explanation of class and status formation in its particularity has usually been the work of historians and anthropologists, whereas the work of generalizing from this array of evidence and explanatory detail has been taken on by sociologists, who risk seeking to order it in some more systematic fashion.

5. Although no one has spelled out the consequences for class and status relations of, for example, a change in favour of a more 'sex-neutral' allocation of persons to positions in the division of labour. Consequently the whole question of whether any such change would alter class and status relations significantly remains a matter of speculation.

6. And have usually had as much to do with status as class considerations. For example, middle-class suffragettes were very conscious of their status disqualification *vis-à-vis* working-class men, who were sometimes among their servants. (I owe this example to Leonore Davidoff). More generally, the view that class conflicts are not substantially motivated by status interests must now be quite anachronistic.

7. See Ortner and Whitehead (1981: p. 16):

In the simplest societies, there are often only two principles of status differentiation: one that distinguishes between senior (or "elder" or "initiated") men and juniors, ranking the former over the latter; and one that distinguishes between male and female, ranking men over women. In such simple systems, needless to say, gender as a prestige system has enormous social salience, and is interwoven with the political-economic fabric of the society in direct and transparent ways. In more complex societies, in which larger systems of nongender-based ranking (ranked lineages, castes, classes) attain asocial structural prominence and historical dynamism, and in which gender recedes into the background as a formal organizational principle, the genders remain nonetheless among the most psychologically salient of status groups.

8. Even in an imaginary society consisting entirely of male and female homosexuals, the a priori reasons for thinking that, in the absence of other differences, gender would be the basis of either class or status formation are not immediately evident; as opposed to an equally imaginary society in which all male homosexuals were capitalists and all female homosexuals proletarians (or vice versa).

9. So, as one authority puts it, 'there is no need for there to be "class consciousness" or autonomous political organization for the class struggle to take

place, and to take place in every domain of social reality.' (Poulantzas 1978: p. 17).

10. An early proponent of this comparison was Myrdal (1944: Appendix 5). Following Weber, ethnic groups are considered here to include all those who 'entertain a subjective belief in their common descent because of similarities of physical type or customs or both, or because of memories of colonization and migration'. Weber also includes 'language' groups and stresses the 'ritual regulation of social life' (1968: pp. 389–90).

11. 'The struggle for suffrage imposed a spurious unity. Once gained, there was nothing to take the vote's place as a rallying point' (O'Neill 1969: p. 93).

12. What it sometimes does reveal, however, is the existence of residual categories. For example, a recent critic of the idea of domestic labour (Molyneux, 1979: p. 14) introduces the notion of 'social display' quite adventitiously into her argument in order to distinguish the work of the bourgeois housewife from that of the proletarian. This lapse is illuminating in two ways. First, it displays ignorance of the extent to which proletarian action is oriented to status interests (the distinction between the 'rough' and the 'respectable' working class being only the most obvious example); and secondly, and much more importantly, the whole idea of status has no place within the Marxist action schema.

The role of women in negotiating and maintaining status boundaries is a much-neglected topic; but one that in the present intellectual climate will not be a popular field of research.

13. And even when it is argued that women do not constitute a class, but that 'those engaged in unpaid domestic labour' do 'share a common class position', it is still concluded that 'housewives as a group do not see themselves as a class or have the basis for organizing collectively to defend their interests, because they are isolated and dependent on the male breadwinner' (Gardiner 1976: p. 119). Note that the same conclusion is arrived at from the rather different premises of 'patriarchy': it 'appears as if each woman is oppressed by her own man alone' and 'it is hard to recognize relations among men and between men and women as systematically patriarchal' (Hartmann 1981: p. 19).

14. For example 'Patriarchal power can be characterized in terms of organizing and rationalizing social relations based on male superiority and female inferiority which, *at one and the same time,* take an economic and familial form, and which pervade the major institutions and belief systems of the society.' (Lown 1983: p. 33).

15. Still exemplary in this respect is Elizabeth Bott's (1957) analysis of the relations between conjugal roles and social networks. See also Whitehead (1976), for empirical typology of gender relations.

16. Weber does not dwell on the role of illegal or extra-legal violence (or the threat of it) in maintaining status boundaries, although it has always been a major means of keeping the lower orders in their place. Even today, in rural India, such sanctions against 'untouchables' are commonplace. In this respect too, the situation of women is analogous to that of a status group, although the incidence of domestic violence, rape, and sexual harrassment is difficult to determine.

17. As opposed to being unintended consequences of action, a possibility raised by Walby (1983: p. 165) who argues that "If a structure or set of practices is patriarchal in its effects, then it is useful to describe it as a patriarchical structure or set of patriarchal practices.'

18. Schoolteaching and white-collar work are the only two major occupations whose sexual composition has undergone a substantial and fairly rapid change in recent times. Yet in neither case would it be easy to prove that fluctuations in the relative social standing of the occupation was due primarily to the extent of its 'feminization', as opposed to the effects of other factors such as the rationalization of office work, the professionalization of the teaching profession and changes in the supply and social origins of qualified labour—not to mention the status-enhancing features of the occupations with which it had traditionally been compared.

19. One rather crucial piece of evidence, much cited, but apparently not equally well scrutinized, is a paper by Haavio-Mannila (1969). The major finding of this study is that people's estimations of the status of occupations (especially 'traditional', in contrast with 'modern' occupations) is affected to a statistically significant degree by the sex of their incumbents—though not to such an extent as to affect the normal rank ordering of these occupations. Moreover, this finding could well have been an artefact of the research methods, as the author readily admits when she writes that her questions (which prevented interviewees from ranking any category the equal of any other) 'may have somewhat influenced the results. For example, male and female representatives of the same occupational group were not allowed to be given the same rank. Thus the inequality of the sexes is, perhaps, accentuated'. This careful qualification seems to have been ignored by commentators on the original, for example, by Murgatroyd (1982b: p. 578).

References

Beechey, V. 1979. "On Patriarchy," *Feminist Review,* no. 3.

Beteille, A. 1956. *Caste, Class and Power.* Berkeley: University of California Press.

Bott, E. 1957. *Family and Social Network.* London: Tavistock.

Britten, N., and Heath, A. 1983. "Women, Men, and Social Class," in E. Gamarnikow *et. al.* (eds.), *Gender, Class, and Work.* London: Hutchinson.

Eliasberg, G. 1974. *Der Ruhrkreig von 1920.* Bonn: Bad Godesberg.

Elshtein, J. B. 1981. *Public Man, Private Woman.* Oxford: Martin Robertson.

Erikson, R. 1984. "Social Class of Men, Women, and Families," *Sociology,* vol. 18, No. 4.

Gardiner, J. 1976. "Domestic Labour in Capitalist Society," in D. Barker and S. Allen (eds.) *Dependence and Exploitation in Work and Marriage.* London: Longman.

Geary, D. 1981. "Identifying Militancy: The Assessment of Working-Class Attitudes Towards State and Society," in R. Evans (ed.). *The German Working Class 1888–1933: The Politics of Everyday Life*. London: Croom Helm.

Goldthorpe, J. H., (with Llewellyn, C., and Payne, C.). 1980. *Social Mobility and Class Structure in Modern Britain*. Oxford: Clarendon Press.

Goldthorpe, J. H. 1983. "Women and Class Analysis: In Defence of the Conventional View," *Sociology*, vol. 17, no. 4.

———. 1984. "Women and Class Analysis: A Reply to the Replies," *Sociology*, vol. 18, no. 4.

Haavio-Mannila, E. 1969. "Some Consequences of Women's Emancipation." *Journal of Marriage and the Family*, vol. 31.

Hartmann, H. 1981. "The Unhappy Marriage of Marxism and Feminism: Towards a More Progressive Union," in L. Sargent (ed.), *Women and Revolution*. London: Pluto Press.

Heath, A., and Britten, N. 1984. "Women's Jobs Do Make a Difference," *Sociology*, vol. 18, no. 4.

Kuper, L. 1974. *Race, Class and Power*. London: Duckworth.

Kuper, L., and Smith, M. J. 1971. *Pluralism in Africa*. Berkeley: University of California Press.

Lown, J. 1983. "Not So Much a Factory, More a Form of Patriarchy: Gender and Class During Industrialization," in E. Garmarnikow, *et. al.* (eds.), *Gender Class and Work*. London: Heinemann.

Mills, C. W. 1963. "Women: The Darling Little Slaves," in *Power, Politics and People*. New York: Oxford University Press.

Molyneux, M. 1979. "Beyond the Domestic Labour Debate." *New Left Review*, no. 116.

Murgatroyd, L. 1982b. "Gender and Occupational Stratification, *Sociological Review*, vol. 30, no. 4.

O'Neill, W. 1969. *The Woman Movement: Feminism in the United States and England*. London: George Allen and Unwin.

Ortner, S., and Whitehead, H. 1981. *Sexual Meanings: The Cultural Construction of Gender and Sexuality*. Cambridge: Cambridge University Press.

Poulantzas, N. 1978. *Classes in Contemporary Capitalism*. London: New Left Books.

Reid, I., and Wormald, E. 1982. *Sex Differences and Britain*. London: Grant McIntyre.

Shils, E. 1967. "Deference," in J. Jackson (ed.), *Social Stratification*. Cambridge. Cambridge University Press.

Shils, E. 1982. *Centre and Periphery: Essays in Macrosociology*. Chicago: Chicago University Press.

Stanworth, M. 1984. "Women and Class Analysis: A Reply to John Goldthorpe," *Sociology*, vol. 18, no. 2.

Walby, S. 1985. *Patriarchy at Work*. Oxford: Polity Press.

Weber, M. 1968. Ed. by G. Roth and C. Wittich, *Economy and Society*. New York: Bedminster Press; 2 vols.

Whitehead, A. 1976. "Sexual Antagonism in Hertfordshire," in D. L. Barker and S. Allen (eds.), *Sexual Divisions and Society: Process and Change*. London: Tavistock.

❖ 13 ❖

Double-Consciousness and the Veil

W. E. B. Du Bois

O water, voice of my heart, crying in the sand,
    All night long crying with a mournful cry,
  As I lie and listen, and cannot understand
    The voice of my heart in my side or the voice of the sea,
  O water, crying for rest, is it I, is it I?
    All night long the water is crying to me.

Unresting water, there shall never be rest
  Till the last moon droop and the last tide fail,
And the fire of the end begin to burn in the west;
    And the heart shall be weary and wonder and cry like the sea,
  All life long crying without avail,
    As the water all night long is crying to me.

                          —Arthur Symons

B etween me and the other world there is ever an unasked question: unasked by some through feelings of delicacy; by others through the difficulty of rightly framing it. All, nevertheless, flutter round it. They approach me in a half-hesitant sort of way, eye me curiously or compassionately, and then, instead of saying directly, How does it feel to be a problem? they say, I know an excellent colored man in my town; or, I fought at Mechanicsville; or, Do not these Southern outrages make your blood boil? At these I smile, or am interested, or reduce the boiling to a simmer, as the occasion may require. To the real question, How does it feel to be a problem? I answer seldom a word.

And yet, being a problem is a strange experience,—peculiar even for one who has never been anything else, save perhaps in babyhood and in

---

Reprinted from W. E. B. Du Bois, *The Souls of Black Folk* (New York: Bantam, 1989): 1–9.

Europe. It is in the early days of rollicking boyhood that the revelation first bursts upon one, all in a day, as it were. I remember well when the shadow swept across me. I was a little thing, away up in the hills of New England, where the dark Housatonic winds between Hoosac and Taghkanic to the sea. In a wee wooden schoolhouse, something put it into the boys' and girls' heads to buy gorgeous visiting-cards—ten cents a package—and exchange. The exchange was merry, till one girl, a tall newcomer, refused my card,—refused it peremptorily, with a glance. Then it dawned upon me with a certain suddenness that I was different from the others; or like, mayhap, in heart and life and longing, but shut out from their world by a vast veil. I had thereafter no desire to tear down that veil, to creep through; I held all beyond it in common contempt, and lived above it in a region of blue sky and great wandering shadows. That sky was bluest when I could beat my mates at examination-time, or beat them at a foot-race, or even beat their stringy heads. Alas, with the years all this fine contempt began to fade; for the words I longed for, and all their dazzling opportunities, where theirs, not mine. But they should not keep these prizes, I said; some, all, I would wrest from them. Just how I would do it I could never decide: by reading law, by healing the sick, by telling the wonderful tales that swam in my head,—some way. With other black boys the strife was not so fiercely sunny: their youth shrunk into tasteless sycophancy, or into silent hatred of the pale world about them and mocking distrust of everything white; or wasted itself in a bitter cry. Why did God make me an outcast and a stranger in mine own house? The shades of the prison-house closed round about us all: walls strait and stubborn to the whitest, but relentlessly narrow, tall, and unscalable to sons of night who must plod darkly on in resignation, or beat, unavailing palms against the stone, or steadily, half hopelessly, watch the streak of blue above.

After the Egyptian and Indian, the Greek and Roman, the Teuton and Mongolian, the negro is a sort of seventh son, born with a veil, and gifted with second-sight in this American world,—a world which yields him no true self-consciousness, but only lets him see himself through the revelation of the other world. It is a peculiar sensation, this double-consciousness, this sense of always looking at one's self through the eyes of others, of measuring one's soul by the tape of a world that looks on in amused contempt and pity. One ever feels his twoness,—an American, a Negro; two souls, two thoughts, two unreconciled strivings; two warring ideals in one dark body, whose dogged strength alone keeps it from being torn asunder.

The history of the American Negro is the history of this strife,—this longing to attain self-conscious manhood, to merge his double self into a better and truer self. In this merging he wishes neither of the older selves to be lost. He would not Africanize America, for America has too much to teach the world and Africa. He would not bleach his Negro soul in a flood of white Americanism, for he knows that Negro blood has a message for the world. He simply wishes to make it possible for a man to be both a Negro and an American, without being cursed and spit upon by his fellows, without having the doors of Opportunity closed roughly in his face.

This, then, is the end of his striving: to be a co-worker in the kingdom of culture, to escape both death and isolation, to husband and use his best powers and his latent genius. These powers of body and mind have in the past been strangely wasted, dispersed, or forgotten. The shadow of a mighty Negro past flits through the tale of Ethiopia the Shadowy and of Egypt the Sphinx. Through history, the powers of single black men flash here and there like falling stars, and die sometimes before the world has rightly gauged their brightness. Here in America, in the few days since Emancipation, the black man's turning hither and thither in hesitant and doubtful striving has often made his very strength to lose effectiveness, to seem like absence of power, like weakness, and yet it is not weakness,—it is the contradiction of double aims. The double-aimed struggle of the black artisan—on the one hand to escape white contempt for a nation of mere hewers of wood and drawers of water, and on the other hand to plough and nail and dig for a poverty-stricken horde—could only result in making him a poor craftsman, for he had but half a heart in either cause. By the poverty and ignorance of his people, the Negro minister or doctor was tempted toward quackery and demagogy; and by the criticism of the other world, toward ideals that made him ashamed of his lowly tasks. The would-be black *savant* was confronted by the paradox that the knowledge of his people needed was a twice-told tale to his white neighbors, while the knowledge which would teach the white world was Greek to his own flesh and blood. The innate love of harmony and beauty that set the ruder souls of his people a-dancing and a-singing raised but confusion and doubt in the soul of the black artist; for the beauty revealed to him was the soul-beauty of a race which his larger audience despised, and he could not articulate the message of another people. This waste of double aims, this seeking to satisfy two unreconciled ideals, has wrought sad havoc with the courage and faith and deeds of ten thousand thousand people,—has sent them often wooing false gods and invoking false means of salvation, and at times has even seemed about to make them ashamed of themselves.

Away back in the days of bondage they thought to see in one divine event the end of all doubt and disappointment; few men ever worshiped Freedom with half such unquestioning faith as did the American Negro for two centuries. To him, so far as he thought and dreamed, slavery was indeed the sum of all villainies, the cause of all sorrow, the root of all prejudice; Emancipation was the key to a promised land of sweeter beauty than ever stretched before the eyes of wearied Israelites. In song and exhortation swelled one refrain—Liberty; in his tears and curses the God he implored had Freedom in his right hand. At last it came,— suddenly, fearfully, like a dream. With one wild carnival of blood and passion came the message in his own plaintive cadences:—

> "Shout, O children!
> Shout, you're free!
> For God has bought your liberty!"

Years have passed away since then,—ten, twenty, forty; forty years of national life, forty years of renewal and development, and yet the swarthy spectre sits in its accustomed seat at the Nation's feast. In vain do we cry to this our vastest social problem:—

> "Take any shape but that, and my firm nerves
> Shall never tremble!"

The Nation has not yet found peace from its sins; the freedman has not yet found in freedom his promised land. Whatever of good may have come in these years of change, the shadow of a deep disappointment rests upon the Negro people,—a disappointment all the more bitter because the unattained ideal was unbounded save by the simple ignorance of a lowly people.

The first decade was merely a prolongation of the vain search for freedom, the boon that seemed ever barely to elude their grasp,—like a tantalizing will-o'-the-wisp, maddening and misleading the headless host. The holocaust of war, the terrors of the Ku-Klux Klan, the lies of carpetbaggers, the disorganization of industry, and the contradictory advice of friends and foes, left the bewildered serf with no new watchword beyond the old cry for freedom. As the time flew, however, he began to grasp a new idea. The ideal of liberty demanded for its attainment powerful means, and these the Fifteenth Amendment gave him. The ballot, which before he had looked upon as a visible sign of freedom, he now regarded as the chief means of gaining and perfecting the liberty with which war had partially endowed him. And why not? Had not votes made war and emancipated millions? Had not votes enfranchised the freedmen? Was anything impossible to a power that had done all this? A million black men started with renewed zeal to vote themselves into the kingdom. So the decade flew away, the revolution of 1876 came, and left the half-free serf weary, wondering, but still inspired. Slowly but steadily, in the following years, a new vision began gradually to replace the dream of political power,—a powerful movement, the rise of another ideal to guide the unguided, another pillar of fire by night after a clouded day. It was the ideal of "book-learning"; the curiosity, born of compulsory ignorance, to know and test the power of the cabalistic letters of the white man, the longing to know. Here at last seemed to have been discovered the mountain path to Canaan; longer than the highway of Emancipation and law, steep and rugged, but straight, leading to heights high enough to overlook life.

Up the new path the advance guard toiled, slowly, heavily, doggedly; only those who have watched and guided the faltering feet, the misty minds, the dull understandings, of the dark pupils of these schools know how faithfully, how piteously, this people strove to learn. It was weary work. The cold statistician wrote down the inches of progress here and there, noted also where here and there a foot had slipped or some one had fallen. To the tired climbers, the horizon was ever dark, the mists were often cold, the Canaan was always dim and far away. If, however, the vistas disclosed as yet no goal, no resting-place, little but flattery and criticism, the journey at least gave leisure for reflection and self-examination; it changed the child of Emancipation to the youth with dawning self-consciousness, self-realization, self-respect. In those sombre forests of his striving his own soul rose before him, and he saw himself,—darkly as through a veil; and yet he saw in himself some faint revelation of his power, of his mission. He began to have a dim feeling that, to attain his place in the world, he must be himself, and not another. For the first time he sought to analyze the burden he bore upon his back, that dead-weight of social degradation partially masked behind a half-named Negro problem. He felt his poverty; without a cent, without a home, without land, tools, or savings, he had entered into competition with rich, landed, skilled neighbors. To be a poor man is hard, but to be a poor race in a land of dollars is the very bottom of hardships. He felt the weight of his ignorance,—not simply of letters, but of life, of business, of the humanities; the accumulated sloth and shirking and awkwardness of decades and centuries shackled his hands and feet. Nor was his burden all poverty and ignorance. The red stain of bastardy, which two centuries of systematic legal defilement of Negro women had stamped upon his race, meant not only the loss of ancient African chastity, but also the hereditary weight of a mass of corruption from white adulterers, threatening almost the obliteration of the Negro home.

A people thus handicapped ought not to be asked to race with the world, but rather allowed to give all its time and thought to its own social problems. But alas! while sociologists gleefully count his bastards and his prostitutes, the very soul of the toiling, sweating black man is darkened by the shadow of a vast despair. Men call the shadow prejudice, and learnedly explain it as the natural defence of culture against barbarism, learning against ignorance, purity against crime, the "higher" against the "lower" races. To which the Negro cries Amen! and swears that to so much of this strange prejudice as is founded on just homage to civilization, culture, righteousness, and progress, he humbly bows and meekly does obeisance. But before that nameless prejudice that leaps beyond all this he stands helpless, dismayed, and well-nigh speechless; before that personal disrespect and mockery, the ridicule and systematic humiliation, the distortion of fact and wanton license of fancy, the cynical ignoring of the better and the boisterous welcoming of the worse, the all-pervading desire to inculcate disdain for everything black, from Toussaint to the devil,—before this there rises a sickening despair that would disarm and discourage any nation save that black host to whom "discouragement" is an unwritten word.

But the facing of so vast a prejudice could not but bring the inevitable self-questioning, self-disparagment, and lowering of ideals which ever accompany repression and breed in an atmosphere of contempt and hate. Whisperings and portents came borne upon the four winds: Lo! we are diseased and dying, cried the dark hosts, we cannot write, our voting is vain; what need of education, since we must always cook and serve? And the Nation echoed and enforced this self-criticism, saying: Be content to be servants, and nothing more; what need of higher culture for half-men? Away with the black man's ballot, by force or fraud,—and behold the suicide of a race! Nevertheless, out of the evil came something of good,— the more careful adjustment of education to real life, the clearer perception of the Negroes' social responsibilities, and the sobering realization of the meaning of progress.

So dawned the time of *Sturm und Drang:* storm and stress to-day rocks our little boat on the mad waters of the world-sea; there is within and without the sound of conflict, the burning of body and rending of soul; inspiration strives with doubt, and faith with vain questionings. The bright ideals of the past,—physical freedom, political power, the training of brains and the training of hands,—all these in turn have waxed and waned, until even the last grows dim and overcast. Are they all wrong,— all false? No, not that, but each alone was over-simple and incomplete,— the dreams of a credulous race-childhood, or the fond imaginings of the other world which does not know and does not want to know our power. To be really true, all these ideals must be melted and welded into one. The training of the schools we need to-day more than ever,—the training of deft hands, quick eyes and ears, and above all the broader, deeper, higher culture of gifted minds and pure hearts. The power of the ballot we need in sheer self-defence,—else what shall save us from a second slavery? Freedom, too, the long-sought, we still seek,—the freedom of life and limb, the freedom to work and think, the freedom to love and aspire. Work, culture, liberty,—all these we need, not singly but together, not successively but together, each growing and aiding each, and all striving toward that vaster ideal that swims before the Negro people, the ideal of human brotherhood, gained through the unifying ideal of Race; the ideal of fostering and developing the traits and talents of the Negro, not in opposition to or contempt for other races, but rather in large conformity to the greater ideals of the American Republic, in order that some day on American soil two world-races may give each to each those characteristics both so sadly lack. We the darker ones come even now not altogether empty-handed: there are to-day no truer exponents of the pure human spirit of the Declaration of Independence than the American Negroes; there is no true American music but the wild sweet melodies of the Negro slave; the American fairy tales and folklore are Indian and African; and, all in all, we black men seem the sole oasis of simple faith and reverence in a dusty desert of dollars and smartness. Will America be poorer if she replace her brutal dyspeptic blundering with light-hearted but determined Negro humility? or her coarse and cruel wit with loving jovial good-humor? or her vulgar music with the soul of the Sorrow Songs?

Merely a concrete test of the underlying principles of the great republic is the Negro Problem, and the spiritual striving of the freedmen's sons is the travail of souls whose burden is almost beyond the measure of their strength, but who bear it in the name of an historic race, in the name of this the land of their fathers' fathers, and in the name of human opportunity.

⇥ 14 ⇤

Facets of the Negro Problem

Gunnar Myrdal

It was important to compare the Negro problem with American minority problems in general because both the similarities and the dissimilarities are instructive. Comparisons give leads, and they furnish perspective.

This same reason permits us to point out that the consideration of the Negro problem as one minority problem among others is far too narrow. The Negro has usually the same disadvantages and some extra ones in addition. To these other disadvantaged groups in America belong not only the groups recognized as minorities, but all economically weak classes in the nation, the bulk of the Southern people, women,[1] and others. This country is a "white man's country," but, in addition, it is a country belonging primarily to the elderly, male, upper class, Protestant Northerner. Viewed in this setting the Negro problem in America is but one local and temporary facet of that eternal problem of world dimension—how to regulate the conflicting interests of groups in the best interest of justice and fairness. The latter ideals are vague and conflicting, and their meaning is changing in the course of the struggle.

There seems to be a general structure of social relations between groups on different levels of power and advantage. From a consideration of our exaggeratedly "typical" case—the Negro—we may hope to reach some suggestions toward a more satisfactory general theory about this social power structure in general. Our hypothesis is that in a society where there are broad classes and, in addition, more minute distinctions and splits in the lower strata, *the lower class groups will, to a great ex-*

Reprinted from Gunnar Myrdal, *An American Dilemma: The Negro Problem and Modern Democracy* (New York: Harper & Row, 1944): 67–78, by permission of HarperCollins Publishers, Inc. Copyright © 1944, 1962 by Harper & Row Publishers, Inc.

tent, take care of keeping each other subdued, thus relieving, to that extent, the higher classes of this otherwise painful task necessary to the monopolization of the power and the advantages.

It will be observed that this hypothesis is contrary to the Marxian theory of class society, which in the period between the two World Wars has been so powerful, directly and indirectly, consciously and unconsciously, in American social science thinking generally. The Marxian scheme assumes that there is an actual solidarity between the several lower class groups against the higher classes, or, in any case, a potential solidarity which as a matter of natural development is bound to emerge. The inevitable result is a "class struggle" where all poor and disadvantaged groups are united behind the barricades.

Such a construction has had a considerable vogue in all discussions on the American Negro problem since the First World War. We are not here taking issue with the political desirability of a common front between the poorer classes of whites and the Negro people who, for the most part, belong to the proletariat. In fact, we can well see that such a practical judgment is motivated as a conclusion from certain value premises in line with the American Creed. But the thesis has also been given a theoretical content as describing actual trends in reality and not only political *desiderata*. A solidarity between poor whites and Negroes has been said to be "natural" and the conflicts to be due to "illusions." This thesis has been a leading one in the field and much has been made of even the faintest demonstration of such solidarity.

In partial anticipation of what is to follow later in this volume, we might be permitted to make a few general, and perhaps rather dogmatic, remarks in criticism of this theory. Everything we know about human frustration and aggression, and the displacement of aggression, speaks against it. For an individual to feel interest solidarity with a group assumes his psychological identification with the group. This identification must be of considerable strength, as the very meaning of solidarity is that he is prepared to set aside and even sacrifice his own short-range private interests for the long-range interests of his group. Every vertical split within the lower class aggregate will stand as an obstacle to the feeling of solidarity. Even within the white working class itself, as within the entire American nation, the feeling of solidarity and loyalty is relatively low. Despite the considerable mobility, especially in the North, the Negroes are held apart from the whites by caste, which furnishes a formidable bar to mutual identification and soldarity.

It has often occurred to me, when reflecting upon the responses I get from white laboring people on this strategic question, that my friends among the younger Negro intellectuals, whose judgment I otherwise have learned to admire greatly, have perhaps, and for natural reasons, not had enough occasion to find out for themselves what a bitter, spiteful, and relentless feeling often prevails against the Negroes among lower class white people in America. Again relying upon my own observations, I have become convinced that the laboring Negroes do not resent whites in any degree comparable with the resentment shown in the opposite direction by the laboring whites. The competitive situation is, and is likely to remain, highly unstable.

It must be admitted that, in the midst of harsh caste resentment, signs of newborn working class solidarity are not entirely lacking; we shall have to discuss these recent tendencies in some detail in order to evaluate the resultant trend and the prospects for the future. On this point there seems, however, to be a danger of wishful thinking present in most writings on the subject. The Marxian solidarity between the toilers of all the earth will, indeed, have a long way to go as far as concerns solidarity of the poor white Americans with the toiling Negro. This is particularly true of the South but true also of the communities in the North where the Negroes are numerous and competing with the whites for employment.

Our hypothesis is similar to the view taken by an older group of Negro writers and by most white writers who have touched this crucial question: that the Negro's friend—or the one who is least unfriendly—is still rather the upper class of white people, the people with economic and social security who are truly a "noncompeting group." There are many things in the economic, political, and social history of the Negro which are simply inexplicable by the Marxian theory of class solidarity but which fit into our hypothesis of the predominance of internal lower class struggle. Du Bois, in *Black Reconstruction,* argues that it would have been desirable if after the Civil War the landless Negroes and the poor whites had joined hands to retain political power and carry out a land reform and a progressive government in the Southern states; one sometimes feels that he thinks it would have been a possibility. From our point of view such a possibility did not exist at all, and the negative outcome was neither an accident nor a result of simple deception or delusion. These two groups, illiterate and insecure in an impoverished South, placed in an intensified competition with each other, lacking every trace of primary solidarity, and marked off from each other by color and tradition, could not possibly be expected to clasp hands. There is a Swedish proverb: "When the feed-box is empty, the horses will bite each other."

That part of the country where, even today, the Negro is dealt with most severely, the South, is also a disadvantaged and, in most respects, backward region in the nation. The Negro lives there in the midst of other relatively subordinated groups. Like the Negro, the entire South is a problem. We do not want to minimize other obvious explanations of the harsher treatment of the Negro in the South: his concentration there in large numbers, the tradition of subordination retained from slavery, and the traumatic effect of the Civil War and Reconstruction; but we do want to stress the fact that the masses of white Southerners are poor and to keep in mind the tendency of lower class groups to struggle against each other.[2]

A few remarks are now relevant on the internal social stratification of the Negro group itself. The stratification of the Negro caste into classes is well developed and the significance attached to class distinctions is great. This is not surprising in view of the fact that caste barriers, which prevent individuals of the lower group from rising out of it, force all social climbing to occur within the caste and encourage an increase in internal social competition for the symbols of prestige and power. Caste consigns the overwhelming majority of Negroes to the lower class. But at the same time as it makes higher class status rarer, it accentuates the desire for prestige and social distance within the Negro caste. In fact it sometimes causes a more minute class division than the ordinary one, and always invests it with more subjective importance. The social distinctions within a disadvantaged group for this reason become a fairly adequate index of the group's social isolation from the larger society.

Caste produces, on the one hand, a strong feeling of mutuality of fate, of in-group fellowship—much stronger than a general low class position can develop. The Negro community is a protective community, and we shall, in the following chapters, see this trait reflected in practically all aspects of the Negro problem. But, on the other hand, the interclass strivings, often heightened to vigorous mutual repulsion and resentment, are equally conspicuous.

Negro writers, especially newspapermen, particularly when directing themselves to a Negro audience, have always pointed out, as the great fault of the race, its lack of solidarity. The same note is struck in practically every public address and often in sermons when the preacher for a moment leaves his other-worldliness. It is the campaign cry of the organizations for Negro business. Everywhere one meets the same endless complaints: that the Negroes won't stick together, that they don't trust each other but rather the white man, that they can't plan and act in common, that they don't back their leaders, that the leaders can't agree, or that they deceive the people and sell out their interests to the whites.

In order not to be dogmatic in a direction opposite to the one criticized, we should point out that the principle of internal struggle in the lower classes is only one social force among many. Other forces are making for solidarity in the lower classes. In both of the two problems raised—the solidarity *between* lower class whites and Negroes and the internal solidarity *within* the Negro group—there can be any degree of solidarity, ranging between utter mistrust and complete trustfulness. The scientific problem is to find out and measure the degree of solidarity and the social forces determining it, not just to assume that solidarity will come about "naturally" and "inevitably." The factors making for solidarity are both irrational and rational. Among the irrational factors are tradition, fear, charisma, brute force, propaganda. The main rational factors are economic and social security and a planned program of civic education.

While visiting in Southern Negro communities, the writer was forced to the observation that often the most effective Negro leaders—those with a rational balance of courage and restraint, a realistic understanding of the power situation, and an unfailing loyalty to the Negro cause—were federal employees (for example, postal clerks), petty railway officials, or other persons with their economic basis outside the local white or Negro community and who had consequently a measure of economic security and some leisure time for thinking and studying. They were, unfortunately, few. Generally speaking, whenever the masses, in any part of the world, have permanently improved their social, economic, and political status through orderly organizations founded upon solidarity, these masses have not been a semi-illiterate proletariat, but have already achieved a measure of economic security and education. The vanguards of such mass reform movements have always belonged to the upper fringe of the lower classes concerned.

If this hypothesis is correct and if the lower classes have interests in common, the steady trend in this country toward improved educational facilities and toward widened social security for the masses of the people will work for increased solidarity between the lower class groups. But changes in this direction will probably be slow, both because of some general factors impeding broad democratic mass movements in America and—in our special problems, solidarity between whites and Negroes— because of the existence of caste.

In this connection we must not forget the influence of ideological forces. And we must guard against the common mistake of reducing them solely to secondary expressions of economic interests. Independent (that is, independent of the economic interests involved in the Negro problem) ideological forces of a liberal character are particularly strong in America because of the central and influential position of the American Creed in people's valuations.

It may be suggested as an hypothesis, already fairly well substantiated by research and by common observation, that those liberal ideological forces tend to create a tie between the problems of all disadvantaged groups in society, and that they work for solidarity between these groups. A study of opinions in the Negro problem will reveal, we believe, that persons who are inclined to favor measures to help the underdog generally, are also, and as a part of this attitude, usually inclined to give the

Negro a lift. There is a correlation between political opinions in different issues, which probably rests upon a basis of temperamental personality traits and has its deeper roots in all the cultural influences working upon a personality. If this correlation is represented by a composite scale running from radicalism, through liberalism and conservatism, to reactionism, it is suggested that it will be found that all subordinate groups —Negroes, women, minorities in general, poor people, prisoners, and so forth—will find their interests more favored in political opinion as we move toward the left of the scale. This hypothesis of a system of opinion correlation will, however, have to be taken with a grain of salt, since this correlation is obviously far from complete.

In general, poor people are not radical and not even liberal, though to have such political opinions would often be in their interest. Liberalism is not characteristic of Negroes either, except, of course, that they take a radical position in the Negro problem. We must guard against a superficial bias (probably of Marxian origin) which makes us believe that the lower classes are naturally prepared to take a broad point of view and a friendly attitude toward all disadvantaged groups. A liberal outlook is much more likely to emerge among people in a somewhat secure social and economic situation and with a background of education. The problem for political liberalism—if, for example, we might be allowed to pose the problem in the practical, instead of the theoretical mode—appears to be first to lift the masses to security and education and then to work to make them liberal.

The South, compared to the other regions of America, has the least economic security, the lowest educational level, and is most conservative. The South's conservatism is manifested not only with respect to the Negro problem but also with respect to all the other important problems of the last decades—woman suffrage, trade unionism, labor legislation, social security reforms, penal reforms, civil liberties—and with respect to broad philosophical matters, such as the character of religious beliefs and practices. Even at present the South does not have a full spectrum of political opinions represented within its public discussion. There are relatively few liberals in the South and practically no radicals.

The recent economic stagnation (which for the rural South has lasted much more than ten years), the flood of social reforms thrust upon the South by the federal government, and the fact that the rate of industrialization in the South is higher than in the rest of the nation, may well come to cause an upheaval in the South's entire opinion structure. The importance of this for the Negro problem may be considerable.

The Manifoldness and the Unity of the Negro Problem

The Negro problem has the manifoldness of human life. Like the women's problem, it touches every other social issue, or rather, it represents an angle of them all. A glance at the table of contents of this volume shows that in our attempt to analyze the Negro problem we have not been able to avoid anything: race, culture, population, breadwinning, economic and social policy, law, crime, class, family, recreation, school, church, press, organizations, politics, attitudes.

The perplexities and manifoldness of the Negro problem have even increased considerably during the last generation. One reason is migration and industrialization. The Negro has left his seclusion. A much smaller portion of the Negro people of today lives in the static, rather inarticulate folk society of the old plantation economy. The Negro people have increasingly stepped into the midst of America's high-geared metropolitan life, and they have by their coming added to the complication of these already tremendously complicated communities. This mass movement of Negroes from farms to cities and from the South to the North has, contrary to expectation, kept up in bad times as in good, and is likely to continue.

Another and equally important reason why the Negro problem shows an increasing involvement with all sorts of other special problems is the fact that America, especially during the last ten years, has started to use the state as an instrument for induced social change. The New Deal has actually changed the whole configuration of the Negro problem. Particularly when looked upon from the practical and political viewpoints, the contrast between the present situation and the one prior to the New Deal is striking.

Until then the practical Negro problem involved civil rights, education, charity, and little more. Now it has widened, in pace with public policy in the new "welfare state," and involves housing, nutrition, medicine, education, relief and social security, wages and hours, working conditions, child and woman labor, and, lately, the armed forces and the war industries. The Negro's share may be meager in all this new state activity, but he has been given a share. He has been given a broader and more variegated front to defend and from which to push forward. This is the great import of the New Deal to the Negro. For almost the first time in the history of the nation the state has done something substantial in a social way without excluding the Negro.

In this situation it has sometimes appeared as if there were no longer a Negro problem distinct from all the other social problems in the United States. In popular periodicals, articles on the general Negro problem gave way to much more specific subjects during the 'thirties. Even on the theoretical level it has occurred to many that it was time to stop studying the Negro problem in itself. The younger generation of Negro intellectuals have become tired of all the talk about the Negro problem on which they were brought up, and which sometimes seemed to them so barren of real deliveries. They started to criticize the older generation of Negroes for their obsession with the Negro problem. In many ways this was a movement which could be considered as the continuation, during the 'thirties, of the "New Negro Movement" of the 'twenties.

We hear it said nowadays that there is no "race problem," but only a "class problem." The Negro sharecropper is alleged to be destitute not because of his color but because of his class position—and it is pointed out that there are white people who are equally poor. From a practical angle there is a point in this reasoning. But from a theoretical angle it contains escapism in new form. It also draws too heavily on the idealistic Marxian doctrine of the "class struggle." And it tends to conceal the whole system of special deprivations visited upon the Negro only because he is not white. We find also that as soon as the Negro scholar, ideologist, or reformer leaves these general ideas about how the Negro should think, he finds himself discussing nothing but Negro rights, the Negro's share, injustices against Negroes, discrimination against Negroes, Negro interests—nothing, indeed, but the old familiar Negro problem, though in some new political relations. He is back again in the "race issue." And there is substantial reason for it.

The reason, of course, is that there is really a common tie and, therefore, a unity in all the special angles of the Negro problem. All these specific problems are only outcroppings of one fundamental complex of human valuations—that of American caste. This fundamental complex derives its emotional charge from the equally common race prejudice, from its manifestations in a general tendency toward discrimination, and from its political potentialities through its very inconsistency with the American Creed.

The Theory of the Vicious Circle

A deeper reason for the unity of the Negro problem will be apparent when we now try to formulate our hypothesis concerning its dynamic causation. The mechanism that operates here is the "principle of cumulation," also commonly called the "vicious circle."[3] This principle has a much wider application in social relations. It is, or should be developed into, a main theoretical tool in studying social change.

Throughout this inquiry, we shall assume a general interdependence between all the factors in the Negro problem. White prejudice and discrimination keep the Negro low in standards of living, health, education, manners and morals. This, in turn, gives support to white prejudice. White prejudice and Negro standards thus mutually "cause" each other. If things remain about as they are and have been, this means that the two forces happen to balance each other. Such a static "accommodation" is, however, entirely accidental. If either of the factors changes, this will cause a change in the other factor, too, and start a process of interaction where the change in one factor will continuously be supported by the reaction of the other factor. The whole system will be moving in the direction of the primary change, but much further. This is what we mean by cumulative causation.

If, for example, we assume that for some reason white prejudice could be decreased and discrimination mitigated, this is likely to cause a rise in Negro standards, which may decrease white prejudice still a little more, which would again allow Negro standards to rise, and so on through mutual interaction. If, instead, discrimination should become intensified, we should see the vicious circle spiraling downward. The original change can as easily be a change of *Negro standards* upward or downward. The effects would, in a similar manner, run back and forth in the interlocking system of interdependent causation. In any case, the initial change would be supported by consecutive waves of back-effects from the reactions of the other factor.

The same principle holds true if we split one of our two variables into component factors. A rise in Negro employment, for instance, will raise family incomes, standards of nutrition, housing, and health, the possibilities of giving the Negro youth more education, and so forth, and all these effects of the initial change, will, in their turn, improve the Negroes' possibilities of getting employment and earning a living. The original push could have been on some other factor than employment, say, for example, an improvement of health or educational facilities for Negroes. Through action and interaction the whole system of the Negro's "status" would have been set in motion in the direction indicated by the first push. Much the same thing holds true of the development of white prejudice. Even assuming no changes in Negro standards, white prejudice can change, for example, as a result of an increased general knowledge about biology, eradicating some of the false beliefs among whites concerning Negro racial inferiority. If this is accomplished, it will in some degree censor the hostile and derogatory valuations which fortify the false beliefs, and education will then be able to fight racial beliefs with more success.

By this we have only wanted to give a hint of an explanatory scheme of dynamic causation which we are going to utilize throughout this inquiry. The interrelations are in reality much more complicated than in our abstract illustrations, and there are all sorts of irregularities in the reaction of various factors. But the complications should not force us to give up our main hypothesis that a cumulative principle is working in social change. It is actually this hypothesis which gives a theoretical meaning to the Negro problem as a special phase of all other social problems in America. Behind the barrier of common discrimination, there is unity and close interrelation between the Negro's political power; his civil rights; his employment opportunities; his standards of housing, nutrition and clothing; his health, manners, and law observance; his ideals and ideologies. The unity is largely the result of cumulative causation binding them all together in a system and tying them to white discrimination. It is useful, therefore, to interpret all the separate factors from a central vantage point—the point of view of the Negro problem.

Another corollary from our hypothesis is practical. In the field of Negro politics any push upward directed on any one of those factors—if our main hypothesis is correct—moves all other factors in the same direction and has, through them, a cumulative effect upon general Negro status. An upward trend of Negro status in general can be effected by any number of measures, rather independent of where the initial push is localized. By the process of cumulation it will be transferred through the whole system.

But, as in the field of economic anti-depression policy, it matters a lot how the measures are proportioned and applied. The directing and proportioning of the measures is the task of social engineering. This engineering should be based on a knowledge of how all the factors are actually interrelated: what effect a primary change upon each factor will have on all other factors. It can be generally stated, however, that it is likely that *a rational policy will never work by changing only one factor,* least of all if attempted suddenly and with great force. In most cases that would either throw the system entirely out of gear or else prove to be a wasteful expenditure of effort which could reach much further by being spread strategically over various factors in the system and over a period of time.

This—and the impracticability of getting political support for a great and sudden change of just one factor—is the rational refutation of so-called panaceas. Panaceas are now generally repudiated in the literature on the Negro problem, though usually without much rational motivation. There still exists, however, another theoretical idea which is similar to the idea of panacea: the idea that there is *one* predominant factor, a "basic factor." Usually the so-called "economic factor" is assumed to be this basic factor. A vague conception of economic determinism has, in fact, come to color most of the modern writings on the Negro problem far outside the Marxist school. Such a view has unwarrantedly acquired the prestige of being a particularly "hard-boiled" scientific approach.

As we look upon the problem of dynamic social causation, this approach is unrealistic and narrow. We do not, of course, deny that the conditions under which Negroes are allowed to earn a living are tremendously important for their welfare. But these conditions are closely interrelated to all other conditions of Negro life. When studying the variegated causes of discrimination in the labor market, it is, indeed, difficult to perceive what precisely is meant by "the economic factor." The Negro's legal and political status and all the causes behind this, considerations by whites of social prestige, and everything else in the Negro problem belong to the causation of discrimination in the labor market, in exactly the same way as the Negro's low economic status is influential in keeping down his health, his educational level, his political power, and his status in other respects. Neither from a theoretical point of view—in seeking to explain the Negro's caste status in American society—nor from a practical point of view—in attempting to assign the strategic points which can most effectively be attacked in order to raise his status—is there any reason, or, indeed, any possibility of singling out "the economic factor" as basic. In an interdependent system of dynamic causation there is no "primary cause" but everything is cause *to* everything else.

If this theoretical approach is bound to do away in the practical sphere with all panaceas, it is, on the other hand, equally bound to encourage the reformer. The principle of cumulation—in so far as it holds true—promises final effects of greater magnitude than the efforts and costs of the reforms themselves. The low status of the Negro is tremendously wasteful all around—the low educational standard causes low earnings and health deficiencies, for example. The cumulatively magnfied effect of a push upward on any one of the relevant factors is, in one sense, a demonstration and a measure of the earlier existing waste. In the end, the cost of raising the status of the Negro may not involve any "real costs" at all for society, but instead may result in great "social gains" and actual savings for society. A movement downward will, for the same reason, increase "social waste" out of proportion to the original saving involved in the push downward of one factor or another.

These dynamic concepts of "social waste," "social gain," and "real costs" are mental tools originated in the practical man's workshop. To give them a clearer meaning—which implies expressing also the underlying social value premises—and to measure them in quantitative terms represents from a practical viewpoint a main task of social science. Fulfilling that task in a truly comprehensive way is a stage of dynamic social theory still to be reached but definitely within vision.

Notes

1. The parallel between the status of Negroes and of women, who are neither a minority group nor a low social class, is particularly instructive.

2. The great similarity in cultural situation—on a different level—between the Negro people in all America and the white South should not be overlooked. Many of the general things which can be said about the Negroes hold true, in large measure, of the white Southerners, or something quite similar can be asserted. Thus, just as the Negro sees himself economically excluded and exploited, so the Southern white man has been trained to think of his economy as a colony for Yankee exploitation. As the Negro has been compelled to develop race pride and a "protective" community, so the white South has also a strong group feeling. The white South is also something of a nation within a nation. It is certainly no accident that a "regional approach" in social science has been stressed in the South. The Southerner, like the Negro, is apt to be sensitive and to take any personal remark or observation as a rebuke, and a rebuke not only against himself but against the whole South. In analyzing himself, he finds the same general traits of extreme individualism and romanticism which are ascribed to the Negro. His educators and intellectual leaders find it necessary to complain of the same shortcomings in him as he finds in the Negro: violence, laziness, lack of thrift, lack of rational efficiency and respect for law and social order, lack of punctuality and respect for deadlines. The rickety rocking-chair on the porch has a symbolic meaning in the South not entirely different from that of the Negro's watermelon, although there is more an association of gloom and dreariness around the former stereotype, and happy-go-lucky carefreeness around the latter. The expression "C.P.T."—colored people's time—is often referred to in the South, but nearly as frequently it is jestingly suggested that it fits the folkways also of the white Southerners. The casual carrying of weapons, which is so associated in the Northerners' minds with the Negro, is commonplace among white Southerners. Both groups are on the average more religious than the rest of America, and the preacher is, or has been, more powerful in society. In both groups there is also a tendency toward fundamentalism and emotionalism, the former characteristic more important for the whites, the latter for the Negroes. The general educational level in the South has, for lack of school facilities, been lower than the national norm, and as a result an obvious double standard in favor of Southerners is actually being applied by higher educational institutions and by such organizations as foundations awarding fellowships and encouraging research projects. The Yankee prejudice against the South often takes the form of a paternalistic favoring of a weaker group. The white writers of the South, like the Negro writers, are accustomed to work mainly for a "foreign" public of readers. And they have, for the benefit of the out-group, exploited the in-group's romance and oddness. During the 'twenties both groups had a literary renaissance, commonly described in both cases as an emancipation from outside determinants and as a new earthbound realism. This list could be continued to a considerable length, but it has already been made understandable both why the Negro in a way feels so much at home in the South and why his lot there sometimes becomes so sad and even tragic.

3. We call the principle the "principle of cumulation" rather than "vicious circle" because it can work in an "upward" desirable direction as well as in a "downward" undesirable direction.

⇥ 15 ⇤

Race and Class

Oliver Cox

We may restate in simple *outline* form the nexus between capitalism and race relations, with special reference to the American scene.

Capitalist, bourgeois society is modern Western society, which, as a social system, is categorically different from any other contemporary or previously existing society.

Capitalism developed in Europe exclusively; in the East it is a cultural adoption.

In order that capitalism might exist it must proletarianize the masses of workers; that is to say, it must "commoditize" their capacity to work.

To "commoditize" the capacity of persons to work is to conceptualize, consciously or unconsciously, as inanimate or subhuman, these human vehicles of labor power and to behave toward them according to the laws of the market; that is to say, according to the fundamental rules of capitalist society. The capitalist is constrained to regard his labor power "as an abstract quantity, a purchasable, *impersonal* commodity, an item in the cost of production rather than a great mass of human beings."

Labor thus becomes a factor of production to be bought and sold in a non-sentimental market and to be exploited like capital and land, according to the economic interest of producers, for a profit. In production a cheap labor supply is an immediate and *practical* end.

To the extent to which labor can be manipulated as a commodity void of human sensibilities, to that extent also the entrepreneur is free from hindrance to his sole purpose of maximizing his profits. Therefore, capitalism cannot be primarily concerned with human welfare. Slavery, in a capitalist society, presents an ideal situation for easy manipulation of labor power; but it is against free competition, a powerful desideratum of capitalism. Labor, under slavery, is of the nature of capital. It should be observed, however, that long-continued contact between slave and master may develop personal sympathies which tend to limit good business practice in the exploitation of slave labor.

It becomes, then, the immediate pecuniary interest of the capitalists, the bourgeoisie, not only to develop an ideology and world view which facilitate proletarianization, but also, when necessary, to use force in accomplishing this end.

So far as ideology is concerned, the capitalists proceed in a normal way; that is to say, they develop and exploit ethnocentrism and show by any irrational or logical means available that the working class of their own race or whole peoples of other races, whose labor they are bent upon exploiting, are something apart: (a) not human at all, (b) only part human, (c) inferior humans, and so on. The bouregeoisie in Europe are faced both with the problem of wresting the power from the agricultural landlords and at the same time keeping the workers from snatching any part of that power. Among the peoples of color, however, the Europeans had only the problem of converting virtually the whole group to worker status.

So far as force is concerned, we might illustrate. In the unrestrained process of "commoditizing" the labor of the American Indians the early European capitalist adventurers accomplished their complete extermination in the West Indies and decimated them on the continent.

The rationalizations for their doing this were that the Indians were not human; they were heathens; they could not be converted to Christianity; therefore, they were exploited, like the beasts of burden, without compunction for infringements of natural human rights. At that time also the argument for the exploitation of the labor of white women and white children in Europe was that the long hours of labor kept them from the concern of the devil, from idleness, and that their supposed suffering was part of the price all human beings must pay for their sins either here or hereafter.

When the great resource of African black labor became available, Indians in the West were not so much relied upon. They were largely pushed back as far as possible from exploitable natural resources.

Slavery became the means by which African labor was used most profitably; hence Negroes were considered producers' capital.

As the tendency to question such overt capitalist exploitation of human beings increased, principally among some articulate persons ordinarily not immediately engaged in business, the rationalizations about the non-human character of Negroes also increased. Moreover, the priests, on the whole, pointed out that God amply sanctioned the ways of the capitalists. The greater the immediacy of the exploitative need, the more insistent were the arguments supporting the rationalizations.

At this time, the early nineteenth century, many white workers in Europe and in America were being killed, beaten, or jailed for attempting to organize themselves so that they might limit their free exploitation by the entrepreneurs. Their unions were considered conspiracies against "society," and thus against the bourgeois state.

In 1861 the Civil War was commenced partly as a reaction to certain social pressures to break the monopoly on black labor in the South and to open up the natural resources of that region for freer exploitation.

At length, however, the Southern agricultural capitalists initiated a counterrevolution and re-established a high degree of control over their labor supply. To do this they had to marshal every force, including the emotional power of the masses of poor whites, in a fanatical campaign of race hatred, with sexual passion as the emotional core.

In support of this restoration the ruling class enacted black codes in which the principal offenses were attempts to whiten the black labor force by sexual contacts and tampering with the labor supply by union organizers or labor recruiters. All sympathetic contact between the white and black masses was scrupulously ruled out by a studied system of segregation. The whole Negro race was defined as having a "place," that of the freely exploitable worker—a place which it could not possibly keep if intermarriage was permitted.

At this time, also, the last quarter of the nineteenth century, the labor movement in the North was being driven underground. Labor had to organize in secret societies—sometimes terroristic societies. Troops, sometimes Federal troops, were being called out from east to west to put down strikes, and the Knights of Labor became a proletarian movement.

Today the ruling class in the South effectively controls legislation in the national Congress favorable to the continued exploitation of the Negro masses mainly by diplomatic bargaining with the politicians of the Northern capitalist exploiters of white labor. The guardians of the racial system in the South control or spend millions of dollars to maintain segregation devices—the most powerful illusory contrivance for keeping poor whites and Negroes antagonized—and to spread anti-color propaganda all over the nation and the world. For this expenditure they expect a return more or less calculable in dollars and cents.

Today it is of vital consequence that black labor and white labor in the South be kept glaring at each other, for if they were permitted to come together in force and to identify their interests as workers, the difficulty of exploiting them would be increased beyond calculation. Indeed, the persistence of the whole system of worker exploitation in the United States depends pivotally upon the maintenance of an active race hatred between white and black workers in the South.

The rationalizations of the exploitative purpose which we know as race prejudice are always couched in terms of the ideology of the age. At first it is mainly religious, then histroico-anthropological, then Darwinian-anthropometrical, and today it is sexual, *laissez faire,* and mystical. The intent of these rationalizations, of course, must always be to elicit a collective feeling of more or less ruthless antagonism against and contempt for the exploited race or class. They could never have the meaning that, since the race or class is supposed to be inferior, superior persons ought to be humane toward it—ought to help it along the rugged road whereby full superior stature might be achieved. On the contrary, they must always have the intent and meaning that, since the race is inferior, superior people have a natural right to suppress and to exploit it. The more "inferior" the race is, the more securely the yoke should be clamped around its neck and the saddle fixed upon its back. The rationalizations are thus a defense; race prejudice is a defensive attitude. The obtrusiveness of certain social ideals developed under capitalism as concessions to the masses makes the rationalizations of racial exploitation necessary.

⇸ 16 ⇷

Toward a New Vision:
Race, Class, and Gender
as Categories of
Analysis and Connection

Patricia Hill Collins

> The true focus of revolutionary change is never merely the oppressive
> situations which we seek to escape, but that piece of the oppressor
> which is planted deep within each of us.
>
> —*Audre Lorde,* Sister Outsider, *123*

A udre Lorde's statement raises a troublesome issue for scholars and activists working for social change. While many of us have little difficulty assessing our own victimization within some major system of oppression, whether it be by race, social class, religion, sexual orientation, ethnicity, age or gender, we typically fail to see how our thoughts and actions uphold someone else's subordination. Thus, white feminists routinely point with confidence to their oppression as women but resist seeing how much their white skin privileges them. African-Americans who possess eloquent analyses of racism often persist in viewing poor White women as symbols of white power. The radical left fares little better. "If only people of color and women could see their true class interests," they argue, "class solidarity would eliminate racism and sexism." In essence, each group identifies the type of oppression with

Reprinted from Patricia Hill Collins, "Toward a New Vision: Race, Class, and Gender as Categories of Analysis and Connection," *Race, Sex, and Class,* Vol. 1, No. 1 (Fall 1993): 25–45, by permission of Patricia Hill Collins and the Center for Research on Women at the University of Memphis.

which it feels most comfortable as being fundamental and classifies all other types as being of lesser importance.

Oppression is full of such contradictions. Errors in political judgment that we make concerning how we teach our courses, what we tell our children, and which organizations are worthy of our time, talents and financial support flow smoothly from errors in theoretical analysis about the nature of oppression and activism. Once we realize that there are few pure victims or oppressors, and that each one of us derives varying amounts of penalty and privilege from the multiple systems of oppression that frame our lives, then we will be in a position to see the need for new ways of thought and action.

To get at that "piece of the oppressor which is planted deep within each of us," we need at least two things. First, we need new visions of what oppression is, new categories of analysis that are inclusive of race, class, and gender as distinctive yet interlocking structures of oppression. Adhering to a stance of comparing and ranking oppressions—the proverbial, "I'm more oppressed than you"—locks us all into a dangerous dance of competing for attention, resources, and theoretical supremacy. Instead, I suggest that we examine our different experiences within the more fundamental relationship of domination and subordination. To focus on the particular arrangements that race or class or gender take in our time and place without seeing these structures as sometimes parallel and sometimes interlocking dimensions of the more fundamental relationship of domination and subordination may temporarily ease our consciences. But while such thinking may lead to short term social reforms, it is simply inadequate for the task of bringing about long term social transformation.

While race, class and gender as categories of analysis are essential in helping us understand the structural bases of domination and subordination, new ways of thinking that are not accompanied by new ways of acting offer incomplete prospects for change. To get at that "piece of the oppressor which is planted deep within each of us," we also need to change our daily behavior. Currently, we are all enmeshed in a complex web of problematic relationships that grant our mirror images full human subjectivity while stereotyping and objectifying those most different than ourselves. We often assume that the people we work with, teach, send our children to school with, and sit next to . . . will act and feel in prescribed ways because they belong to given race, social class or gender categories. These judgments by category must be replaced with fully human relationships that transcend the legitimate differences created by race, class and gender as categories of analysis. We require new categories of connection, new visions of what our relationships with one another can be. . . .

[This discussion] addresses this need for new patterns of thought and action. I focus on two basic questions. First, how can we reconceptualize race, class and gender as categories of analysis? Second, how can we transcend the barriers created by our experiences with race, class and gender oppression in order to build the types of coalitions essential for social exchange? To address these questions I contend that we must acquire both new theories of how race, class and gender have shaped the experiences not just of women of color, but of all groups. Moreover, we must see the connections between these categories of analysis and the personal issues in our everyday lives, particularly our scholarship, our teaching and our relationships with our colleagues and students. As Audre Lorde points out, change starts with self, and relationships that we have with those around us must always be the primary site for social change.

How Can We Reconceptualize Race, Class and Gender as Categories of *Analysis?*

To me, we must shift our discourse away from additive analyses of oppression (Spelman 1982; Collins 1989). Such approaches are typically based on two key premises. First, they depend on either/or, dichotomous thinking. Persons, things and ideas are conceptualized in terms of their opposites. For example, Black/White, man/woman, thought/feeling, and fact/opinion are defined in oppositional terms. Thought and feeling are not seen as two different and interconnected ways of approaching truth that can coexist in scholarship and teaching. Instead, feeling is defined as antithetical to reason, as its opposite. In spite of the fact that we all have "both/and" identities, (I am both a college professor and a mother—I don't stop being a mother when I drop my child off at school, or forget everything I learned while scrubbing the toilet), we persist in trying to classify each other in either/or categories. I live each day as an African-American woman—a race/gender specific experience. And I am not alone. Everyone has a race/gender/class specific identity. Either/or, dichotomous thinking is especially troublesome when applied to theories of oppression because every individual must be classified as being either oppressed or not oppressed. The both/and position of simultaneously being oppressed and oppressor becomes conceptually impossible.

A second premise of additive analyses of oppression is that these dichotomous differences must be ranked. One side of the dichotomy is typically labeled dominant and the other subordinate. Thus, Whites rule Blacks, men are deemed superior to women, and reason is seen as being preferable to emotion. Applying this premise to discussions of oppression leads to the assumption that oppression can be quantified, and that some groups are oppressed more than others. I am frequently asked, "Which has been most oppressive to you, your status as a Black person or your status as a woman?" What I am really being asked to do is divide myself into little boxes and rank my various statuses. If I experience oppression as a both/and phenomenon, why should I analyze it any differently?

Additive analyses of oppression rest squarely on the twin pillars of either/or thinking and the necessity to quantify and rank all relationships in order to know where one stands. Such approaches typically see African-American women as being more oppressed than everyone else because the majority of Black women experience the negative effects of race, class and gender oppression simultaneously. In essence, if you add together separate oppressions, you are left with a grand oppression greater than the sum of its parts.

I am not denying that specific groups experience oppression more harshly than others—lynching is certainly objectively worse than being held up as a sex object. But we must be careful not to confuse this issue of the saliency of one type of oppression in people's lives with a theoretical stance positing the interlocking nature of oppression. Race, class and gender may all structure a situation but may not be equally visible and/or important in people's self-definitions. In certain contexts, such as the antebellum American South and contemporary South America, racial oppression is more visibly salient, while in other contexts, such as Haiti, El Salvador and Nicaragua, social class oppression may be more apparent. For middle class White women, gender may assume experiential primacy unavailable to poor Hispanic women struggling with the ongoing issues of low paid jobs and the frustrations of the welfare bureaucracy. This recognition that one category may have salience over another for a given time and place does not minimize the theoretical importance of assuming that race, class and gender as categories of analysis structure all relationships.

In order to move toward new visions of what oppression is, I think that we need to ask new questions. How are relationships of domination and subordination structured and maintained in the American political economy? How do race, class and gender function as parallel and interlocking systems that shape this basic relationship of domination and subordination? Questions such as these promise to move us away from futile theoretical struggles concerned with ranking oppressions and towards analyses that assume race, class and gender are all present in any given setting, even if one appears more visible and salient than the others. Our task becomes redefined as one of reconceptualizing oppression by uncovering the connections among race, class and gender as categories of analysis.

1. The Institutional Dimension of Oppression

Sandra Harding's contention that gender oppression is structured along three main dimensions—the institutional, the symbolic, and the individual—offers a useful model for a more comprehensive analysis encompassing race, class and gender oppression (Harding 1989). Systemic relationships of domination and subordination structured through social institutions such as schools, businesses, hospitals, the work place, and government agencies represent the institutional dimension of oppression. Racism, sexism and elitism all have concrete institutional locations. Even though the workings of the institutional dimension of oppression are often obscured with ideologies claiming equality of opportunity, in actuality, race, class and gender place Asian-American women, Native American men, White men, African-American women, and other groups in distinct institutional niches with varying degrees of penalty and privilege.

Even though I realize that many . . . would not share this assumption, let us assume that the institutions of American society discriminate, whether by design or by accident. While many of us are familiar with how race, gender and class operate separately to structure inequality, I want to focus on how these three systems interlock in structuring the institutional dimension of oppression. To get at the interlocking nature of race, class and gender, I want you to think about the antebellum plantation as a guiding metaphor for a variety of American social institutions. Even though slavery is typically analyzed as a racist institution, and occasionally as a class institution, I suggest that slavery was a race, class, gender specific institution. Removing any one piece from our analysis diminishes our understanding of the true nature of relations of domination and subordination under slavery.

Slavery was a profoundly patriarchal institution. It rested on the dual tenets of White male authority and White male property, a joining of the political and the economic within the institution of the family. Heterosexism was assumed and all Whites were expected to marry. Control over affluent White women's sexuality remained key to slavery's survival because property was to be passed on to the legitimate heirs of the slave owner. Ensuring affluent White women's virginity and chastity was deeply intertwined with maintenance of property relations.

Under slavery, we see varying levels of institutional protection given to affluent White women, working class and poor White women, and enslaved African women. Poor White women enjoyed few of the protections held out to their upper class sisters. Moreover, the devalued status of Black women was key in keeping all White women in their assigned places. Controlling Black women's fertility was also key to the continuation of slavery, for children born to slave mothers themselves were slaves.

African-American women shared the devalued status of chattel with their husbands, fathers and sons. Racism stripped Blacks as a group of legal rights, education, and control over their own persons. African-Americans could be whipped, branded, sold, or killed, not because they were poor, or because they were women, but because they were Black. Racism ensured that Blacks would continue to serve Whites and suffer economic exploitation at the hands of all Whites.

So we have a very interesting chain of command on the plantation—the affluent White master as the reigning patriarch, his White wife help-mate to serve him, help him manage his property and bring up his heirs, his faithful servants whose production and reproduction were tied to the requirements of the capitalist political economy, and largely propertyless, working class White men and women watching from afar. In essence, the foundations for the contemporary roles of elite White women, poor Black women, working class White men, and a series of other groups can be seen in stark relief in this fundamental American social institution. While Blacks experienced the most harsh treatment under slavery, and thus made slavery clearly visible as a racist institution, race, class and gender interlocked in structuring slavery's systemic organization of domination and subordination.

Even today, the plantation remains a compelling metaphor for institutional oppression. Certainly the actual conditions of oppression are not as severe now as they were then. To argue, as some do, that things have not changed all that much denigrates the achievements of those who struggled for social change before us. But the basic relationships among Black men, Black women, elite White women, elite White men, working class White men and working class White women as groups remain essentially intact.

A brief analysis of key American social institutions most controlled by elite White men should convince us of the interlocking nature of race, class and gender in structuring the institutional dimension of oppression. For example, if you are from an American college or university, is your campus a modern plantation? Who controls your university's political economy? Are elite White men over represented among the upper administrators and trustees controlling your university's finances and policies? Are elite White men being joined by growing numbers of elite White women helpmates? What kinds of people are in your classrooms grooming the next generation who will occupy these and other decision-making positions? Who are the support staff that produce the mass mailings, order the supplies, fix the leaky pipes? Do African-Americans, Hispanics or other people of color form the majority of the invisible workers who feed you, wash your dishes, and clean up your offices and libraries after everyone else has gone home?

If your college is anything like mine, you know the answers to these questions. You may be affiliated with an institution that has Hispanic women as vice-presidents for finance, or substantial numbers of Black men among the faculty. If so, you are fortunate. Much more typical are colleges where a modified version of the plantation as a metaphor for the institutional dimension of oppression survives.

2. The Symbolic Dimension of Oppression

Widespread, societally-sanctioned ideologies used to justify relations of domination and subordination comprise the symbolic dimension of oppression. Central to this process is the use of stereotypical or controlling images of diverse race, class and gender groups. In order to assess the power of this dimension of oppression, I want you to make a list, either on paper or in your head, of "masculine" and "feminine" characteristics. If your list is anything like that compiled by most people, it reflects some variation of the following:

Masculine	Feminine
aggressive	passive
leader	follower
rational	emotional
strong	weak
intellectual	physical

Not only does this list reflect either/or dichotomous thinking and the need to rank both sides of the dichotomy, but ask yourself exactly which men and women you had in mind when compiling these characteristics. This list applies almost exclusively to middle class White men and women. The allegedly "masculine" qualities that you probably listed are only acceptable when exhibited by elite White men, or when used by Black and Hispanic men against each other or against women of color. Aggressive Black and Hispanic men are seen as dangerous, not powerful, and are often penalized when they exhibit any of the allegedly "masculine" characteristics. Working class and poor White men fare slightly better and are also denied the allegedly "masculine" symbols of leadership, intellectual competence, and human rationality. Women of color and working class and poor White women are also not represented on this list, for they have never had the luxury of being "ladies." What appear to be universal categories representing all men and women instead are unmasked as being applicable to only a small group.

It is important to see how the symbolic images applied to different race, class and gender groups interact in maintaining systems of domination and subordination. If I were to ask you to repeat the same assignment, only this time, by making separate lists for Black men, Black women, Hispanic women and Hispanic men, I suspect that your gender symbolism would be quite different. In comparing all of the lists, you might begin to see the interdependence of symbols applied to all groups. For example, the elevated images of White womanhood need devalued images of Black womanhood in order to maintain credibility.

While the above exercise reveals the interlocking nature of race, class and gender in structuring the symbolic dimension of oppression, part of its importance lies in demonstrating how race, class and gender pervade a wide range of what appears to be universal language. Attending to diversity in our scholarship, in our teaching, and in our daily lives provides a new angle of vision on interpretations of reality thought to be natural, normal and "true." Moreover, viewing images of masculinity and femininity as universal gender symbolism, rather than as symbolic images that are race, class and gender specific, renders the experiences of people of color and of non-privileged White women and men invisible. One way to dehumanize an individual or a group is to deny the reality of their experiences. So when we refuse to deal with race or class because they do not appear to be directly relevant to gender, we are actually becoming part of some one else's problem.

Assuming that everyone is affected differently by the same interlocking set of symbolic images allows us to move forward toward new analyses. Women of color and White women have different relationships to White male authority and this difference explains the distinct gender symbolism applied to both groups. Black women encounter controlling images such as the mammy, the matriarch, the mule and the whore, that encourage others to reject us as fully human people. Ironically, the negative nature of these images simultaneously encourages us to reject them. In contrast, White women are offered seductive images, those that promise to reward them for supporting the status quo. And yet seductive images can be equally controlling. Consider, for example, the views of Nancy White, a 73-year old Black woman, concerning images of rejection and seduction:

> My mother used to say that the black woman is the white man's mule and the white woman is his dog. Now, she said that to say this: we do the heavy work and get beat whether we do it well or not. But the white woman is closer to the master and he pats them on the head and lets them sleep in the house, but he ain't gon' treat neither one like he was dealing with a person. (Gwaltney, 148)

Both sets of images stimulate particular political stances. By broadening the analysis beyond the confines of race, we can see the varying levels of rejection and seduction available to each of us due to our race, class and gender identity. Each of us lives with an allotted portion of institutional privilege and penalty, and with varying levels of rejection and seduction inherent in the symbolic images applied to us. This is the context in which we make our choices. Taken together, the institutional and symbolic dimensions of oppression create a structural backdrop against which all of us live our lives.

3. The Individual Dimension of Oppression

Whether we benefit or not, we all live within institutions that reproduce race, class and gender oppression. Even if we never have any contact with members of other race, class and gender groups, we all encounter images of these groups and are exposed to the symbolic meanings attached to those images. On this dimension of oppression, our individual biographies vary tremendously. As a result of our institutional and symbolic statuses, all of our choices become political acts.

Each of us must come to terms with the multiple ways in which race, class and gender as categories of analysis frame our individual biographies. I have lived my entire life as an African-American woman from a working class family and this basic fact has had a profound impact on my personal biography. Imagine how different your life might be if you had been born Black, or White, or poor, or of a different race/class/gender group than the one with which you are most familiar. The institutional treatment you would have received and the symbolic meanings attached to your very existence might differ dramatically from what you now consider to be natural, normal and part of everyday life. You might be the same, but your personal biography might have been quite different.

I believe that each of us carries around the cumulative effect of our lives within multiple structures of oppression. If you want to see how much you have been affected by this whole thing, I ask you one simple question—who are your close friends? Who are the people with whom you can share your hopes, dreams, vulnerabilities, fears and victories? Do they look like you? If they are all the same, circumstance may be the cause. For the first seven years of my life I saw only low income Black people. My friends from those years reflected the composition of my community. But now that I am an adult, can the defense of circumstance explain the patterns of people that I trust as my friends and colleagues? When given other alternatives, if my friends and colleagues reflect the homogeneity of one race, class and gender group, then these categories of analysis have indeed become barriers to connection.

I am not suggesting that people are doomed to follow the paths laid out for them by race, class and gender as categories of analysis. While these three structures certainly frame my opportunity structure, I as an individual always have the choice of accepting things as they are, or trying to change them. As Nikki Giovanni points out, "we've got to live in the real world. If we don't like the world we're living in, change it. And if we can't change it, we change ourselves. We can do something" (Tate 1983, 68). While a piece of the oppressor may be planted deep within each of us, we each have the choice of accepting that piece or challenging it as part of the "true focus of revolutionary change."

How Can We Transcend the Barriers Created by Our Experiences with Race, Class and Gender Oppression in Order to Build the Types of Coalitions Essential for Social Change?

Reconceptualizing oppression and seeing the barriers created by race, class and gender as interlocking categories of analysis is a vital first step. But we must transcend these barriers by moving toward race, class and gender as categories of connection, by building relationships and coalitions that will bring about social change. What are some of the issues involved in doing this?

1. Differences in Power and Privilege

First, we must recognize that our differing experiences with oppression create problems in the relationships among us. Each of us lives within a system that vests us with varying levels of power and privilege. These differences in power, whether structured along axes of race, class, gender, age or sexual orientation, frame our relationships. African-American writer June Jordan describes her discomfort on a Caribbean vacation with Olive, the Black woman who cleaned her room:

> . . . even though both "Olive" and "I" live inside a conflict neither one of us created, and even though both of us therefore hurt inside that conflict, I may be one of the monsters she needs to eliminate from her universe and, in a sense, she may be one of the monsters in mine (1985, 47).

Differences in power constrain our ability to connect with one another even when we think we are engaged in dialogue across differences. Let me give you an example. One year, the students in my course "Sociology of the Black Community" got into a heated discussion about the reasons for the upsurge of racial incidents on college campuses. Black students complained vehemently about the apathy and resistance they felt most

White students expressed about examining their own racism. Mark, a White male student, found their comments particularly unsettling. After claiming that all the Black people he had ever known had expressed no such beliefs to him, he questioned how representative the view points of his fellow students actually were. When pushed further, Mark revealed that he had participated in conversations over the years with the Black domestic worker employed by his family. Since she had never expressed such strong feelings about White racism, Mark was genuinely shocked by class discussions. Ask yourselves whether that domestic worker was in a position to speak freely. Would it have been wise for her to do so in a situation where the power between the two parties was so unequal?

In extreme cases, members of privileged groups can erase the very presence of the less privileged. When I first moved to Cincinnati, my family and I went on a picnic at a local park. Picnicking next to us was a family of White Appalachians. When I went to push my daughter on the swings, several of the children came over. They had missing, yellowed and broken teeth, they wore old clothing and their poverty was evident. I was shocked. Growing up in a large eastern city, I had never seen such awful poverty among Whites. The segregated neighborhoods in which I grew up made White poverty all but invisible. More importantly, the privileges attached to my newly acquired social class position allowed me to ignore and minimize the poverty among Whites that I did encounter. My reactions to those children made me realize how confining phrases such as "well, at least they're not Black," had become for me. In learning to grant human subjectivity to the Black victims of poverty, I had simultaneously learned to demand White victims of poverty. By applying categories of race to the objective conditions confronting me, I was quantifying and ranking oppressions and missing the very real suffering which, in fact, is the real issue.

One common pattern of relationships across differences in power is one that I label "voyeurism." From the perspective of the privileged, the lives of people of color, of the poor, and of women are interesting for their entertainment value. The privileged become voyeurs, passive onlookers who do not relate to the less powerful, but who are interested in seeing how the "different" live. Over the years, I have heard numerous African-American students complain about professors who never call on them except when a so-called Black issue is being discussed. The students' interest in discussing race or qualifications for doing so appear unimportant to the professor's efforts to use Black students' experiences as stories to make the material come alive for the White student audience. Asking Black students to perform on cue and provide a Black experience for their White classmates can be seen as voyeurism at its worst.

Members of subordinate groups do not willingly participate in such exchanges but often do so because members of dominant groups control the institutional and symbolic apparatuses of oppression. Racial/ethnic groups, women, and the poor have never had the luxury of being voyeurs of the lives of the privileged. Our ability to survive in hostile settings has hinged on our ability to learn intricate details about the behavior and world view of the powerful and adjust our behavior accordingly. I need only point to the difference in perception of those men and women in abusive relationships. Where men can view their girlfriends and wives as sex objects, helpmates and a collection of stereotypes categories of voyeurism—women must be attuned to every nuance of their partners' behavior. Are women "naturally" better in relating to people with more power than themselves, or have circumstances mandated that men and women develop different skills? . . .

Coming from a tradition where most relationships across difference are squarely rooted in relations of domination and subordination, we have much less experience relating to people as different but equal. The classroom is potentially one powerful and safe space where dialogues among individuals of unequal power relationships can occur. The relationship between Mark, the student in my class, and the domestic worker is typical of a whole series of relationships that people have when they relate across differences in power and privilege. The relationship among Mark and his classmates represents the power of the classroom to minimize those differences so that people of different levels of power can use race, class and gender as categories of analysis in order to generate meaningful dialogues. In this case, the classroom equalized racial difference so that Black students who normally felt silenced spoke out. White students like Mark, generally unaware of how they had been privileged by their whiteness, lost that privilege in the classroom and thus became open to genuine dialogue. . . .

2. Coalitions around Common Causes

A second issue in building relationships and coalitions essential for social change concerns knowing the real reasons for coalition. Just what brings people together? One powerful catalyst fostering group solidarity is the presence of a common enemy. African-American, Hispanic, Asian-American, and women's studies all share the common intellectual heritage of challenging what passes for certified knowledge in the academy. But politically expedient relationships and coalitions like these are fragile because, as June Jordan points out:

> It occurs to me that much organizational grief could be avoided if people understood that partnership in misery does not necessarily provide for part-

nership for change: When we get the monsters off our backs all of us may want to run in very different directions (1985, 47).

Sharing a common cause assists individuals and groups in maintaining relationships that transcend their differences. Building effective coalitions involves struggling to hear one another and developing empathy for each other's points of view. The coalitions that I have been involved in that lasted and that worked have been those where commitment to a specific issue mandated collaboration as the best strategy for addressing the issue at hand.

Several years ago, masters degree in hand, I chose to teach in an inner city, parochial school in danger of closing. The money was awful, the conditions were poor, but the need was great. In my job, I had to work with a range of individuals who, on the surface, had very little in common. We had White nuns, Black middle class graduate students, Blacks from the "community," some of whom had been incarcerated and/or were affiliated with a range of federal anti-poverty programs. Parents formed another part of this community, Harvard faculty another, and a few well-meaning White liberals from Colorado were sprinkled in for good measure.

As you might imagine, tension was high. Initially, our differences seemed insurmountable. But as time passed, we found a common bond that we each brought to the school. In spite of profound differences in our personal biographies, differences that in other settings would have hampered our ability to relate to one another, we found that we were all deeply committed to the education of Black children. By learning to value each other's commitment and by recognizing that we each had different skills that were essential to actualizing that commitment, we built an effective coalition around a common cause. Our school was successful, and the children we taught benefitted from the diversity we offered them.

. . . None of us alone has a comprehensive vision of how race, class and gender operate as categories of analysis or how they might be used as categories of connection. Our personal biographies offer us partial views. Few of us can manage to study race, class and gender simultaneously. Instead, we each know more about some dimensions of this larger story and less about others. . . . Just as the members of the school had special skills to offer to the task of building the school, we have areas of specialization and expertise, whether scholarly, theoretical, pedagogical or within areas of race, class or gender. We do not all have to do the same thing in the same way. Instead, we must support each other's efforts, realizing that they are all part of the larger enterprise of bringing about social change.

3. Building Empathy

A third issue involved in building the types of relationships and coalitions essential for social change concerns the issue of individual accountability. Race, class and gender oppression form the structural backdrop against which we frame our relationship—these are the forces that encourage us to substitute voyeurism . . . for fully human relationships. But while we may not have created this situation, we are each responsible for making individual, personal choices concerning which elements of race, class and gender oppression we will accept and which we will work to change.

One essential component of this accountability involves developing empathy for the experiences of individuals and groups different than ourselves. Empathy begins with taking an interest in the facts of other people's lives, both as individuals and as groups. If you care about me, you should want to know not only the details of my personal biography but a sense of how race, class and gender as categories of analysis created the institutional and symbolic backdrop for my personal biography. How can you hope to assess my character without knowing the details of the circumstances I face?

Moreover, by taking a theoretical stance that we have all been affected by race, class and gender as categories of analysis that have structured our treatment, we open up possibilities for using those same constructs as categories of connection in building empathy. For example, I have a good White woman friend with whom I share common interests and beliefs. But we know that our racial differences have provided us with different experiences. So we talk about them. We do not assume that because I am Black, race has only affected me and not her or that because I am a Black woman, race neutralizes the effect of gender in my life while accenting it in hers. We take those same categories of analysis that have created cleavages in our lives, in this case, categories of race and gender, and use them as categories of connection in building empathy for each other's experiences.

Finding common causes and building empathy is difficult, no matter which side of privilege we inhabit. Building empathy from the dominant side of privilege is difficult, simply because individuals from privileged backgrounds are not encouraged to do so. For example, in order for those of you who are White to develop empathy for the experiences of people of color, you must grapple with how your white skin has privileged you. This is difficult to do, because it not only entails the intellectual process of seeing how whiteness is elevated in institutions and symbols, but it also involves the often painful process of seeing how your whiteness has shaped your personal biography. Intellectual stances against the institutional and symbolic dimensions of racism are generally easier to maintain than sustained self-reflection about how racism has shaped all of our individual biographies. Were and are your fathers, uncles, and grandfathers really more capable than mine, or can their accomplishments be explained in part by the racism members of my family experienced? Did your mothers stand silently by and watch all this happen? More importantly, how have they passed on the benefits of their whiteness to you?

These are difficult questions, and I have tremendous respect for my colleagues and students who are trying to answer them. Since there is no compelling reason to examine the source and meaning of one's own privilege, I know that those who do so have freely chosen this stance. They are making conscious efforts to root out the piece of the oppressor planted within them. To me, they are entitled to the support of people of color in their efforts. Men who declare themselves feminists, members of the middle class who ally themselves with anti-poverty struggles, heterosexuals who support gays and lesbians, are all trying to grow, and their efforts place them far ahead of the majority who never think of engaging in such important struggles.

Building empathy from the subordinate side of privilege is also difficult, but for different reasons. Members of subordinate groups are understandably reluctant to abandon a basic mistrust of members of powerful groups because this basic mistrust has traditionally been central to their survival. As a Black woman, it would be foolish for me to assume that White women, or Black men, or White men or any other group with a history of exploiting African-American women have my best interests at heart. These groups enjoy varying amounts of privilege over me and therefore I must carefully watch them and be prepared for a relation of domination and subordination.

Like the privileged, members of subordinate groups must also work toward replacing judgments by category with new ways of thinking and acting. Refusing to do so stifles prospects for effective coalition and social change. Let me use another example from my own experiences. When I was an undergraduate, I had little time or patience for the theorizing of the privileged. My initial years at a private, elite institution were difficult, not because the coursework was challenging (it was, but that wasn't what distracted me), or because I had to work while my classmates lived on family allowances (I was used to work). The adjustment was difficult because I was surrounded by so many people who took their privilege for granted. Most of them felt entitled to their wealth. That astounded me.

I remember one incident of watching a White woman down the hall in my dormitory try to pick out which sweater to wear. The sweaters were piled up on her bed in all the colors of the rainbow, sweater after sweater. She asked my advice in a way that let me know that choosing a sweater was one of the most important decisions she had to make on a daily basis. Standing knee-deep in her sweaters, I realized how different our lives were. She did not have to worry about maintaining a solid academic average so that she could receive financial aid. Because she was in the majority, she was not treated as a representative of her race. She did not have to consider how her classroom comments or basic existence on campus contributed to the treatment her group would receive. Her allowance protected her from having to work, so she was free to spend her time studying, partying, or in her case, worrying about which sweater to wear. The degree of inequality in our lives and her unquestioned sense of entitlement concerning that inequality offended me. For a while, I categorized all affluent White women as being superficial, arrogant, overly concerned with material possessions, and part of my problem. But had I continued to classify people in this way, I would have missed out on making some very good friends whose discomfort with their inherited or acquired social class privileges pushed them to examine their position.

Since I opened with the words of Audre Lorde, it seems appropriate to close with another of her ideas. . . .

> Each of us is called upon to take a stand. So in these days ahead, as we examine ourselves and each other, our works, our fears, our differences, our sisterhood and survivals, I urge you to tackle what is most difficult for us all, self-scrutiny of our complacencies, the idea that since each of us believes she is on the side of right, she need not examine her position (1985).

I urge you to examine your position.

References

Butler, Johnnella. 1989. "Difficult Dialogues." *The Women's Review of Books* 6, no. 5.

Collins, Patricia Hill. 1989. "The Social Construction of Black Feminist Thought." *Signs.* Summer 1989.

Harding, Sandra. 1986. *The Science Question in Feminism.* Ithaca, New York: Cornell University Press.

Gwaltney, John Langston. 1980. *Drylongso: A Self-Portrait of Black America.* New York: Vintage.

Lorde, Audre. 1984. *Sister Outsider.* Trumansberg, New York: The Crossing Press.

————. 1985 "Sisterhood and Survival." Keynote address, conference on the Black Woman Writer and the Diaspora, Michigan State University.

Jordan, June. 1985. *On Call: Political Essays.* Boston: South End Press.

Spelman, Elizabeth. 1982. "Theories of Race and Gender: The Erasure of Black Women." *Quest* 5: 26–32.

Tate, Claudia, ed. 1983. *Black Women Writers at Work.* New York: Continuum.

Part IV: Related Readings

Acker, Joan. 1973. "Women and Social Stratification: A Case of Intellectual Sexism," *American Journal of Sociology* 78:936–45.

Barrett, Michele. 1980. *Women's Oppression Today*. London: Verso.

Chodorow, Nancy. 1978. *The Reproduction of Mothering*. Berkeley: University of California Press.

Collins, Patricia Hill. 1990. *Black Feminist Thought: Knowledge, Consciousness, and the Politics of Empowerment*. Boston: Unwin Hyman.

Firestone, Shulamith. 1971. *The Dialectic of Sex*. New York: Bantam.

Higginbotham, Elizabeth, and Mary Romero, eds. 1997. *Women and Work: Exploring Race, Ethnicity, and Class*. Thousand Oaks, Calif.: Sage Publications.

Lorber, Judith. 1998. *Gender Inequality: Feminist Theories and Politics*. Los Angeles: Roxbury Publishing.

McKee, James B. 1993. *Sociology and the Race Problem: The Failure of a Perspective*. Chicago: University of Illinois Press.

Oliver, Melvin L., and Thomas M. Shapiro. 1995. *Black Wealth/White Wealth: New Perspectives on Racial Inequality*. New York: Routledge.

Omi, Michael, and Howard Winant. 1986. *Racial Formation in the United States: From the 1960s to the 1980s*. New York: Routledge and Kegan Paul.

Romero, Mary, Pierrette Hondagneu-Sotelo, and Vilma Ortiz, eds. 1997. *Challenging Fronteras: Structuring Latina and Latino Lives in the U.S.* New York: Routledge.

Wilson, William Julius. 1978. *The Declining Significance of Race: Blacks and Changing American Institutions*. Chicago: University of Chicago Press.

———. 1987. *The Truly Disadvantaged: The Inner City, the Underclass, and Public Policy*. Chicago: University of Chicago Press.

———. 1997. *When Work Disappears*. New York: Knopf.

Conclusion

No one would disagree that valued resources are unequally distributed in contemporary society. The most significant indicator of inequality is wealth and income. How we conceptualize who has access to wealth and income and other valued resources involves developing categories of analysis. Although Karl Marx and Max Weber clearly have had a great influence on stratification theory, and most social scientists would agree that class and status are central categories for understanding stratification, it is now necessary to ask if the classic statements on social inequality can help us to understand other forms of inequality, especially those based on gender and race. Can the new concern with understanding the intersection of race, class, and gender be illuminated by older ways of explaining inequality, which tended to treat class separately from race and gender? Simply put, are the classics still relevant to the study of inequality? The answer is an unequivocal yes.

Level of Analysis

The Abstract versus the Concrete

One of the main concerns of Marx and Weber was to understand the root of inequality in industrial capitalist society. Both Marx and Weber approached the issue on a rather abstract level. For Marx, an analysis of class was conceptualized theoretically at the level of the mode of production, meaning that class was conceptualized in relation to property relations and relations of exploitation. For Weber, class and status were conceptualized on the level of society, extending Marx's view to include the political and sociocultural levels of separate but interacting spheres with the economic foundation of society (Marx's "mode of production").

Whereas Marx and Weber approached social inequality within capitalism at a high level of abstraction and analyzed the contours of inequality at the level of the social system, most analyses of gender and racial inequality—and especially new work that calls for an analysis of the intersection of race, class, and gender—have been pitched at a different level of abstraction and analyze various aspects of inequality at the more empirical level of the social structure. For both Marx and Weber, capitalism is based on a fundamental inequality between social classes. On the most abstract level, nothing about capitalism requires gender or racial inequality. This does not mean, however, that the specific form of gender inequality and racial inequality occurring at a given historical moment can be understood separate from an understanding of capitalism itself. In other words, the conceptualizations of both Marx and Weber are compatible with the view that the specific historical development of capitalism has embedded within it certain structures and institutions that help explain various forms of racial and gender inequality. The fact that neither Marx nor Weber addressed the specific issues of gender and race in the same manner as issues of class has more to do with the politics of the time and what "issues" were defined as centrally important.[1] Race and gender issues were seen as secondary to broader class issues.

Few class analysts today, as Erik Olin Wright so clearly points out, would argue that one form of stratification is more "important" than another. Such a determination depends on the issue at hand. The task, as Wright argues, is to sort out the interaction of class stratification with gender stratification, and we can add race stratification to the list (Wright 1997, 242). Following this line of reasoning, the classic perspectives remain relevant for studying social inequality because class, gender, and race are analytically distinct categories. Although they can be theorized separately on a certain level of abstraction, the intersection of class, gender, and race can only be studied on the concrete, historical level. The experience of the combined weight of class, gender, and racial inequality varies by the constantly changing nature of race relations and gender relations. There is no theoretical linkage, no inherent relationship, for example, between class at the most abstract level and gender and/or race at the most abstract level. All three forms of inequality can be conceptualized quite abstractly on their own terms. But the intersection between, for example, the effects of class on gender and vice versa, or race on class, or race on gender, or any combination of the three, can be discerned only on the basis of the specific historical setting that takes into account how various institutional arrangements and the like came into being and are further developed and maintained.

Nonclass Forms of Inequality

Gender Stratification

An ascribed status is something we are born with, a biological fact, so to speak. Gender, although an ascribed status, is socially defined. That is, "maleness" and "femaleness" are socially constructed even though we are biologically either male or female. Gender stratification is neither natural nor biological. Differential opportunities, rewards, and privileges are based on social definitions that involve a power dimension. The behavior and ideology of sexism serve to create and reinforce the system of gender inequality. "Institutionalized" forms of sexism are most relevant for understanding gender stratification, which means that the normal functioning of institutions (social, economic, political) results in the systematic subordination of a particular gender. This subordination is usually justified on the basis of biological differences. These beliefs and practices become part of the normal functioning of society. Gender inequality involves not only an understanding of power differences between men and women, but how these power relations result in gender stratification within the larger institutions of society. As such, although gender relations can be theorized on an abstract level, most analyses of gender inequality are approached on the level of actually existing societies.

Feminist scholars emerging from the women's movement of the 1970s challenged existing paradigms of class analysis and stratification for not paying due attention to gender inequality and the subordination of women to men in both the public and personal spheres. Feminists working within the Marxist tradition sought to explain the subordination of women in the context of the contradictions of capitalism.[2] Marxist feminists focused on three basic issues. The first is the relationship between women's work in the home and their paid work in the labor force. Society's dominant ideology stressed that women's place was in the home, meaning that working women had two jobs. The burden of women's domestic responsibilities put strain on job performance and was used to legitimate women's relatively low wages and concentration in low-wage, nonunionized jobs.

Marxist feminists next focused on the role women played in providing the conditions for maintaining and continuing existing property relations by biologically reproducing future generations of workers and capitalists. Discussion here centered on reproductive rights, the availability of birth control, and the development of the nuclear family. With little control over reproductive rights, women were tied to the home and had primary responsibility for raising children and taking care of basic necessities such as food, clothing, and shelter. Thus, the nuclear family enabled working-class men to get up in the morning, go to work, and produce profits for the capitalists without having to take care of the household or children. The unpaid domestic labor of women aided in the creation of more surplus value for the capitalist. If the worker had to pay for all household maintenance, then the capitalist would have to pay higher wages so that the worker could sustain himself and his family. According to this line of argument, women's unpaid labor in the home contributed to the creation of surplus value.

Third, Marxist feminists describe women's role in the continual accumulation of capital, focusing primarily on women's labor-force participation and an explanation of the low wages received by women workers. Juliet Mitchell provides the clearest example of a Marxist feminist approach that sought to understand gender inequality in the context of capitalist class relations (Mitchell 1971). Other feminists, both Marxist and non-Marxist, focus on the issue of patriarchy, arguing that the control of women by men was manifested in the legal sanctioning of men to assign women's position in a wide variety of tasks. The issue of patriarchy and the concerns it raises reveal the dual nature of contemporary gender stratification. Today, gender stratification is not only built into society's public institutions but also maintained and reproduced within the family and personal relationships.

Gender relations and gender inequality cannot be understood solely in terms of economic relations. The ideological forces behind gender inequality cannot be reduced to economic "needs." The persistence of male dominance calls into question the narrow view of a purely economic analysis of gender relations. Yet, gender relations are tied to broader class issues. For example, although all women share a certain "gendered position" in society, not all women are subordinated in the same way. Social class and race create significant differences among women. Gender as an analytical category is distinct from class and cannot be subsumed totally within a class analysis. Gender relations can affect class relations as much as class relations can affect gender relations.[3] For example, gender can be a form of class relations, a sorting mechanism into class relations, and/ or a causal interaction with class in determining outcomes. Engels, for example, argued that the first form of class antagonism was between men and women in monogamous marriages, and the first form of class oppression was that of the female sex by the male sex. Gender relations can sort men and women into certain types of jobs, such as domestic service, where certain expectations for women as nurturer and homemaker play an important role in creating house-cleaning and child-care services. Moreover, gender socialization can affect the aspirations of men and women to pursue certain types of jobs over others, and the various forms of gender discrimination can affect access to certain occupational pursuits. Through marriage and other kinship relationships, individuals are linked to class structures. Finally, one's views on affirmative action policies, or the availability of adequate child care, or even comparable worth, for example, may be affected by both one's gender and class relations.

Saying that gender is socially defined means that there is nothing biological that determines men's and women's position within the economic, sociocultural, or political spheres of society. Moreover, there is nothing essential to the development of capitalism that requires the subordination of women to men. After all, how property is appropriated and distributed is a matter of power, not gender. The unique aspect of gender stratification is that gender inequality intrinsically links the domestic sphere with the public sphere. We have seen that women's and men's position in the family and the responsibility assigned to the raising of children have a direct relationship with gender inequality in the workforce. Women's role in the home can also affect the types of jobs and wages available to women. The more gendered the division of household work, the more likely women will occupy subordinated positions in the workforce. A simple example can illustrate this point. To become "successful" as a university professor, one must not only teach well but also do research and publish—in other words, be "productive." Women professors are put at a distinct disadvantage for upward mobility in the academy if they are married, have children, and experience much gendered division of labor in their home. If the female professor is primarily responsible for raising the children and maintaining the household, then less of her time is going into the "productive" labor of research and publishing, something that wages and promotions depend upon. Hence, gender plays a distinctive role even in the privileged academic hierarchy, with more men attaining the rank of full professor and far fewer women achieving even the basic credentials needed to compete. The gendered division of labor, therefore, is socially constructed, not innate.

Racial Stratification

Like gender, race is both an ascribed status and a socially defined category. Although we are born with a certain race (or mixture of races), all that is necessary for a race to exist is for it to be defined by society as such. Races are viewed as biologically or culturally different from the dominant group, yet races can appear and disappear over time. In the late nineteenth century in the United States, southern and eastern Europe immigrants were defined as a separate race by the dominant Anglo-Saxons. Italians were sometimes perceived of as a "criminal" race; eastern

European Jews were thought to be "Negro on the inside"; and even the Irish, earlier in that century, were not perceived as "white" until they politically supported slavery.[4] In the United States people who have varying degrees of African ancestry are defined as "black," but most societies have a multitude of "racial" categories to which they assign people of African descent. To say that race is socially defined highlights the very real socioeconomic and political origins and consequences of that definition. Racial inequality results from the way racism is built into society's institutions. Institutionalized forms of racism include beliefs and behaviors that result in the systematic exclusion of a group of people defined as a race from the resources, power, and privilege more readily bestowed on dominant groups.

Like gender, the category of race is theorized on a very different level of abstraction from class or status. Unlike gender, however, racial inequality is located solely within the public sphere. Nevertheless, classical social theorists such as Marx and Weber were more concerned with the relationship of ownership and work shaping the new capitalist order than with issues of race per se. For Marx and many generations of Marxists, racial inequality was subsumed within class analysis. Classical Marxism addressed issues of race in terms of divisions within the working class. It also saw the nature of racial oppression as distinct from class oppression and, in many ways, secondary to it.[5] Writing in 1948, Oliver Cox developed a truly class-based theory of racial stratification, locating racial inequality within the development of capitalism on a world scale. For Cox, race prejudice developed with European expansion and reached its acme with the institutionalization of a racist ideology to justify the economic exploitation of people of color throughout the world. Still, there is nothing essential about racial inequality for the development of capitalism. Yet, like gender, the concrete historical development of capitalism cannot be understood without understanding the systematic oppression of and discrimination against people of color. For Cox, racial stratification in capitalist societies is an aspect of class relations (Cox 1959).

An understanding of racial inequality in relation to class stratification did not become prevalent until the civil rights movement of the 1960s. Most work on race relations in American sociology viewed racial inequality as either a product of misguided prejudicial attitudes (Myrdal 1944) or part of the process of assimilation. Like other immigrant groups, "racial minorities" were at a disadvantage due to their lack of skills or specialized knowledge. Once these skills were required, earlier observers argued, racial stratification would give way to class stratification.[6] The movement for racial equality in the 1960s made clear that previous work on race was simply misguided. Racial inequality was alive and well in the United States even after African Americans had been in the paid labor force for nearly a century. Empirical work documenting the disadvantaged position of people of color within the class structure began to take seriously the relationship between class exploitation and racial oppression.

Debates during the past twenty years have addressed the question of whether race or class position is more significant in determining the position of people of color within the overall social structure. Wilson (1978), for example, argued that depending on the historical period one can detect which is more important, race or class, in determining life chances. For Wilson, the political rights gained by African Americans and other people of color in the 1960s led to growing class differentiation, causing class to be a more significant indicator of life chances than race. The fact, for example, that African Americans are disproportionately represented among the jobless and most "truly disadvantaged" can be explained more in terms of their class position and the changes in the U.S. economy than by racial oppression (Wilson 1987; 1996).

But race cannot be understood solely in relation to the economic sphere. The social and political sphere, as Du Bois ([1903], 1989) has pointed out, is relevant in understanding the processes of social closure that have excluded people on the basis of the social definition of race from full access to resources and full political participation. Racism has a real impact on the life chances of people of color; even for those who have risen in the class structure, racism is a fact of life. Even people of color who have financial resources are often excluded from buying homes in certain neighborhoods, getting served in certain restaurants, and acquiring membership in certain exclusive social clubs.[7] As Pettigrew (1981) argued almost twenty years ago, it is the interaction of race and class *systems* of inequality that needs to be addressed. For Pettigrew, aspects of racial stratification operate differently across class lines. Similarly, class stratification effects vary according to race. A study conducted on political attitudes in Atlanta among white and black students from different social class backgrounds revealed the significance of the interaction of race and class effects. Social class did not have an effect on differentiating black and white students' views on the sense of political belonging except for students in the highest class. On the one hand, social class had a significant effect on differences between poor white students and white students from other class groupings on student views of political trust. On the other hand, social class had little effect on the views of political trust for black students from all class backgrounds. For Pettigrew, the effects of race and class added together do not account for a wide range of significant socioeconomic and political outcomes. It is the interaction effect that is most telling of similarities and differences.

New Directions in the Study of Social Inequality

Black social scientists such as Du Bois and Cox in the early twentieth century were the first to analyze the relationship of race to the class system. Similarly, women of color have been in the forefront of writing on the intersection of race, class, and gender (Collins 1990; Romero 1992). The civil rights movement made it clear to white society that racism was still a strong presence in the United States. New work on race developed to explain and document the nature and extent of racial inequality. Much of the work on both race and gender debated the importance of class over gender analysis, or race over class analysis or vice versa. The new social movements of the 1980s and 1990s—particularly those concerned with the rights of various disadvantaged groups such as people of various racial and ethnic backgrounds, women, the physically challenged, and gays and lesbians—and the development of identity politics brought an interest in the diverse and multicultural nature of American society. These movements and concerns stimulated some scholars to go beyond old frameworks and debates. As Wright (1997, 242) maintains, few even within the Marxist paradigm would argue that class is always more important than gender. We can extend this view to the study of race. In early stratification textbooks, race and gender were hardly considered. Today it is rare to find a single textbook without some reference to the "intersection of race, class, and gender."[8] Even the American Sociological Association formed a section called the Section on Race, Gender, and Class, in addition to the sections concerned with Sex and Gender, Race and Ethnic Minorities, and Marxist Sociology.

Patricia Hill Collins's call for study of the intersection of race, class, and gender speaks to the issues raised by these new social movements. For Collins, race, class, and gender interact to form various systems of inequality and domination. No one system is more salient than another. Additive models of oppression are replaced with interlocking ones, which, according to Collins, represents a paradigmatic shift and offers new possibilities for conceptualizing inequality. This "matrix of domination" approach holds that there are multiple, interlocking levels of domination structured along axes such as race, class, and gender and also structured on several levels—the level of the individual, the level of the group, and the level of social institutions (Collins 1990, 222–30).

Collins's call for a paradigmatic shift in our thinking about class and racial and gender stratification has affected research agendas more than theory. This, in itself, is a major contribution to the study of social stratification. When gender and race are treated simply as variables added on to a class analysis, the experience and structural position of women of color are submerged into either a race or a gender category. Moreover, the study of racial stratification in the United States is often modeled on a binary paradigm, classifying people as either black or white. By classifying people by race alone, the unique experience of women of color, often obscured in add-on approaches, is revealed.[9] As Romero (1997, 243) has so lucidly pointed out, by understanding the intersection of race, class, and gender, one can fully appreciate the disadvantaged experience of women of color in the workforce. Simply adding gender and race to existing theories of class obscures the experience and position of women of color within the class structure, since race as a general category often refers to men of color and gender refers predominantly to white women.

Recent controversies over affirmative action and attempts to roll back certain civil rights legislation can also benefit from an analysis of how gender and race intersect with class. Opponents of affirmative action often argue that discrimination based on race and/or gender is a thing of the past and point to aggregate data that suggest that the income gap is closing. They also state that there is much more racial and gender diversity within the occupational structure. Although national data may bear this out, studies that seek to understand the unique ways in which gender and race impact on class experience provide a fuller appreciation of the role of both race and gender on the life chances of people throughout the class structure. This mode of analysis also can lead to surprising findings. Stanglein (1997) found that while the decline of manufacturing in the 1980s led to a decrease in male employment, there was no significant change in women's employment among people with no college education. In fact, shifts in family structure are argued to be a more plausible explanation of declining female employment. Moreover, Black women's employment was found to be negatively affected by increases in white women's employment.

The differing impact of racial differences can also be seen when researchers test for race while holding gender and class constant in their study of data. For example, Hanson and Palmer-Johnson (1997) found that because of certain resources African American women receive in terms of unique gender ideologies and work expectations, these women tend to do better in science-related fields than their white counterparts or African American men. Unlike white women, African American women are found to have more familial and kinship support to enter traditionally male areas of study; they also have very high work expectations, since women in the African American community have always worked outside of the home. Gender can intersect with race to produce different class outcomes as well. In a study of Latin American and Caribbean individuals in Massachusetts, Levitt and Gomez (1997) found that race played an important role in mediating men's socioeconomic status but was less salient among women. All of these examples suggest that the intersection of race, class, and gender can be grasped only in the actual historical and social context where they come together.

But at its theoretical root, this new research is still based on the foundations established by Marx and Weber. Gender, race, and class are still conceptualized as distinct social categories and structures. The work of Marx on class and Weber on status groups provides the theoretical foundations for understanding class in capitalist societies and status stratification. Whereas class relations have a material basis in terms of property relations and/or life chances, gender relations and race relations are best understood within particular historical contexts that take into account not only structural arrangements but ideological ones as well. Although gender and race clearly have an impact on class relations, it is possible to theorize a situation in which the basic contours of class relations remain the same and gender and race relations are much more egalitarian. In order to understand race, gender, and class as a matrix of domination or subordination, we are still compelled to return to the classics to find a firm basis for the understanding of power and conflict in the contemporary world.

Notes

1. See Connell 1997 and R. Collins 1997 for a debate on why the classics asked the questions they did.

2. For an excellent review of Marxist feminist writing on gender, see Morrisey and Stoecker 1994.

3. For an excellent elaboration of the possible effects of gender on class and class on gender, see Wright 1997, 239–48.

4. For excellent historical accounts on how race is socially defined, see Ignatiev 1995; Roediger 1991; Allen 1994.

5. For an overview of the Marxist analysis of race and ethnicity, see Geschwender and Levine 1994.

6. For an extensive critique of this perspective, see Geschwender 1978, 39–69.

7. Several books document how race still operates in the lives of upper-income people of color. See, for example, Feagin and Sikes 1994; Feagin and Vera 1995; Feagin, Vera, and Imani 1996; Zweigenhaft and Domhoff 1998; Collins 1997.

8. The number of textbooks written with race, class, gender either in the title or subtitle is astounding. See Anderson and Collins 1995, Cyrus 1997, Rosenblum and Travis 1996, and Grusky 1994 for only a few examples of this growing trend.

9. For an excellent set of articles that explores the intersection of race, class, and gender as it pertains to women's work, see Higginbotham and Romero 1997.

References

Allen, Theodore W. 1994. *The Invention of the White Race*. London: Verso.

Anderson, Margaret, and Patricia Hill Collins. 1995. *Race, Class, and Gender: An Anthology*. Boston: Wadsworth.

Collins, Patricia Hill. 1990. *Black Feminist Thought: Knowledge, Consciousness, and the Politics of Empowerment*. Boston: Unwin Hyman.

Collins, Randall. 1997. "A Sociological Guilt Trip: Comment on Connell." *American Sociological Review* 102: 1558–64.

Collins, Sharon. 1997. *Black Corporate Executives: The Making and Breaking of a Black Middle Class*. Philadelphia: Temple University Press.

Connell, R. W. 1997. "Why Is Classical Theory Classical?" *American Journal of Sociology* 102: 1511–57.

Cox, Oliver C. 1959. *Caste, Class, & Race*. New York: Monthly Review Press.

Cyrus, Virginia. 1997. *Experiencing Race, Class, and Gender in the United States*, 2nd ed. Mountain View, Calif.: Mayfield.

Du Bois, W. E. B. 1989. *Souls of Black Folk*. New York: Bantam.

Feagin, Joe, and Melvin Sikes. 1994. *Living with Racism: The Black Middle Class Experience*. Boston: Beacon Press.

Feagin, Joe, and Hernan Vera. 1995. *White Racism*. New York: Routledge.

Feagin, Joe, Hernan Vera, and Nikitah Imani. 1996. *The Agony of Education*. New York: Routledge.

Geschwender, James A. 1978. *Racial Stratification in America*. Dubuque, Iowa: William C. Brown.

Geschwender, James A., and Rhonda F. Levine. 1994. "Classical and Recent Theoretical Developments in the Marxist Analysis of Race and Ethnicity," in *From the Left Bank to the Mainstream: Historical Debates and Contemporary Research in Marxist Sociology*, ed. Patrick McGuire and Donald McQuarie. Dix Hills, N.Y.: General Hall.

Grusky, David B. 1994. *Social Stratification in Sociological Perspective: Class, Race & Gender*. Boulder, Colo.: Westview Press.

Hanson, Sandra L., and Elizabeth Palmer-Johnson. 1997. "Expecting the Unexpected: African American Women in Science." Paper presented at the annual meetings of the American Sociological Association, August, Toronto, Ontario.

Higginbotham, Elizabeth, and Mary Romero, eds. 1997. *Women and Work: Exploring Race, Ethnicity and Class*. Thousand Oaks, Calif.: Sage Publications.

Ignatiev, Noel. 1995. *How the Irish Became White*. New York: Routledge.

Levitt, Peggy, and Christina Gomez. 1997. "The Intersection of Race and Gender among Dominicans in the U.S." Paper presented at the annual meetings of the American Sociological Association, August, Toronto, Ontario.

Mitchell, Juliet. 1971. *Woman's Estate*. New York: Random House.

Morrissey, Marietta, and Randy Stoecker. 1994. "Marxist Theory and the Oppression of Women," in *From the Left Bank to the Mainstream: Historical Debates and Contemporary Research in Marxist Sociology*, ed. Patrick McGuire and Donald McQuarie. Dix Hills, N.Y.: General Hall.

Myrdal, Gunnar. 1944. *An American Dilemma*. New York: Harper and Row.

Pettigrew, Thomas F. 1981. "Race and Class in the 1980s: An Interactive View." *Daedalus* 110:233–55.

Roediger, David. 1991. *Wages of Whiteness: Race and the Making of the American Working Class*. London: Verso.

Romero, Mary. 1992. *Maid in the U.S.A.* New York: Routledge.

———. 1997. "Epilogue," in *Women and Work: Exploring Race, Ethnicity, and Class*, ed. Elizabeth Higginbotham and Mary Romero. Thousand Oaks, Calif.: Sage Publications.

Rosenblum, Karen E., and Toni-Michelle C. Travis. 1996. *The Meaning of Difference: American Constructions of Race, Sex and Gender, and Social Class, and Sexual Orientation*. New York: McGraw-Hill.

Stanglein, Gena M. 1997. "The Employment of Black Women with Low Skills, 1980–1990: Industrial Restructuring, Crowding, and Shifts in Family Structure." Paper presented at the annual meetings of the American Sociological Association, August, Toronto, Ontario.

Wilson, William Julius. 1978. *The Declining Significance of Race: Blacks and Changing American Institutions*. Chicago: University of Chicago Press.

———. 1987. *The Truly Disadvantaged: The Inner City, the Underclass, and Public Policy*. Chicago: University of Chicago Press.

———. 1996. *When Work Disappears*. New York: Knopf.

Wright, Erik Olin. 1997. *Class Counts: Comparative Studies in Class Analysis*. Cambridge: Cambridge University Press.

Zweigenhaft, Richard L., and G. William Domhoff. 1998. *Diversity and the Power Elite: Are Women and Minorities Reaching the Top?* New Haven: Yale University Press.

Index

academic hierarchy, 253
advertising, social class and, 82–83
affirmative action, 257
African-Americans, 168, 163n.15; cumulative principle and, 222–25, 226n.3; economic issues, 224–25; education, 223; history, 208–14; image of, 212–13; labor and, 228–30; minority problem comparison, 215–16; problems of, 221–22; strife for recognition, 210–14; talents of, 110n.6; treatment in South, 217–18, 226n.6; women, 257–58; *see also* race; race relations; racism; slavery
Africa, women as laborers, 176
American dream, social class and, 60–64
American Sociological Association, 256
Antiquity, class struggles of, 48
Ariés, Philippe, 190
authority positions, 202–203
automation, 177

Bales, Robert F., 190n.22
Berg, I., 130
Black Reconstruction, 217
blue-collar workers, 120–21
Bott, Elizabeth, 205n.15
bourgeois; collision with proletariats, 20–21; competition among, 19;

definition, 39n.1; development of, 14–16; family systems, 26; freedom and, 24–25; historical overview, 13–18; housewife, 205n.12; kinship link to, 133–37; marriage, 27; Marx's theory of, 121–23; social closure and, 128–33; socialism and, 34–35; sociological analysis of, 119–21; status of women in, 183
Bowlby, John, 186
Bowles, Samuel, 145
Braverman, H., 123
Busfield, Joan, 203n.1

Caldwell, Erskine, 62
capital, 3–5, 22; relationship to possession, 128; as social power, 24–25
capital-labor relations, 24–25, 144–45
capitalism; analysis of, 250; authority role, 146–47, 149–50, 162n.10; composition of, 3; exclusionary practices, 125–26, 133–37; exploitation of workers, 144–45; family structure and, 151–53, 163n.14; gender relationships and, 251–53; labor and, 227–28; Marx's views on, 115–16; middle-class locations map, 149–50; status of women in, 183; underclass and, 152–53; Weber's views on, 114–16
capitalists, 3–4, 143–44
Carchedi, G., 122, 129

caste endogamy, 73–75
caste systems, 50–52, 73–75
Caucasians, 73, 217. *see also* race; race
 relations; racism
children; socialization of, 184–88,
 190n.22, 190n.23, 190n.24; social
 class and, 81
China, 182, 189
Christian Socialism, 31
citizenship, 201, 202
civil rights movement, 254–55, 257
class; American Dream and, 60–64;
 analysis of, 233–40, 256–58; authority role, 146–47, 149–50,
 162n.10; as bases for social action,
 44; changes in attitude toward,
 240–46; common cause coalitions
 in, 242–43; concrete vs. abstract
 analysis, 249–50; definition, 2, 4,
 117, 155; democracy and, 61–62;
 economic factors involved in,
 44–45; empathy building in,
 244–46; exclusionary practices of,
 141–42, 161n.2; history of, 13; in-
 come-leisure relationship, 155–56;
 leadership in, 63–64; Marx analysis
 of, 5–7, 8–9, 41–42, 114–18, 141,
 197–200, 249–50; Marx vs. Weber
 analysis, 153–60, 164n.17; mobility of, 76–77, 82, 83, 85n.16,
 117–18; non-paid labor force, 151–
 53, 163n.14; parties and, 55–56;
 property and, 115; race and,
 227–30; racial inequality and,
 254–55; ranking systems, 204n.7;
 references in literature, 60, 62–63;
 research, 79; role in society, 77–84;
 skills and expertise role, 147–49,
 150–51; social action and, 47; social perspectives of, 74; strata
 within, 159; structure within,
 64–67; studies of, 2, 63–64, 67–75;
 types of struggle within, 47–48;
 United States, 66–77; Weber on,
 5–6, 114–18, 249–50; women and,
 199; *see also* stratification

class antagonisms, market situation
 and, 48
class conflict, 138
class inequality, 250
class interest, social action and, 45–47
class structure, analysis of, 193–94,
 204n.4
*The Class Structure of the Advanced
 Societies*, 118n.9
class struggle, 35–36, 114–18, 196,
 204n.6
class subordination, 133–37
class wars, 65
classless societies, 65–66
collectivism, 6, 127, 135
Collins, Patricia Hill, 8, 168, 231–47,
 256
color-caste system, 73–75
commerce, 14, 15
commodities, production of, 171
communes, 39–40n.4, 135–37, 197
Communism, 12, 35–37
Communist Party; Manifesto of the,
 11, 12–40; oligarchical roles, 134
communists, opposition parties and,
 38–39; working-class differences,
 22–23
conscience collective, 126–27
conservative socialism, 34–35
contraception, 179–80
Council for National Academic
 Awards, 140n.30
Cox, Oliver, 8, 168, 227–30, 254, 256
credentialism, 129–33, 148, 163n.13
critical-utopian socialism, 35–37
culture, 25–26
cumulation, principle of, 222–25,
 226.3

Davidoff, Leonore, 203n.1 Davis, Allison, 73
Davis, Kingsley, 7, 59, 86–98, 99–107,
 126
De Beauvoir, Simone, 177
democracy, social status and, 61–62
direct class locations, 151–52
discrimination, 201, 222–23

domestic labor, 175, 198–99, 189n.3, 205n.12, 205n.13, 252
Dore, R., 130
Du Bois, W. E. B., 8, 168, 208–14, 217, 255, 256
Durkheim, Emile, 126–27, 128
dynamic causation, 223–24

economic issues, African-Americans and, 224–25; class determination and, 44–45; class structure and, 114–18; effects of stratification on, 53–55; gender relations and, 252–53; social class and, 65–66, 75–76; social honor and, 43–44
Economy and Society, 116
education, 5, 6, 26; African-Americans, 223; higher, 82; lower-class groups, 219; as professional credential, 130; social class and, 69; social mobility and, 77–82
Eells, Kenneth, 7, 59, 60–85
efficiency wage theory, 162n.12
empathy, social changes and, 244–46
employment, 257–58
employment rents, 162n.12
Engels, Friedrich, 8, 167, 169–72
England, polygamy and, 182–83
entertainment professions, 130–31
Erickson, Robert, 159
Eros Denied, 181–82
ethnic groups, 197, 201–202, 205n.10; segregation of, 50–52; the South, 75
exchange relations, 3, 5–6
exclusion principles, 71
exploitation, 5; of African-Americans, 228–30; civilization and, 171–72; class relations and, 158–59; forms of, 162n.10; historical perspective, 28; interaction patterns, 142–43; life chances and, 164n.21; Marx's views on, 154, 156–58; nature of, 3; nonexploitative oppression and, 142–45; of petty-bourgeois, 144, 162n.7; principle criteria of,

141–42; rate of, 4; of workers, 128–29, 132, 136–37
extra-economic coercion, 164n.22

Family and the Sexual Revolution, 184
family systems, 252–53, 257; adult roles, 185–86; bourgeois, 26; capitalism and, 151–53, 163n.14; female role in, 169–70; gender role in, 170–72; lineage, 170–71; patterns of, 187–88; propertyless families, 144, 162n.8; Russia, 188; sexual relations and, 184; status of men and, 171–72; true family, 174; women's role in, 174, 178–79
federal employees, 219
females, class structure and, 197–98; rank in society, 204n.7; role in family, 170–72; traits of, 237–38; feminism, 173, 188, 197–98, 251–52
feudal society, 13, 22, 30–31, 158, 164n.22
France, 31–32, 38

Gardner, Burleigh B., 73
Gardner, Mary R., 73
gender, analysis of, 233–40, 250, 256–58; changes in attitudes toward, 240–46; common cause coalitions in, 242–43; empathy building in, 244–46; Marx theory, 197–200; oppression and, 234, 235; role in family, 170–72; status groups and, 200–203; stratification theory and, 193, 194, 195–97, 251–53
gender inequality, 8–9, 168, 250, 251–53
Genealogy of Morals, 51–52
German socialism, 32–34
Germany, 38, 40n.6
Gerth, H. H., 114
Giddens, Anthony, 113
Gintis, Herb, 145
Giovanni, Nikki, 240
Goldthorpe, John, 150–51, 159
Gomez, Christina, 257

Goode, W. J., 109–110
goods and services, 45, 106, 110n.2;
 consumption of, 54; distribution of,
 44; ownership of, 93–94; stratification and, 100
government and stratification, 92
gradational class concept, 154, 157,
 164n.19
Great Britain, aristocracy, 40n.6
Grun, Herr Karl, 40n.7
guild-masters, 39n.3

Haavio-Mannila, E., 206n.19
Hanson, Sandra L., 257
Harding, Sandra, 235
Hegel, Georg, 127
history, recorded, 39n.2
home colonies, 40n.8
homelessness, 141, 161n.1
homemakers, 151, 163n.14, 205n.12,
 205n.13

Icaria, 37, 40n.8
income, 93; efficiency wage theory,
 162n.12; leisure and, 155–56,
 164n.20; training and, 103–104
India, status groups, 205n.16
individualism, 134–37
industrial revolution, 13–14
inequality, views of, 7–8
infancy, 186–87
inherited wealth, 126
invidious systems, 95, 96

job satisfaction, 105
Jordan, June, 242–43

kinship relations, 133–37, 203
Klein, Melanie, 186
Klein, Viola, 178
Kovalevsky, M., 171
Ku-Klux Klan, 211

labor, 144–45, African-Americans,
 228–30; appropriation of, 143–44;
 authority over, 146–47, 149–50;
 capital relationship, 3–5; capitalism

and, 227–28; division of, 176, 194,
 198–99, 201, 203, 253; managerial
 authority, 121–23; manual trades,
 131–32; manual vs. nonmanual,
 119–40; Marx on, 125–26; non-
 paid, 151–53, 163n.14; physical
 demands of, 175–77; production
 and, 227–28; productively saleable,
 152–53; scarcity of, 89, 100; skills
 and expertise of, 101, 147–49,
 150–51; status of, 53; stratification
 and, 92–94; wage relationship,
 24–25; Weber on, 125–26; see also
 domestic labor
labor theory of value, 161n.3
learned professions, 131–32
legal order, 43–44
leisure, 155–56, 164n.20
Lévi-Strauss, Claude, 185
Levitt, Peggy, 257
Lewis, Sinclair, 62
liberalism, 219–20
liberation of women, 188–89
life chances, 5–6, 46, 154–57, 201,
 164n.21
lifestyle, 49, 53
List, F. 42n.1
Lockwood, David, 168, 192–207
Lorde, Audre, 231, 246
lower-class groups, education and, 78–
 82, 219; membership, 218; New
 England, 69–70; social perspectives
 of, 74; social relations and, 215–16;
 solidarity of, 218–19; the South,
 73–75; the West, 72
loyalty rents, 151, 156–57

McIntosh, Mary, 203n.1
males, labor demands, 175–77; rank in
 society, 204n.7; role in family,
 170–72; traits of, 237–38
managers, 121–23; class location of,
 156–57; contradictory roles of,
 146–47, 162n.11 "Manifesto of the
 Communist Party," 11, 12–40
market situation, 5–6, 44–45, 48
marriage, 27, 181, 184, 188, 203

Marx, Karl, 1–2, 59, 113; on bourgeois, 134; class analysis, 2–3, 5–6, 8–9, 41–42, 141, 249–50; class structure, 114–18, 153–60, 164n.17; class struggle, 4; class theory, 119–40, 197–200, 216; on feminists, 251; gender theory, 197–200; on labor, 176, 177; "Manifesto of the Communist Party," 11, 12–40; "On Classes," 11, 41–42; patriarchy, 197–200; on property, 125–26; on racial inequality, 254–55; role of authority in class structure, 121–23; on sexuality, 181; social conflict and, 196–97; on social closure, 137–38; Weber class structure and, 114–18
mass behavior, 46
material interests, 143–44
Mead, Margaret, 185
mediated class locations, 152
Meeker, Marchia, 7, 59, 60–85
men. see gender; males
meritocracy, 135
Middle Ages, class struggles of, 48
middle-class groups, class locations map, 149–51; concept of, 145–46; education and, 78–82; New England, 69; social perspectives of, 74; the West, 72
Mills, C.W., 114, 136–37, 200
minorities, 21
Mitchell, Juliet, 167–68, 173–91
monogamy, 182–84
monopolies, 132–33
Moore, Wilbert, 7, 59, 86–98, 99–107, 126
moral judgments, 143–44
morality, Soviet Union, 181
Morley, Christopher, 62
motherhood, 169, 187
motivation, 87–88, 102, 105
Myrdal, Gunnar, 215–26, 8168

nationality, 27
Native Americans, 142, 161n.5, 163n.16; family heritage and, 170–71; labor and, 228
Neugarten, Bernice L., 81
Neuwirth, G., 124
New England, social class studies, 67–70
Nietzsche, Friedrich, 51–52
nonexploitative economic oppression, 142

occupations, authority hierarchy and, 203, 206n.18; pursuit of, 201; status of, 203, 206n.19
old-family class, 84n.2; New England, 67–70; the West, 70–72
opportunity, degree of, 96, 155–56
oppression, additive analyses of, 231–34; individual dimension of, 239–40; institutional dimension of, 235–37; nonexploitative economic, 142; symbolic dimension of, 237–39
Ortner, S., 204n.7
Orwell, G., 134
Ossowski, Stanislaw, 164n.19
ownership. see private property

Palmer-Johnson, Elizabeth, 257
parenthood, 180
Parkin, Frank, 113, 119–40, 158
Parsons, Talcott, 127, 185–86, 200, 190n.22, 190n.23, 190n.24
parties, 55–56
patriarchy, 197–200, 203, 205n.13, 205n.14, 206n.17, 235–37
periodicals, social class and, 82
personality, social class and, 82, 83, 85n.16
Pettigrew, Thomas F., 255
petty-bourgeois, 31–32, 145–46; class locations, 150; exploitation of, 144, 162n.7
Phalansteres, 40n.8
Philosophie de la Misere, 35
physical labor, 53
Plamenatz, J., 127
Poland, communists, 38

political opinions, cultural influences of, 219–20
political power, 29 politics, African-American, 224
polygamy, 182–83
positions in society, distribution of, 87–88; motivation for, 87; privileged, 103–104; rank determinants, 88–89, 97–98n.3, 99–101; societal functions and, 90–95; status relevance, 202–203; value of, 100–101
power, sources of, 6
prejudice, 213
price wars, 48
private property, 23–26, 29, 115, 122, 154; as class determinant, 44–45, 125–27; class struggle and, 47–48; concepts of, 127–28; Durkheim on, 126, 128; Hegel on, 127; marriage and, 181; opportunities and, 155–56; Parsons on, 127; Plamenatz on, 127; possession vs. capital, 128; Rose on, 127–28; status and, 49, 53–54; stratification and, 92–94
privileges of status groups, 52–53, 241–42, 245–46
production, 3; class locations map, 149–51; costs of, 18; historical overview, 15–17; labor and, 227–28; process of, 177; reproduction and, 179, 180–81; social relations of, 3; socio-economic relationships of, 117; tributary mode of, 161n.4; women's role in, 175–78
productivity, 4, 54, 110n.6
profits, 3–4, 143, 144–45; see also surplus value
proletarians, bourgeois housewife and, 205n.12; Communists and, 22–30; development of, 17–19; exclusionary practices, 136; measures necessary for supremacy of, 28–30
propertyless families, 144, 162n.8

public policy, support for, 224

race, analysis of, 233–40, 256–58; changes in attitude toward, 240–46; class stratification and, 254–55; common cause coalitions in, 242–43; empathy building in, 244–46; power and privilege differences in, 240–42; stratification and, 253–55; symbolic images of, 237–38
race relations, 168, 222–23, 227–32, 254–55
racial inequality, 8–9, 250, 254–55
racism, 235–37, 241
radicalism, 220
radio, social class and, 83
relational class concept, 154, 157, 164n.19
religion and stratification, 90–92
reproduction of children, 178–81, 187, 251–52
Roemer, John, 162n.7, 164n.21
Romero, Mary, 257
Rose, D., 127
Russia, 65–66, 188

sacred matters, 95–96
schoolteaching, 206n.18
Scott, Alison, 203n.1
segregation, ethnic, 50–52
self-sufficient economies, 42n.1
sense of dignity, 51
service class, 150
sexual inequality, 193, 201, 203, 206n.19
sexual relations, 184, 196, 204n.7, 204n.8
sexuality, 181–84
Shils, E., 201, 202
six-class systems, 73–74
skills and expertise of employees, 147–49, 150–51
slavery, 176, 177, 235–37; see also African-Americans
social action, 44–47
social class. see class

social closure, 6, 9, 123–33; credentialism, 129–33; exclusionary practices
of, 123–26, 128–33, 139n.11; kinship link, 133–37; modes of, 125;
power and, 125; property and,
125–27, 128; socially ineligibles,
124; usurpation practices, 124–25,
139n.11; Weber defines, 123–24
social conflict, 196–97
social engineering, 224
social formation, 194
social honor, 43–44 social inequality,
100, 107, 168; analysis of, 250;
definition, 109; study of, 256–58
social interaction, 193
social relations of production, 3
social stratification. see stratification
Social-Democrats, 38, 40n.9
socialism, conservative, 34–35; feudal,
30–31; German, 32–34; petty-
bourgeois, 31–32; utopian, 35–37
socialization of children, 184–88,
190n.22, 190n.23, 190n.24
solidarity, 96, 139n.11, 197, 216, 217,
218–19
Souls of Black Folk, 168, 208–14
the South, African-Americans, 217–
18, 226n.2; characteristics of, 220;
education and social class, 79–80;
social class studies, 72–75
specialization, degree of, 95
spending, social class and, 69–70
sporting professions, 130–31, 140n.30
Stanglein, Gena M., 257
status formation, gender role, 195–96,
204n.5; sexual relations, 196,
204n.8
status groups, 6, 115; class and,
54–55; exclusiveness of, 201; formation of, 52; gender and, 200–
203; parties and, 56; privileges of,
52–53; sense of dignity and, 51–52;
violence role, 205n.16
status honor, 49–50, 53
status situation, 49, 200–201
stratification, access restriction, 102–

103; African-Americans, 218; analysis of, 192–95, 250; by status
groups, 49–50; composite types,
97; early American theories of, 7;
economic conditions and, 53–56;
exclusionary practices of, 123–26,
128–33, 139n.11; functions of,
107–109; gender and, 168, 195–97,
204n.5, 251–53; goods and, 106,
107; government and, 92; influence
of external conditions on, 96–97;
necessity for, 87–88; nonclass
forms, 8; principles of, 99–110; racial, 253–55; ranking within,
110n.1; religion and, 90–92; rewards of, 106–107; societal functions and, 90–95; study of, 1–2;
system types, 95–96; talents of population, 101–102; theories of, 193;
wealth and, 92–93; Weber's view
of, 6–7; see also positions in society
suffrage, 188, 204n.6, 205n.11
surplus, 3–4, 147, 161n.11, 162n.11
survival value, 100–101
Switzerland, communists, 38
Symons, Arthur, 208

technology, social structure and,
65–66; stratification and, 94–95;
women and, 177–78
Thomas, Keith, 183
training, 100, 102–106; see also education
tributary mode of production, 161n.4
true socialism, 32–34
Tumin, Melvin, 7–8, 59, 99–110

underclass, 152–53, 163n.15, 163n.16
unions, development of, 19–20
United States, social class and, 66–77
upper-class groups, characteristics, 68,
69; education and, 78–82; New England, 68; social perspectives of, 74;
social relations and, 215–16; the
South, 73–75; the West, 72
upward mobility, 61, 76–77, 78, 253
utopian socialism, 35–37

utopias, 35–37, 40n.8

wage-labor relations, 115, 117–18
wages, 3–4, 24
Walby, S., 206n.17
Warner, Lloyd, 7, 59, 60–85
wealth, status of women and, 170–72;
    stratification and, 92–93
Weber, Max, 1–2, 113; class analysis,
    249–50; class definition, 5–6;
    "Class, Status, Party," 11, 43–56;
    class structure, 114–18, 153–60,
    164n.17; on credentialism, 129,
    130; on learned professions, 132;
    Marx class structure and, 114–18;
    on property, 125–26; on racial in-
    equality, 254–55; role of authority
    in class status, 121–23; on social
    closure, 134, 138; status formation,
    196; on status
situation, 200–201; on stratification
    theory, 192–93
the West, social class studies, 70–72

White, Nancy, 238
white-collar workers, 120–23, 130–
    32, 206n.18
Whitehead, H., 204n.7
Wilson, William Julius, 255, 163n.15
women, African-American, 257–58;
    China, 182, 189; inherited status,
    201; liberation of, 177, 251; love
    and marriage, 184; oppression of,
    173–75; physical capabilities,
    175–77; production capability,
    175–78; reproduction role,
    178–81; role in society, 167–68;
    sexuality and, 181–84; socializa-
    tion of children, 184–88, 190n.22,
    190n.23, 190n.24; status of, 26–
    27, 203; *see also* gender
workforce. *see* labor; proletarians
Wright, Arthur, 169
Wright, Erik Olin, 113, 250, 256; class
analysis, 141–65; exploitation and,
    4–5

Young, Wayland, 181–82

About the Editor

Rhonda F. Levine is associate professor of sociology at Colgate University, where she has taught since 1982. She is the author of *Class Struggle and the New Deal: Industrial Labor, Industrial Capital and the State* (1988), and coeditor of *Recapturing Marxism: An Appraisal of Recent Trends in Sociological Theory* (1987), *Bringing Class Back In: Contemporary and Historical Perspectives* (1991), and *Radical Sociologists and the Movement: Experiences, Lessons, and Legacies* (1991). She has been on the board of directors of the Society for the Study of Social Problems. She has also has sat on numerous committees of the American Sociological Association, including the council of the Political Sociology Section, and is past chair of the Section on Marxist Sociology.